IN
EUROPE'S
IMAGE

IN EUROPE'S IMAGE

The Need for American Multiculturalism

O. R. Dathorne

BERGIN & GARVEY
Westport, Connecticut • London

Library of Congress Cataloging-in-Publication Data

Dathorne, O. R.
     In Europe's image : the need for American multiculturalism / O. R.
Dathorne.
          p.   cm.
     Includes bibliographical references (p.) and index.
     ISBN 0–89789–397–2
     1. United States—Civilization—European influences.   2. United
States—Relations—Europe.   3. Europe—Relations—United States.
4. Pluralism (Social sciences)—United States.   5. Multiculturalism—
United States.   I. Title.
E169.1.D29   1994
305.8′00973—dc20   94–4754

British Library Cataloguing in Publication Data is available.

Library of Congress Catalog Card Number: 94–4754
ISBN: 0–89789–397–2

First published in 1994

Bergin & Garvey, 88 Post Road West, Westport, CT 06881
An imprint of Greenwood Publishing Group, Inc.

Printed in the United States of America

The paper used in this book complies with the
Permanent Paper Standard issued by the National
Information Standards Organization (Z39.48–1984).

10 9 8 7 6 5 4 3 2 1

For
Hilde Ostermaier Dathorne
who provided me with the time, space, and climate to make this possible
and who gave unstintingly of her time and effort

Contents

Acknowledgments ————————————————————

I first became interested in this topic some fifteen years ago when an unsuspecting dean, not knowing what to do with an unfortunate stepchild called "American Studies," asked me to head the program. It seemed only logical to me (in my folly) that I should try to establish it as a program that would deal with all the ramifications of American culture—Native American, African American, Latino American, Asian American, and Euro American. But this was not to be—my decision called down the fury of the professional "Americanists." My tenure as director, dramatically brief, did not outlast my interest.

On reflection, I recalled that it really was not possible to live in the Western hemisphere and be oblivious to the presence of the United States. Despite the fact that the British, with typical arrogance, had taught their colonials to ignore the United States, American presence came to us during the war years at the American bases, through radio and cinema, comic books, and even with the Bobbsey Twins and hair straightening. We fell in love to Patti Page and Louis Armstrong, being not quite old enough to establish the rigid color distinctions that applied in the United States. Furthermore, we had "rich" aunts and uncles who were constantly returning from the United States on visits, complete with a new way of speaking, sunglasses, and chewing gum—all of which we felt had something to do with the America of which they spoke so fondly.

Like all good colonials, I went to study in Britain, where I learned from the best minds that there was really no such thing as American culture. It was, they assured me, a branch of English letters. After all, T. S. Eliot was living proof to my undergraduate mind that this must indeed be true. And when, as a nineteen-year-old, I actually met the great man, I came away convinced that he too had recognized just how wonderful and superior the British were—Eliot had become English.

It was several years later that I met my second well-known American. This was no less a personage than Malcolm X, who wanted me to see in him what was clearly invisible and lost to us both: to wit, an African exterior. He had spoken at the University of Ibadan about the joys of breathing freely in Nigeria, to much loud applause from the students who neither thought of themselves as Nigerian nor African. They were quite pleased though that this American had come all the way from overseas to tell them how wonderful their country was. I can be forgiven, I think, for pretending to have the same feelings. Rising, I gave them a stirring speech, reminiscent of my debating days, about the joys of living in Africa—only to reveal at the end, "Do you see how easily you can be fooled?" Mr. X was not pleased, as he made abundantly clear in his *Autobiography*.

Apart from these delightful personal experiences, on the more serious side, there are certain books that were invaluable to me in assisting me to formulate some of the ideas expressed here—in particular, David Dimbleby and David Reynolds, *An Ocean Apart: The Relationship between Britain and America in the Twentieth Century*; Christopher Hitchens, *Blood, Class and Nostalgia: Anglo-American Ironies*; John U. Nef, *The United States and Civilization*; and Robert Weisbuch, *Atlantic Double-Cross: American Literature and British Influence in the Age of Emerson*. These helped me in varying degrees, since I often wanted either to agree desperately or react quite strongly. In any event, I often felt that in many instances they seemed to pull back a little. Hence, the question that pervades this book, and the one I always asked myself is, Why is there the constant concentration on the Europeanization of the United States, and why has so little of other cultures filtered through?

I could not have accomplished the research and wring for this book without the help and cooperation of the University of Kentucky. I am particularly indebted to the Department of English, which provided me with the time and the opportunity, and to the graduate school, which aided me with small grants. Now that I am no longer engaged in fighting academe's small wars, I can truthfully say that I prefer the peace.

In particular, I should like to thank Ms. Lucy Combs and Ms. Emily Carpenter for helping with the arduous task of preparing the manuscript for publication. Lucy Combs has willingly undertaken to assist me with the mundane labors that make up a professor's life, thereby providing me with the time to research, write, and rewrite this work. Emily Carpenter has been most patient and considerate, taking the time to locate material for me, as well as to check and doublecheck. Again, I have to thank her for her dedication and her willingness to explore new avenues.

Finally, I must yet again thank Hilde Ostermaier Dathorne, my wife of thirty-four years. Because she takes on so much, I have the time and the opportunity to work—especially now that, thankfully, our two children have bidden their fond farewells. To her, I remain eternally grateful.

As the disclaimer always states, I alone must accept the responsibility for what is written here. I hope that not all my readers will feel like the graduate student in California who asked after I had lectured on the subject, "So, why don't you like America?" Or, even more damning, the erstwhile acquaintance who, when asked by me to read over the manuscript, cast the offending thing into the garbage! I did not ponder for long on the matter of exactly what his thoughts in so doing might be.

IN
EUROPE'S
IMAGE

1
Search for the Classic Past ──────────────

Locating past American experience must, of necessity, begin with an examination of negatives. For, from the country's inception (as any colony can only hold up a mirror image of the metropolis), definitions of being American require an admission of colonial historical legacy. Independence is itself dependent on the "positive" attributes of the conqueror, whose offspring the colony is. True, ex-colonial states emerge with their own indigenous format, but strains and strands of the imperial presence continue to exist.

For a long time the assumption had been held in England—and continued in America until the early part of the twentieth century—either that American culture did not exist as a separate entity or that any literature evolved from it was clearly at most a province of English letters. Henry James's famous dicta indicate how a Europeanized American could actually visualize his own American present in terms of an alien European past:

No State, in the European sense of the word, and indeed, barely a specific national name. No sovereign, no court, no personal loyalty, no aristocracy, no church, no clergy, no army, no diplomatic service, no country gentlemen, no palaces, no castles, nor manors, nor old country houses, nor parsonages, nor thatched cottages, nor ivied ruins; no cathedrals, nor abbeys, nor little Norman churches; no great universities nor public schools—no Oxford, nor Eton, nor Harrow; no literature, no novels, no museums, no pictures, no political society, no sporting class—no Epsom nor Ascot![1]

Clearly, for James, in 1880, the negatives arise out of a failure created by the mere fact of being different.

James's negatives enumerate a series of pointers that may be further discussed. For him the state must be European or cease to exist. Yet this is a most literal rendition of what constitutes a state. Recall that, particularly in Italy and Germany, the concept of the state comes about only in the nineteenth century. The frightening effects of Garibaldi's welding of disparate groups might be seen as the ultimate cause of Mussolini's Fascist dogma. Equally, Bismarck's insistence on cementing different German-speaking peoples may be the early progenitor of Hitler's *Herrenvolk*. One does not suggest that James would have approved of such later excesses, but they must be borne in mind when Europe is held up as the cultural example.

Even more worrisome is the winsome harkening back to Divine Right, and the vicious contentions of European kings, which produced a large sector of parasitic dependents. These aristocratic forerunners were merely those who had fought well, obeyed the royal dictate, and succeeded in court intrigue. There is no inherent, God-conferred aristocracy in Europe. Class merely sanctions the excesses of human greed and ambition, rewarding those who succeed at the expense of those who do not.

The American response was quick and practical, yet clearly erring in its simplicity, for it was an apparent explanation of what was perceived and accepted as a negative. Charles Brockden Brown wrote in 1806, expressing what could have been a national opinion: "A people," he asserted, "must secure a provision of absolute necessities before they think of conveniences; and must enjoy conveniences before they can indulge in the agreeable arts of life."[2] Hence, he contends, even before James, that culture has to be a practical matter.

These assertions do not fully answer James's condemnations. For James seemingly demands the impossible, that a culture be gift-wrapped, mothballed, and rendered appropriately antiquated before it can be acknowledged. Although such a culture was indigenous to the American continent, it was not one that its European inhabitants recognized. The very petulance of his outcry exposes James's Americanness, for he demands instant redress—an ancient culture, complete with trappings of court, church, education, and art—on demand. In a way, Charles Brockden Brown and Henry James share the same pragmatic approach to culture.

Any acceptance of such a discrepancy between a supposed "nonculture" and a culture, between an absence of tradition and its presence, clearly equates positives with "civilization" and negatives with barbarism. Robert Weisbuch distinguishes these articulators as "the party of mimesis"—those who attempt to fill the supposed cultural gaps with handy equivalents—and "the party of consciousness"—those who reject the notion, opting instead for a disregard of European conventions and a concern with a distinct sensibility capable of

Americanizing European tenets.[3] These constitute the two aspects of the ongoing American debate about the nature of culture.

In the grand debate what was omitted was perhaps the most pertinent factor, namely, that culture evolves from layers of generational impulses and that art (one of its manifestations) asserts itself in two ways: First, it builds as each successive work, consciously or unconsciously, co-opts its predecessors. Second, it discards, refurbishes, redefines, and renews with each new effort. There is no contradiction between the manner in which these two influences function, at times independent of each other, at other times merging, or even colliding. In the process much is borrowed from other cultures.

Even the widely accepted legitimacy of a common heritage may be soundly disputed, for the Graeco-Roman world was at best a convenient tag, a way of fusing differing aspects of a global past. This past had been preserved in Andalusia for nine centuries by foreign conquerors from North Africa. After Europe woke up from its Dark Ages, recovered from the Black Death, and finally stopped squandering its purse on the Saracen "heathens," the tradition was there, intact, preserved by the Moors. But although English visitors did visit Andalusia after 1492 (the year of Moorish expulsion and New World invasion), the Western legacy was really bequeathed to Spain and Portugal, the direct and natural inheritors of Moorish genius. Anglo-speakers had little if any claims to this cultural spoil. One cannot, therefore, begin with the assumption that British culture was somehow part of this classical past.[4]

Another issue was that Graeco/Roman culture had converted itself into a synthesis not entirely authentic. Arnold Toynbee, a conservative and even ethnocentric historian, commented in the BBC Reith Lectures of 1952:

> This disillusioned Greek and Roman dominant minority was, in fact, suffering from the same spiritual starvation as a majority of contemporary mankind, but the new religions which were now being offered to all men and women without respect of persons would have stuck within a philosopher's throat if the missionary had not sugared the strange pill for him; and so, for the sake of accomplishing their last and hardest task of converting a Greek-educated die-hard core of a pagan public, the new religions did clothe themselves in diverse forms of Greek dress. All of them, from Buddhism to Christianity inclusive, presented themselves visually in a Greek style of art, and Christianity took the further step of presenting itself intellectually in terms of Greek philosophy.[5]

For the purpose of this argument, one may safely ignore the contentious comparison to Buddhism and merely note that even Toynbee visualized the Greek past as a synthesis, filtered through the whims and prejudices of the church fathers. Thus, Americans and British dispute over a past that is Graeco-Roman only by revisionist assumptions. In reality, it was preserved within a kind of global marketplace, wherein participants from Africa played an unmistakable role. After the Western European assumption of this legacy, with the aid of texts copiously copied down by hand and translated first into Arabic, then retranslated and laboriously copied into Latin, what is one to make of the cultural muddle? One thing is clear: The Anglo world had little claim to such a heritage. Indeed, the very culture to which America lays claim might itself be more eastern than western, more African than European.

The post–World War II years mark the advent of the United States as donor. With the food parcel enter named American artifacts that must be accepted in Europe as part of the new exchange. The loudest voice of the new venture is the movie industry, for it packages and exports Americana. The result is a bit of gratitude mingled with a deep sense of shame on the part of the British, but they are, at that time, in no position to refuse to be co-opted. Perhaps this feeling was the logical acceptance of American political (even cultural) hegemony: The colonialist was colonized by the colonial. It is a merging that James could not have anticipated and would certainly not have approved.

A new American environment mandated a linguistic division, not merely through naming things but also through responding to a different landscape. This accounts for the debunking of another myth—a shared language. The New World encounter demonstrated both the modification and the alteration of the European experience. It called for and demanded reduction in one way and insisted on expansion in another. The creative process assumed a different dimension, as themes and issues, explanation and change, ran counter to the supposedly nurturing mother culture in Europe.

Presence in a new place, with differing requirements and a new sense of urgency and order, effectively divorced American national aspirations from England's. The colonial experience had manufactured not British islanders nor European nationalists from tiny feuding states, but Atlanticists who ought to have had a new and differing vision, projecting grander realities. The artist, in turn, sought to free himself or herself, based on a conscious choice.

In this new world, the "aristocrat" does not emerge until the late nineteenth, early twentieth century. He (and the new creature is male) would be the first to assert peasant progeny as a cultural justification, whether from slave origins (African) or serf ancestry (Europeans). Therefore, to cite but two examples, Booker T. Washington and Cornelius Vanderbilt, however different, assume a resemblance. The "bootstrap theory" does not arise so much out of American democratic belief as from the archetype of the human, pitted against wilderness. America, John Adams reminds us, "is that Part of the World which is pointed out in the Revelation of God."[6] No greater claim could be made for American authenticity and cultural apartness. Given the authoritative and definitive nature of scriptural text, ultimate vindication of American cultural sovereignty lay in the rigid acceptance of this religious credo.

Nationalizing God was the first act for political liberty. Early settlers in the land were religious exiles who sought, not the much touted religious freedom but the less well understood political liberation. In turn, political independence gave way to literary claim-staking. Weisbuch shows ways in which the opposing sides invent a literature, dependent on each other, yet independently directed:

> Melville himself, watching Dickens apparently steal from Hawthorne's romances and from one of his own, attempts to devastate *Bleak House* in the brief space of "Bartleby the Scrivener." Whitman savages the culture ideal of Matthew Arnold in "Democratic Vistas." Thoreau sets himself in explicit opposition to Coleridge while implicitly contesting Wordsworth in *Walden*. Emerson stands Carlyle on his head in refusing the idea of history as providing emboldening models as he answers *On Heroes, Hero-Worship and the Heroic in History* with *Representative Men*. Whitman's 1855 "Song of Myself" completes and rudely corrects the 1850 *Prelude*.[7]

One does not suggest that American literature merely constitutes a series of rebuttals and responses but that embedded deep with the psychic constitution of the American author is the need for radical alteration—involving a dual process of "reduction" and "expansion."

Response may be in the form of deep, bitter, resentful anger, or it may, through rewriting English text, make the American hero the chief and relevant focal point. American writers may themselves not clearly understand the intentional myth within which they operate—the doubtful Graeco/Roman legacy or its African preservation and transmittal—but they still feel the need to be engaged in it.

Literary responses form part of this larger concept. Therefore, at one level, Melville's "Bartleby the Scrivener" exists quite independently of Dickens's *Bleak House*, for his moroseness confounds us and anticipates Kafka's, moving him beyond anything that Dickens attempted. Likewise, the young Pip in *Great Expectations* is not a mere forerunner of Huck. Because they regard phenomena differently, they respond differently. Pip is embarked on a Victorian rags-to-riches adventure (if one views him at his most superficial), but one cannot see in Huck anything other than clear hints at definitions of what it means to be American. Dickens did not undertake any such task as national self-definition; Pip's Englishness not only caters to an insular audience but also arises out of the author's narrower perception of reality. Dickens was required to do less; Twain was almost mandated to attempt more. Huck cheerfully combines elements of rascal and epic hero, the former for the popular reader, the latter for the cultural record.

Such close accounting by American writers occurs so that work may expand into "universality." But this is a troublesome word, because nearly always it is narrow, conjuring up visions of what only the European world admits. There is an agreed recognition of structures by the two sides, indicating that American and English writers have, albeit silently, admitted to certain mutualities.

Their connectedness is the point of both linkage and separation. In 1787, the English House of Lords had veto power over the House of Commons; so, in 1787, the Senate had to be constructed as a gentleman's club that would oversee the wranglings of the people's deputies. In 1787, the English accepted the Royal prerogative; likewise, Americans substituted the presidential veto. Later on, during World War II, British "orders in council" were the model for expansive American presidential power.[8]

Even though Greek words replaced some English ones, "House" was retained, as was "Speaker." True, their respective functions altered, but only slightly, as the American Revolution was spawned in Europe. Ferdinand Lundberg sums up in *Cracks in the Constitution* that "the British Constitution was a many-splendored thing to the American forerunners."[9] Herbert Horwill further argues that the differences between the English and American Constitution do not exist in fact but are a product of intentional myth-making:

> The distinction between them is not that one is written and the other unwritten, or that one consists of a single document while the other is a composite of many ingredients. The American Constitution has all the ingredients of the English and one more . . . [namely, that it] is not capable of being amended by the legislature.[10]

The latter point is worth emphasizing, for it again shows a degree of infallibility, often associated with divine intervention. In Horwill's words, the American Constitution was often regarded "as though believed to be verbally inspired."[11] The need to inject this degree of supreme sanction lay in the troubled scenario of the time. The humans who assembled on May 28, 1787, for the convention at State House were well aware of the troublesome condition of their European world. Their own United States was being laboriously pieced together, against the European background of the excesses that would ultimately lead to Bastille Day. More important, the model had been proven to have feet of clay; the British Constitution had come under severe pressure with Cromwell and the severance of royalty from the affairs of the English state. Before Restoration it must have seemed as if all the firm assurances of the old world had collapsed. The American Constitution attempted to define in clear and unmistakable terms the imposition of a new order and to safeguard its transmittal, uninterrupted through successive generations.

No true democratic vote was therefore required, not from slaves, free Negroes, Native Americans, or women. Indeed John Herman Randall indicts the signatories in very strong language: The American Declaration of Independence, he opines "was brought about against the wishes and resistance of a formidable minority of the people, and the declaration of independence never had the universal assay of all inhabitants of the country."[12] But the Founding Fathers can scarcely be faulted for assuming a role that Plato had assigned to his philosopher kings. They were not subject to popular approval, and certainly they may be accused of bias, even of elitism, racism, and sexism in current jargon. But their authority was supposedly secure in Greek thought and in the codification of Judaeo-Christian belief.

This is why the Founders became, in a very real sense, myth-makers. Because myths are "concerned with ultimate realities . . . set out outside of historical time . . . and frequently concern the actions of divine or semi-divine characters,"[13] the writers of the Declaration sought for the establishment of a credible mythology. Through mythology, both implicit and explicit in the text of the Declaration, both part of and apart from the writing, the Framers of the Constitution imbued their work with fundamental designs of an order patterned after Europe.

The "narrator" of any text (fictional or nonfictional) attempts to project himself as a negotiator between chaos and order. The finished work is the final document that reconciles conflicting dualities and clarifies apparently opposing truths. This is as true for the Constitution as for later artistic endeavor. For the work to be effective, whether it be a promulgation, pamphlet, or poem, it must acquiesce to the very similarities it seeks to devalue. How else can it be accepted as part of the Western canon?

Yet there is scant agreement as to what constitutes a European model. This made the task of the American creator even more gargantuan. The Euro American lawgiver and writer tried to reconcile polarities, to court a popular audience, and to appeal to a learned group at the same time. This is why John Locke's *Second Treatise on Government* (1690) "was very popular with the more literate of rank-and-file American colonists, as much on account of its brevity and simplicity as for its happy tidings about the people's vital role."[14] Locke's views could be easily understood by the general public and debated by the learned; so should the Constitution. On the other hand, David Hume's *Essays Moral, Political and Literary* (1752) "widely read by the British and American educated classes took a different stance," for it "simply demolished Locke's idea of political consent."[15] Its arguments were, however, restricted to the learned.

Against the background of clashing appeals and ideological points of reference, the task of the Euro American myth-maker became more difficult. For they had to acknowledge disagreement, synthesize disparity, and proclaim a unified stance for all to understand. This is both an invention of new Euro American myth and an extension of old European myth. The former argues for democracy, itself a fiction; the latter is rooted in European aristocratic privilege, admittedly also fictitious, but in a different sense.

Put differently, as Weisbuch contends:

American writers, in their propensity *to turn to England as the nearest most relevant comparative model*, would find themselves in reluctant agreement. They would become aware of absences not only external in America but within the environment of their imaginations. *They could neither pretend to a history that had not occurred nor alter at will the resultant social associational fabric.* They had no choice, then, but to redefine the very meanings of history and society and to reconsider the relation of either to the creation of literature.[16]

This new definition of history itself becomes a reordering, a renewal, almost an invention. Therefore, as American settlers discover a new Rome or Athens, they embark on alternatives within an old framework, much as the writers do. The concept of William Penn's woods or Joseph Smith's Latter-Day Saints actually borrows social, literary, and religious situations for an American context. In addition, and this is more pertinent to the culture, they design new paradigms. Supposedly, at the locus, there existed a new individual who was identified with the nation.

In actuality, no one (least of all "Americans") wanted conflict, and it would seem that the Anglo-French conflict from 1689 to 1763 and the subsequent Treaty of Paris had left the colonists with even stronger feelings of allegiance to England. Naturally, they savored the enormous help they had rendered the mother country. Yet, even though the colonists might have felt victimized by the process, they hesitated to indict parliamentary supremacy. John Dickinson is typical: "We do not complain of these measures. These burdens we bear heavily but gladly, as a token of our affection."[17] At the center of this "affection" was the perceived nurturing agency of the British colonial ruler. Therefore, the argument went, not even the Acts of Trade and Navigation, demonstrating conclusive elements of British overlordship, could or would sever the ties.

Linkages between colonial and colonizer, like those of serf and lord, slave and master, fall within the larger category of victim-and-victor psychological bondings. The colonial experience, providing succor to the fledgling colony, presupposed that an umbilical cord linked the two in an eternal bond. But the appalling and gruesome condition of servitude is indeed part of a larger victim/victor relationship, whereby the two become bound in a kind of pact that neither fully comprehends.

The Declaration of Independence and the Articles of Confederation affirmed an adamant independence within dependence. Adopted on November 15, 1777, the second Article emphasized that "Each state retains its sovereignty, freedom and independence." Distrust of Britain was codified as a way of life between the states. Thus, within the very foundations of nation-building, the earliest stones were set for later civil strife.

At the very bedrock of colonial perception was the need to feel secure within the bonds and boundaries of kinship ties. In a very special sense, therefore, the colonial experience in America is different from India's or Africa's. Colonists in America not only saw themselves as transplanted Europeans, but also for all practical purposes, lived and existed within this cultural ambit. Only England's denial of their locus, of their perceived place at the core of Empire, had struck a harsh note that seemed to deny them their professed loyalty. Imperial reforms, after the Treaty of Paris, were understood as willful British intentions to negate both a personal and collective vision of the American colonists. Jack P. Greene terms these notions, "a kind of sacred, if not entirely explicit, moral order,"[18] which Britain sought to deny and the young American states insisted on affirming.

For such a state of affairs to be preserved, some obvious degree of commitment on Britain's part was necessary. Once the metropolis stopped the nurturing process, the relationship became jarred and expectations could no longer be satisfied. If the association were sacred, then the need for duties to be carried out in good faith existed as a given. Edward S. Morgan demurs, arguing in "Revisions in Need of Revising" that "the British government could not run the empire without bringing on evils that appeared insufferable to men like Washington, Jefferson, John Adams, and Franklin."[19] The reality was that

> the freedom of action left to the colonists was still quite spacious, the degree of internal autonomy that remained was, for colonies, still quite extraordinary. But would the foundations of the colonial position remain secure if the new measures went unresisted? Having succeeded in their initial efforts to tighten imperial ties, would the British then rest content or would they look upon success as an invitation to assert an even greater control?[20]

Speculation certainly did not automatically lead to conflagration, but it is not merely a truism to contend that "tyranny anticipated" led to inevitable strife. Doubly ironical is the manner in which domestic British ideas and parliamentary entanglements gave respectability and validation to the unthinkable.[21] Bernard Bailyn neatly sums up the situation by asserting that the

> bearing of certain eighteenth-century British political ideas on the realities of politics in pre-Revolutionary America . . . provides the sufficient background for understanding why there was a Revolution . . . a pattern of ideas, assumptions, attitudes and beliefs given destructive shape by the opposition elements in English politics.[22]

Nor need one be astounded over the contradictory conclusion that imperialism nurtured both colony and anticolony, both pro- and anti-British feelings, for both ideological formats were part of the British debate. Britain was the superpower, and from it came a plethora of beliefs and ideas that fueled both parts of the controversy.

In a way Britain had reared its own monster. First, it had exported slightly resentful, yet nostalgic, kith and kin. The elites who had prospered had proclaimed a new aristocratic status, copied from, yet independent of, Britain's control. Small farmers, indentured servants, artisans, and shopkeepers imitated a class pattern in England, although they had not yet constituted a recognizable class in America. In turn, the haves were afraid of possible antagonism directed at them by the have-nots, especially as the latter had been placed in this condition partly because of the severity of an indigenous system. However, the new American aristocrats clung to a belief in the possibility of being admitted to the old, closed, upper echelons of British society.

American social order was pressured in an entirely different way by two non-European realities. One was the slave issue, the other the frontier. Decisions could be, and indeed were, made by the metropolitan powers of England, France, and Spain, as they went about their business of carving up the land, exchanging, bidding, conquering, compromising. But land was a local reality in America, and no amount of European conquest could make Euro Americans believe otherwise.

In the final analysis, slave labor and land provided the rift that tore America and Britain apart. The 1772 decision by Chief Justice Mansfield in England had taken the "civilized" view: Slavery was intolerable, but only in England, a fact that Benjamin Franklin both recognized and deplored. In Europe, land as an aristocratic symbol of power had been accepted as such for generations by the landless with an almost sanguine resignation. In eighteenth-century America, Euro Americans were not prepared to assume the status of slaves or landless persons, for they had sought escape from just this. It became almost mandatory to create a downtrodden mass: The Native American and the African American served that purpose.

The new ideas that flowed from Europe and legitimized the thinking of separateness did not contradict the unraveling vision of the new colonist. When Locke preached "natural rights," it was understood in a private sense, as the "inalienable rights" of propertied white males—the rich man in his castle, the poor man at his gate. Montesquieu's demand for a separation of the powers of government in order to prevent tyranny seemed to be a clarion call to respond to historical wrongs. Translated as the separation of church and state, state and states, and the limitation of power, again American response was to codify European philosophy.

Voltaire's attack on superstition and Paine's anti-Christian salvo can also be understood in this way, for the new America existed in a post-Reformation world, which had already seen the destruction of the Roman Catholic monolith. So the framers of the Declaration took great care: "Laws of Nature and of Nature's God" was a nice condensation, for in these words Voltaire, Rousseau, Paine, and late eighteenth-century pantheists were all combined. Adam Smith provided the legitimate answer to the much-hated mercantilism, infusing incipient American thinking with the "rights" of the marketplace. It should hardly be surprising that mercantilism was passed down as a kind of divine right, by which democracy and capitalism became intertwined. Finally, humanitarian idealism was infused into the whole.

Legal charges listed against George III took on the language of a formal summons: "He has abdicated Government here, by declaring us out of his Protection and waging War against us. He has plundered our Seas, ravaged our Coasts, burnt our Towns, and destroyed the Lives of our People." He was "totally unworthy [to be] the Head of a civilized Nation." For, as the charges clearly state, the king had no respect for rights, freedom, or justice. The catalog is long, and the condemnation is directed, not only at royalty, but also at parliamentary inhumanity. However, "Our British Brethren" possess "native Justice and Magnanimity" and are "our common kindred." After all, the colonies had existed under the "free System of English Laws." This sentiment claimed the ordinary British person as kin while denouncing the ruling class. In this way there could still be a union with British people, for only their aristocracy had failed to understand the unique ties that bound the two peoples together.

From its inception until the present, America constitutes appropriations from European (particularly British) law, architecture, music, philosophy, art, and literature. This is surprising only in that it was once a serious debate whether America should or should not be a German-speaking country. Until now, the English stewardship has persisted and continues to alter radically the pattern of growth and change. Long after the thirteen colonies had effectively severed relationships with England and despite the presence of other Europeans, Africans, and Asians, the Anglocentric myth persisted. Broadly speaking, European experience in eighteenth-century America remains theoretical and can be accorded any firm validity only by hindsight. There was no more a "European" frame of reference than there was an "American" one; yet, within such a generalization lies a pronounced reality. "Europe" existed not over there, in Europe, any more than Africa existed in Africa. Both were refashioned, albeit not in their own image, here in America and were given New World identity.

Eighteenth-century European factionalism could not have promoted unified concepts. If there were broad agreement as to what constituted "civilization," then there was equal disagreement as to how it came about and the global influences that had created it. Linguistic, political, and cultural barriers in Europe constituted further barriers toward the perception of Europe as some unified whole.

When American architecture claimed its validity with reference to a Graeco-Roman past and a man-god proximity, this was neither evident nor desirable among the insular British. The domain that permitted for the interaction of God and man was situated here in a new world. This concept arose out of seemingly unlimited space and the predicament of transplanted Europeans adrift in an alien landscape, which dwarfed them and rendered them immensely isolated and vulnerable. True, Shelley later said, "We are all Greeks," but there was a degree of Romantic excessiveness in his assertion. Here the practical demands of hostile landscape forced the newcomers to reach back aggressively into a past to which they felt they could lay claim without compromising their personal identity or natural independence.

What was "Grecian" in Europe (but not in England) was associated with liberty, reason, and justice. This was true particularly of the eighteenth and nineteenth centuries, when Greek sculpture, architecture, and artifacts provided escapism from the tedium of the troublesome realities of landownership and landlessness, trade and tariffs, imperial dominance and internecine repression. Grecian art, then, no longer ritualistic or functional (yet still undeniably "pagan"), became merely decorative and ornamental. These visual images, exported to America, signified rare taste, good cultivation, and excellent breeding. Jefferson's Monticello, therefore, in by-passing England, constructed a fabric which Jeffersonian America could visualize as its own by right and progeny. It was all a delightful fabrication.

For ancient Greeks, neither the Parthenon nor the Acropolis was a mere fantasy etched from the borders of their imagination. Both played important sustaining roles in Hellistic and Hellenistic culture. With the advent of their duplication in Washington, D.C., it almost seems as if American town planners had expressly undertaken the task of reconstructing ruins. Edward K. Spann claims that

> Although based on European practice, this design for America's new capital was, as Pierre L'Enfant boasted, a new plan expressive of the character of American government: it emphasized the constitutional separation of executive and legislative powers by placing the Presidential "Palace" (yet to be called the White House) and the Capitol building at opposite ends of Pennsylvania Avenue; similarly, it displayed the sovereign presence of the states in the American federal system by providing a square for each of the then fifteen states.[23]

The "myth" persisted: Europe could be imported into America. L'Enfant's plan (partially saved by Black town planner Benjamin Banneker, after L'Enfant's dismissal in 1792) imitated what he knew best—French baroque planning. Again, even in the case of Philadelphia, the touch of England was evident. True, the gridiron was modified to suit the new environment, but Thomas Holmes's Philadelphia plan of 1683 owed its origin to the very system proposed in 1666 London after the Great Fire.

American town planning, thus fashioned, bisected at right angles, flowing to the focal point of a central square. It did not anticipate immigration, population growth, and ethnic diversity. Such a design was intended for European rallies at the town center, where townspeople could gather; here, in America, it would in time become necessary to design cities that prevented such gatherings and even facilitated the dispatch of troops into inner-city areas. As Garry Wills bluntly stated, "If you live in any city in America, your home is mapped for defense from its own citizenry. There are elaborate arrangements being formed, codified, revised."[24]

Nor was this new dimension of ethnic reality in American life incorporated into administrative decision making. Exclusion from the Declaration, indeed from history itself, meant that African Americans, Native Americans, and European ethnic groups were all subjected to "ghetto" conditions, directly the result of bad town planning, but more important the direct effect of architectural imitation of Europe.

Not unnaturally, even landscape designers (like city planners, architects, painters, musicians, and writers) fall prey to this intoxication with Europe. Frederick Olmsted's visits to England committed him to what Elbert Peets terms "the English landscape style of gardening." Peets further accused Olmsted of elevating his style of the picturesque and the pastoral into "the holy word of his time, and so [Olmsted] made of it a religion." Peets further asked,

why must Central Park be an amalgam as of Herefordshire sheep walk and the location for a movie version of "Hiawatha"? We know the answers: Central Park is Nature and Nature is man's Great Solace, the only sure antidote to hurdy-gurdies, pool-rooms, factories, tenements, and all the other vicious influences of a great city.[25]

Peets is continuing the debate for autonomy that goes back to the so-called Founding Fathers; equally strident is the other side, Olmsted's, which advocates Eurocentrism. Of course, many contend that Olmsted sought to democratize public space and in this way radically departed from the conservative concerns of European private parks. This is certainly true, but in depicting his public park he was still forced to rely heavily on English models.[26]

Peets dismisses Olmsted's view of landscape art as holy writ, but we have already noted that biblical equation, like Graeco-Roman allusion, was intended to gain total and unequivocal acceptance. It is no accident that the indictments against George III have the ring of the Ten Commandments, nor that before John Hancock's signature appear the words that associate the Revolution with God—a "Firm Reliance on the Protection of divine Providence."

Both sides in the dispute claim to be "American" and to have God on their side. Olmsted himself sees the perfect designer as one who outdoes nature (God?) so that "Nature shall be employed upon it for generations, before the work he [the human designer] had arranged for her shall realize his intentions."[27] Unquestionably Olmsted realized the need to continue the myth. No doubt the Marquis of Westminster would have been a trifle horrified by such a reaction to his estate at Eton. But Olmsted's words relate a Euro American's response to the European world. Americans begin to return their phantoms to Europe.

Americans see the European past in ways through which they can mythicize it. Their conception need have no basis in reality. Yet, in a way, they seem to remain forever free in a total sense: having been removed from the old worlds of Europe (and Africa and Asia), they can invent any past they want. In a way, this is a total if somewhat distorted liberty of the imagination.

NOTES

1. Henry James, "Nathaniel Hawthorne," in *Literary Criticism* (New York: Library of America, 1984).

2. Charles Brockden Brown, "Why the Arts Are Distorted in American Life," *Literary Magazine* (July 1806), 76–77.

3. Robert Weisbuch, *Atlantic Double-Cross* (Chicago: University of Chicago Press, 1986), ix–x. For me, Weisbuch's subtext is more informative than his general thesis. Beneath his main thrust of a culturally independent United States, he shows the extent to which this country relies heavily on a belief in a British aesthetic.

4. Jan Read, *The Moors in Spain and Portugal* (London: Faber and Faber, 1974). This is a thorough and well-researched account of the Moorish cultural contribution.

5. Arnold Toynbee, *The World and the West* (New York: Oxford University Press, 1953), 98–99.

6. As quoted by Benjamin Spencer, *Quest for Nationality* (Syracuse, N.Y.: Syracuse University Press, 1957), 22.

7. Weisbuch, *Double-Cross*, 15.

8. I am relating only the more obvious examples. One could argue, of course, that European American and British people merely shared a common understanding and response to world situations.

9. Ferdinand Lundberg, *Cracks in the Constitution* (New York: Oxford University Press, 1925), 15.

10. Herbert W. Horwill, *The Usages of the American Constitution* (New York: Oxford University Press, 1925), 8–9.

11. Ibid., 22.

12. John Herman Randall, *The Career of Philosophy,* 2 vols. (New York: Columbia University Press, 1962), 634.

13. Elliot Oring, *Folk Groups and Folklore Genres: An Introduction* (Logan: Utah State University Press, 1986), 124.

14. Lundberg, *Cracks*, 19.

15. Ibid., 21.

16. Weisbuch, *Double-Cross*, xiii. Emphasis added.

17. John Dickinson, *Letters from a Farmer in Pennsylvania to the Inhabitants of the British Colonies*, published in the *Pennsylvania Chronicle* (1767–1768). Reprinted in pamphlet form in 1768. Taxation, he argued, was contrary to the principles of English law.

18. Jack P. Greene, "An Uneasy Connection: An Analysis of the Preconditions of the American Revolution," in *Essays on the American Revolution,* ed. Stephen G. Kurtz and James H. Huston (Chapel Hill: University of North Carolina Press, 1973), 55.

19. Edward S. Morgan, "Revisions in Need of Revising," in *The Challenges of the American Revolution* (New York: W. W. Norton, 1976), 51.

20. Robert W. Tucker and David C. Hendrickson, *The Fall of the First British Empire* (Baltimore: Johns Hopkins University Press, 1982), 205.

21. Moses Coit Tyler, *The Literary History of the American Revolution 1763–1783,* 2 vols. (New York: G. P. Putnam's Sons, 1897), 1:100.

22. Bernard Bailyn, *The Origins of American Politics* (New York: Knopf, 1968), 13.

23. Edward K. Spann, "The Greatest Grid: The New York Plan of 1811," in *Two Centuries of American Planning,* ed. Daniel Schaffer (Baltimore: Johns Hopkins University Press, 1988), 11–13.

24. Gary Wills, *The Second Civil War* (New York: New American Library, 1968), 36.

25. Elbert Peets, "The Landscape Design," *American Mercury* 4 (1925), 339. Emphasis added.

26. In Olmsted and his English architect, Calvert Vaux, two new researchers even see alterations in design. The new park was for the New World, and the European formality of statues was discarded for contrasts in light and shade. See Roy Rosenzweig and Elizabeth Blackmar, *The Park and the People: A History of Central Park* (Ithaca, N.Y.: Cornell University Press, 1992).

27. Peets, "Landscape Design," 133.

2
European Mythologies in America ───────────

B ecause, from the viewpoint of European settlers, Europe predates Euro
America, the need for their myth-making becomes evident. European
realities left behind, forgotten, yet partly recollected, are skewed before they
penetrate American shores. When Americans attempt to define themselves, in
whatever field or discipline, they inadvertently opt for a supposedly European
identification. As such a reality did not and does not exist in Europe, a further
process is observable—the manner in which a false past is co-opted by manufacturing fresh emblems and symbols. These products become the new images
of Euro American belief.

In its narrower sense, "myth" admits to a number of interpretations. For
Freud, myth is not collective but the individual expression of unconscious
desires. For Jung, myth typifies a collective human unconscious. Joseph Campbell, the main American articulator of folklore, posits a departure-initiation-
return cycle for what he terms the hero "monomyth." Note that "myth," even
in this sense of oral ethnic accounts, emanates from the consciousness of a
people. Likewise, in a larger sense, social myth (or the social consciousness of
a people) derives from their interpretation of who and what they believe they
are.

American culture therefore responds to foreign myths outside America—
mainly European, but also to a lesser extent African. Colonial European
dependency reinforced cultural dependency, which remained long after official
declarations of independence. The residents of the thirteen colonies, despite
their varied European (and African) origins, viewed England as the source—the
originator of their language, of their very existence.

Within the American context the only term that describes such a cultural process is "creolization," for the inhabitants of the colonies, transplanted English persons and Africans from England, underwent such a creole process in terms of language and culture. They were Anglo Europeans and non–Anglo Europeans, as well as Afro Europeans, existing far away from the nourishing element of the parent host culture.

Language in the New World was therefore "creolized," as English combined with other European tongues and reluctantly borrowed from indigenous Native American and African languages—in the latter instance particularly after the advent of the slave trade. The New World environment was different, and colonists were forced to see themselves as involved in a different encounter, in a strange landscape, featuring non-European animals, trees, and geography as well as different terms of reference—the settler as unwanted alien, subjected to assault by the rightful heirs of the land. The total experience, because it was so different from European origins, required a new way of seeing and hearing. Symbols and myths had to be restated and reordered. Territorial expansion had no European counterpart, as Europe had ended at Constantinople in the east and at the Atlantic to the west. Naming unusual things thus became important in this new challenge. Even the word "prairie" had to be borrowed from the French with the advent of western and southern expansion. Yet there is large-scale rejection by Euro Americans of the indigenous Native American myth, belief, and culture that could more appropriately address the new experience.

In a way, Anglo attitudes mark a significant departure from the colonizing effects of Euro Americans from Spain and Portugal, where the incorporation of indigenous New World myth constituted an essential part of the social fabric. The reasons for this difference may be found in the history of the Iberian peninsula that preceded New World conquest. Although the Moors had been forced to withdraw in 1492, the same year that Columbus's exploration began, they had implanted their culture for over seven hundred years. Furthermore, early Iberian New World settlers were 75 percent Andalusian. It was therefore not difficult for Spaniards and Portuguese to adapt to New World cultures, be they African or indigenous American. They had experienced a long period of cultural adjustment and had taken part in the ethnic and religious tolerance as well as the easy pluralism of the Moorish Muslims. England, a world power, was effectively cut off from this mainspring of civilizing European thought and interaction.[1]

North American experience had to be different because of this intentional attempt at peopling a new country from scratch. From the outset, the country was seen as Anglo. Later, in the nineteenth century, new immigrants were drawn from Europe, but there remained the feeling at the highest levels that British settlers were preferable. Intentional immigration policy even sought to terminate certain types of immigration from less desirable parts of Europe. What the pro-British advocates did not foresee was that the new arrivals, after compulsory sequestration in urban ghettos, would themselves move toward acquiescing to an Anglo version of European culture. The American colonial elites had absorbed the lessons of Britain, not Europe. Now, as the new possessors of power, they projected Anglo European cultural stances, which they laid down as the basis of success for the newcomers.

Both Africans and Europeans viewed their new world with an alien eye. Europeans brought modified French, German, Jewish, and Italian names but anglicized their names and themselves. Euro Americans named their new possessions—towns, land, slaves. Along with place names like Athens, Rome, Greece, and London, they sought to import their own version of Europe, to utilize it as a new image for self-definition. Naming, as they well knew, was a way of owning, of imposing their culture on others. A powerful Anglo European elite thus began the process of control, promulgating a concept of Europe that had never really existed.

Because of the Anglo European power status, a forced primary synthesis took place, which incorporated people from disparate European language groups and ethnicities. Africans as well were involuntarily and voluntarily involved in this change. This synthesis is novel, for both Europe and Africa were still in the process of establishing clearly demarcated boundaries of nation-states. Indeed, not until the nineteenth century, when the Berlin Conference arbitrarily allotted boundaries for Africa, nor until the breakup of the Holy Roman Empire, and the efforts of Garibaldi and Bismarck does one witness the emergence of African and European nations. This is why Americans (Black and White) become the first (and only) pan-Europeans.

America to this day remains linked to the Anglo metropole. As yet, it has not recovered from its dependent status, because it is still involved in justifying its situation in terms set some three hundred years ago by English colonizers. It is well nigh impossible to piece the past together, because it is disjointed and because so much has been made into myth that it becomes difficult to separate truths from falsehoods. Although Max Lerner adamantly states, "America is not a European civilization," he must still concede the following:

> Not that the Americans recoiled from everything European. Jefferson as architect translated Greek forms to the Monticello terrain, just as Jefferson as political thinker adapted the French Physiocrats and philosophes to the American revolutionary struggle. The American stonecutters carved out Greek forms with a Yankee strength and cunning of hand, just as the American shipbuilders fashioned their clipper ships with a tautness of design as economical as any design of the Greeks, yet geared to swiftness and nervous energy. Cooper and Washington Irving copied European forms even while they poured into them the content of a new continent. Emerson was a Platonist who fused the absolutism of the Greek philosopher with a Yankee astringency, and who translated the mysticism of the

Eastern sages into terms of Yankee common sense. Longfellow, Whittier, Lowell, Holmes, were a bookish circle who borrowed their poetic ideas from the library stock of European memories, even when their material was native. The poetry of Poe was the inner flash of a tortured mind whose intellectual (like his acceptance) was in European romantics.[2]

Synthesis brings about the establishment (only in America and Canada) of a European diaspora as a projection of the British coastline. America is constructed in non-Native American, non-African American, neo-Anglo terms and laboriously defined with an Anglophile mythology.

In turn, this construct is fused with an ancient past that bypasses British cultural experience and asserts two additional mythical elements: a political one that is Graeco-Roman, and a religious one that is Judaeo-Christian. These are codified in the Declaration of Independence, the Constitution, and the Articles of Confederation. New and radical European thought further infused the thinking of the Constitution's framers. Religion was not that of the Roman Catholic Church (since the Reformation had sought to render it obsolete) nor that of the Anglican Church (since the American Revolution had made it irrelevant). Instead, Deism and Primitivism combined into a legally enshrined concept of a "creator" and "Nature's God," as the Constitution states.

European icons, the visible evidence of the presence of myth, thus appear in three ways: first, the verbal or spoken text, already noted in the Declaration of Independence, the Articles of Confederation, and the Constitution. Here the word becomes action, legalized, foreshadowing the new way of life and transforming European thought from idea into experience. Throughout American history this practical application will be often observed; William Penn, the Quakers, the Amish, and the more recent Mormons all show how European belief is transformed and given substance.

The other side to the transformation of the "verbal text" is the alteration of the "heard text." The "Star Spangled Banner" and the "Battle Hymn of the Republic" give war a new spirituality and sacredness—the "right to bear arms"—no longer the last resort of contentious and desperate dissenters, but an enshrined constitutional right. Therefore, it does not seem to matter that the "musical" sound of the national anthem is taken from an eighteenth-century English drinking song of the Anacreontic Societies. The "spoken" sound has to do with fire and injustice, as Francis Scott Key witnesses British bombardment of Fort McHenry in 1814. A Congressional Act of 1931 says just that.

At still another level, the red, white, and blue of the Union Jack is replaced by the red, white, and blue of the Stars and Stripes. States are elevated to stars, a claim to their divinely inspired statehood. This is the symbolic, generalized, and thus easily understood subtextual rendering of the European symbol. When the French construct the Statue of Liberty, the total meaning is complete: "Verbal" or "seen" texts in which words become action (the Declaration, the Articles of Confederation, and the Constitution) are blended with the "heard" text in which sounds are elevated to a new martial spirituality (the Star Spangled Banner, the Battle Hymn of the Republic), and further combined with the "visual" or "symbolic" text, with its strong, generalized undertextual meanings (the Stars and Stripes, the Union Jack, and the Statue of Liberty).

Quite naturally, the supertextual public symbols proliferate in the state capitols, Supreme Court buildings, and other architectural constructions. Equally, the role of the artist becomes entirely different from his or her European counterpart for, in general, the American artist speaks for the national well-being. Each new writer sees himself or herself almost as engaged in manufacturing amendments to the Constitution by extending its text into literature.

Adam Smith fits quite neatly into the divine elevation of the state. The "invisible hand" of the marketplace has an almost theological ring to it and, not unnaturally, is adopted wholesale as the economic faith of the new nation. Thus, the evidence remains that unaware American masses were propelled by Westernized European males into the earliest concepts of the country. Ordinary people understood neither the process nor its consequences, but they knew instinctively that

> American resistance in the 1760's and 1770's was a response to acts of power deemed arbitrary, degrading and uncontrollable—a response, in itself objectively reasonable, that was inflamed to the point of explosion by ideological currents generating fears everywhere in America that irresponsible and self-seeking adventurers—what the twentieth century would call political gangsters—had gained the power of the English government and were turning first, for reasons that were variously explained, to that Rhineland of their aggression, the colonies.[3]

This was a script that could be understood by the masses at the gut level. A total appeal could not be made solely through learned sentiments of Anglicized Western-oriented White males.

Indeed, a wide gulf separated the training of the philosopher kings and the ordinary citizens in the American educational system. The problems regarding the average person may be gleaned from this:

> In sum, the task of the reading teacher throughout the entire colonial period was clearly laid out. Both methodology and content were agreed upon; the curriculum was, in effect, standardized. Moreover, no qualifications for teaching reading were necessary other than being able to read oneself. Not only did the child not write in the course of learning to read, as a matter of fact the teacher did not need to know how to write either.[4]

"Democratization" of education meant little more than "educating the individual person in a manner consistent with democratic goals [so as to] educate him for purposes identical with his own interests."[5]

This is indeed a very perverse notion of a democratic process, for it led to serious discrepancies, later on (indeed as late as the twentieth century) advocated by African Americans like W. E. B. Du Bois, when he opted for the training and educating of a "talented tenth." It had never been the intention of the Anglo elite, from the very beginnings of the Republic up until the present, to educate the masses. Hence, the need for the "seen," "heard," and "symbolic" renderings. They survive today in the "bear" and "bullish" representation of Wall Street and in the visualization of the two major parties as two animals— elephant and mule. Seemingly, only thus can the masses comprehend.

At the very center of popular European belief was total belief in the Bible. In 1693, John Locke had laid out the outline for the reading curriculum: from "hornbooks" with their alphabet to the very apex of accomplishment, the ability to read the Bible. Despite Reformation and Counter-Reformation, printing presses in America had served to spread basic religious belief. Nor was the Word of God disturbed by the Revolution, as (again it must be stressed) it had bypassed Englishness, rendering the godhead in quaint Judaeo-Christian terms. Troublesome niceties, such as Christ as olive-skinned Jew, were put aside. After all, Europe had done as much, and the rich, ornate renderings of Catholic and Protestant churches had remade the Christ figure in the recognizable image of a blond blue-eyed male. Americans simply continued the adaptation process. Perhaps it reached its true climax (or nadir) with Joseph Smith's "discovery" and "translation" of the holy texts that he found in New York State. The originals were burned, we are reliably informed: *The Book of Mormon* exists as the supreme supertext fashioned from the American penchant and need for mythmaking.

Americans never departed too far from accepted European "universalities." American concepts of God, democracy, and capitalism were not shifts from European norms, but merely radical points at the extreme of the European parameter. Only with the Marshall Plan does one observe an inversion of this order. Here America becomes the donor to Europe, but the case must not be exaggerated, for America exports only material artifacts.

Persistent voices in America did insist on a vision different from the norm. But there was still a heavy dependency on European thinking. Thoreau lived out Wordsworth's Lake District fantasies at Walden; Emerson, and later Whitman, articulated the need for an American culture, but it would not radically depart from its European parent. For, even as they summon American antithetical responses to European theses, even as they seek to substitute Americana for Europeana, they do so within an agreed prescription. In responding and reacting to Europe, they are arguing for positives where they detect negatives. Such a dialogue could not be maintained on only one side: By its very nature, it must presuppose a knowledge of European reference points. Thus, even though the debate moves out and beyond European parameters, it could hardly have existed without a European paradigm. Only by denying certain European values could American intellectuals, however radical, affirm alternative American ones.

Rousseau's "Noble Savage" is a case in point, for he was conjuring up an imaginary and totally confused version of the New World. Europeans had identified the Noble Savage as Native American and/or African—they could never be sure which, because the two were inextricably bound in the muddle of post-Columbian European exploration. Ancient beliefs obtrude into New World American everyday concerns and, in America, are both doubted and believed at the same time.

The Noble Savage had seemingly honorable origins. In Greece, Homer, among others, had idealized the Arcadians who later appeared in Canada and New Orleans. Latin writers, like Horace, Virgil, and Ovid, equated the Scythians with Homer's Arcadians. They were unlettered sheepherders, who had observed the lessons of life by living close to the natural world. In England, as early as 1673, an Anglo New World version appears in Richard Ligon's *A True and Exact History of the Island of Barbados*, where an "Indian woman," Yarico, is rescued by an English sailor before being sold into slavery. Steele's version, in the *Spectator* of March 3, 1711, is a little different: The sailor is called Inkle and lives with Yarico in America before leaving for Barbados. English poems, novels, and plays abound with name changes and variations of the theme.[6] Aphra Behn's *Oroonoko* gives her African prince the name of the Orinoco River, thereby further illustrating the chaos that arises out of this muddle.

More pertinent for our concerns is Rousseau's *Émile* (1762), the subject of which is the education of a young boy, free from the corrupting effects of European life. Rousseau's dictum was "to prevent anything from being done."[7] Until the age of five, the child should live in the countryside. After five, there would be no dependence on humans, "which is the effect of the society."[8] The child will learn about duty and obligation and should not be taught history, languages, or even how to draw: "Lest through the substitution of strange fantastic shapes for the reality, he should lose his sense of proportion and his taste for the beauties of nature."[9] The wise tutor avoids taking the child away from what is natural, for most academic subjects may be taught by relying on physical and natural representations, not by delving into atlases. Thus the child becomes "Robinson Crusoe on his island, deprived of the help of his fellow men and the instruments of the arts."[10] For reason and intellect, emotions were substituted. At fifteen, when childhood ends, the child will enter society, with his tastes having been formed by nature.

Against the background of widespread illiteracy, this should hardly have appealed to eighteenth-century Americans as a feasible prospect. Yet, despite the American reality of the presence of a lifesize "Indian" Inkle, and a real African Oroonoko, European myth was still borrowed. Its assumption by

Americans showed the defects of a colonized mind, rejecting its own reality in favor of the colonizer's fantasy. Europeans may not have been able to distinguish between Oroonoko, with his Caucasian features, or the "Indian" Yarico. They did not detect that Émile, despite Rousseau's contention, is more recognizable as Friday (a creature of the New World) than as Crusoe (an Englishman). As Americans faced a new reality, they ought to have been able to discard these European fictions.

An enormous problem of cultural transferral thus emerges. How do Americans accept European "universals," even when they clearly conflict with everyday American reality? American thinkers knew their own truths, for they were aware of clear differences (even though their own more "mythical" ones) between "Indian" and "African." The former could be an aggressor, not the passive creature of Nature; the latter could be a suspicious victim and certainly no Arcadian. American thinkers and the general populace could both have agreed that Émile was not a realistic possibility in the New World, given the grave hostility of the natural environment, illiteracy, and the need to improve the practical business of everyday material conditions. Yet this never happened; European myth, with its strong British preference, persisted.

Benjamin Franklin had earlier on pointed out that the consequences of non-English immigration were a sure way of destroying the carefully built-up mythological link with England. Thus his objection to Palatinate settlement in Pennsylvania:

> And since detachments of English from Britain, sent to America, will have their places at home so soon supplied and increase so largely here, why should Palatine boors be suffered to swarm into our settlements and, by herding together, establish their language and manners to the exclusion of ours? Why should Pennsylvania, founded by the English, become a colony of aliens, who will shortly be so numerous as to germanize us instead of our anglifying them, and will never adopt our language or customs any more than they acquire our complexion?[11]

Franklin then concluded:

> Which leads me to add one remark, that the number of purely white people in the world is proportionably very small. All Africa is black or tawny; Asia chiefly tawny; America (exclusive of the newcomers), wholly so. And *in Europe, the Spaniards, Italians, French, Russians, and Swedes are generally of what we call a swarthy complexion; as are the Germans also,* the Saxons only excepted, who, with the English, make the principal body of white people on the face of the earth. I could wish their numbers were increased. And while we are, as I may call it, scouring our planet by clearing America of woods, and so making this side of our globe reflect a

brighter light to the eyes of inhabitants in Mars or Venus, *why should we, in the sight of superior beings, darken its people? Why increase the sons of Africa by planting them in America*, where we have so fair an opportunity, by excluding all blacks and tawnies, of increasing the lovely white and red? But perhaps I am partial to the complexion of my country, for such kind of partiality is natural to mankind.[12]

The last words, *omitted by Franklin in subsequent reprintings of his work*, are the precursor to popular misconceptions of Malthus and Mendel and also embarrassingly echo some of the more extreme present-day racist theories. Fierce ethnocentric attachment to the Anglophilic ideal had to lead to Franklin's conclusions and in turn inevitably seemed to place Native American/African American existence outside the domain of Euro American humanity.

Thomas Jefferson claimed to be an authority on the differences between Native Americans and African Americans, bemoaning the fact "that though for a century and a half we have had under our eyes the races of black and of red men, they have never yet been viewed by us as subjects of natural history."[13] Jefferson further suggests, "as a suspicion only, that the Blacks, whether originally a distinct race, or made distinct by time and circumstances, are inferior to the whites in the endowments both of body and mind."[14] When he compares Native Americans and Blacks, he finds that, even though some Blacks were educated and exposed to the arts and sciences of the West, he was not able to identify any Black person who "had uttered a thought above the level of plain narration," nor had he ever seen "even an elementary trait of painting or sculpture" among them.[15] On the other hand,

The Indians, with no advantages of this kind, will often carve figures on their pipes not destitute of design or merit. They will crayon out an animal, a plant, or a country, so as to prove the existence of a germ in their minds which only wants cultivation. They astonish you with strokes of the most sublime oratory; such as prove their reason and sentiment strong, their imagination glowing and elevated.[16]

Actually, Jefferson is not half as outrageous as he seems. He is accepting the primitivism of his European counterparts, but excluding Blacks from his own consideration. He is putting forward a view in keeping with, yet partly independent of, European theory. He is setting straight the Native American/African American muddle and concluding that the Native American might indeed be an appropriate candidate for the European Noble Savage. Of course, in doing this, he constructs his own mythology. As he himself knew, the very African Americans of whom he spoke so harshly became part of his own extended family and helped him construct and maintain order at Monticello.[17]

Jefferson's acceptance of the "Indian" and rejection of the "Black" affects a compromise between European idealism and American factuality. At that time, Native Americans no longer constituted a serious threat in terms of eastern monoethnic settlement, and African Americans certainly did not. Later on, Native Americans, having been driven south and west, would be housed in reservations; African Americans, not because of state benevolence but because of the need for them in a free work force, had to live among Whites. Their presence as slaves could be seen as positive reinforcement of Euro American claims to Eurocentric hierarchy. Alexis de Tocqueville is most relevant here, pointing out the link between American slaveholder and European aristocrat:

> the position then in all southern families was the same as is still found in noble families in certain parts of Europe, where the younger members, though they do not have the eldest son's wealth, live a life as idle as his. Entirely similar causes produced this same effect both in America and in Europe. In the South of the United States the whole white race formed an aristocratic body having at its head a certain number of privileged persons whose wealth was permanent and leisure hereditary. These leaders of the American nobility perpetuated the traditional prejudices of the white race in the body they represented, making idleness honorable.[18]

However, Tocqueville saw only two clear alternatives:

> Once one admits that white and emancipated Negroes face each other like two foreign peoples on the same soil, it can easily be understood that there are only two possibilities for the future: the Negroes and the whites must either mingle completely or they must part.[19]

Integration was not an option that Jefferson publicly desired. He articulated the view that, should slavery be abolished, African Americans should be forced to live by themselves. On the other hand, Tocqueville thought that Southern Whites might be forced off the land. "Perhaps" he adds "the White race in the South will suffer the fate of the Moors in Spain"—an interesting comparison.

Above all, part of the view of the African American as nonhuman was consistent with European intellectual thought and easily blended with the Eurocentric views of American Anglophiles. In England, from the eighteenth century to the early twentieth century, Africans were confined to one phase—interesting objects of curiosity. As "pets," they were brought to England, officially or unofficially adopted, and then sent to school as part of a grand experiment. The pet is an object, to be nurtured and trained in the master's image. Francis Williams, a pet of the Duke of Montagu, was an eighteenth-century Jamaican, trained at Cambridge. He penned Latin elegies to successive English governors, describing himself as a "white man acting under a black skin."[20] He was as much a product of the Anglocentric colonial world as was Thomas Jefferson.

Quite serious and sincere attempts were made by European aristocrats to ascertain the intellectual capability of Africans, much as Jefferson had done. Even earlier on, in Spain, Juan Latino (1516–1594) was educated in the household of the Duke of Sesa, writing poems in Latin and translating Horace. He also became a university professor.[21] Later on, in a German state, Duke Anton Ulrich von Braunschweig-Wolfenbüttel brought a young African, later called Anton Wilhelm (the names of the duke and his son) Amo (since he too was expected to be a Latin prodigy).[22] Amo proved their point; after his formal education at the University of Halle, he became a professor and wrote several books of logic in Latin. Apparently the experiments did convince Europeans that Blacks could reason. Dr. Johnson enjoined his own "pet," Frances Barber: "You can never be wise unless you love reading."[23] In a way, this was putting Rousseau to the test.

Jefferson dismissed all contemporary Black writers. He seemed to have been especially hard on Phillis Wheatley, whose poems were published in London in 1773.[24] Other Blacks who published in English, including Ignatius Sancho (b. 1729), Ottobah Cugoano (b. 1748), and Olaudah Equiano or Gustavus Vassa (b. 1745), were all condemned.[25] Jefferson derided Sancho's *Letters* of 1784 as imitative, arguing that he was "compelled to enroll him [Sancho] at the bottom of the column."[26]

For people of Jefferson's time, the first truly great schism comes about over Blacks, between total adherence to European cultural reference points and the conflicting claims of a stubborn American prejudice. Blacks were not even what Kipling in 1899 would later term the "white man's burden," whereby Whites were duty bound to turn even ungrateful Blacks away "from bondage" and their "loved Egyptian night" toward civilization. One may contend that Europeans were hypocritical, as their slavocracy gave way to colonialism or even as their pious explanations sought to justify their brutality, but at least their unfamiliarity made their actions a little more understandable than Jefferson and his peers.

For race as an issue did not occur in Britain until recently. Colonialism, with its comforting assurances of the colonizer's benevolent role, kept Black racial problems in colonies, much as slavery, earlier on, had expelled Africans to the colonies. England was good at maintaining a clean house. The colonies, including America, inherited the deleterious effects of metropolitan-mandated policies.

Jefferson, his contemporaries, and those who succeeded him had to wrestle with the consequences of an ill-conceived British policy. Their conclusions were pragmatic, for one's next-door neighbor (the African), especially if he evoked fear of possible reprisals, could not be romanticized as an exotic creature. In fact, he had to be "removed beyond the reach of mixture," as Jefferson made note.[27]

In this way, at least to some extent, Native Americans and African Americans demythologized themselves, or rather were demythicized, from European cultural process. But a newer, differing myth is projected. For instance, concerning the Native American:

> By the late seventeenth century, on the eastern shore of Virginia and Maryland, Indians were hunted like wolves, with a bounty on their heads, as a menace to society. . . . As more and more Indians were displaced by the white westward migration, it became apparent that something had to be done about the Indians who surrendered. Defined as pariahs, they were no longer acceptable within white society.[28]

So, indeed, between the period of Jefferson's *Notes* and the mid-nineteenth century, European images of the Native American and the African American were recreated out of American practical considerations and not out of some noble European impulse. American reality, at least as perceived by early Euro Americans and even later European immigrants, had little occasion or need to sentimentalize Native Americans and African Americans.

Eventually Native American and African American therefore reached a common low ground, dislodged from the legendary European height of Noble Savage to the depths of ignoble barbarian. But examples survive in American literature of attempts by writers such as James Fenimore Cooper and Mark Twain to contest, even to subvert, this view and (not surprisingly) to resuscitate the untainted European concept of nobility and docile savagery. This is even more surprising, since Cooper and Twain were not abstract theorizers but men of the world who intimately knew the reality of American life. Yet, the Noble Savage still lingers in their work, almost as a postscript to European letters.

This reimportation of the Noble Savage into the framework of American thought displays a dual consciousness that speaks to the condition of a divided mind. Actually, the Noble Savage does not emerge until the mid-nineteenth century in American letters, but one must still be shocked and surprised that he is realized at all. If our preceding arguments have any significance, they surely continue to emphasize the important point of the difficulties of true cultural separation. For despite their authors' firm American rootedness, Cooper's *Leather-Stocking Tales* and Melville's *Moby Dick* continued to exhibit the prevalence of European metropolitan myth long after political freedom had affirmed the pragmatic correctness and value of place.

Chingachgook, a Noble Savage chief, and his son Uncas show one side to this problem of a divided American consciousness. Despite the romanticization of the Native American chief, Cooper has his readers witness a realistic clash of cultures, the age-old conflict between settler/homesteader and drifter/cowboy, as well as the tension between human law and natural law. This is done through the eyes of Natty Bumpo, "a sort of type of what

Adam might have been supposed to be before the fall."[29] The biblical equation must not be missed, for it extends the frontier narrative to Europe via the Bible. The point remains that Native Americans are seen, understood, and realized only through Natty's values, through the eyes of White maleness, which is the Euro American embodiment of the rational. Thus, ipso facto, the Native American/African American must be equated with the irrational. Intellectual rationality is the White European male's "reward" (what Virginia Woolf terms his "opiate") for acknowledged supremacy, accorded by the state and arising from his prescribed status within it. In turn, this "right" sustains him in the Eurocentric system's sense of place within a male-centered White universe. Cooper has an English servant in *The Redskins* (1846) say, "The nigger grows uglier and uglier every year, and that is the most of a change I can see in him while I do think, Sir, that the Indian grows 'andsomer and 'andsomer. He's the 'andsomest old gentleman, Sir, as I know of, far and near!"[30] The narrator of this one section can easily agree with both Jefferson and Franklin. Together, they all easily identify villainy in the other, while pinpointing virtue in themselves. The result is an unabashed self-laudation that has to be understood in the ethnic context of the European birthright in the New World diaspora.

In *The Last of the Mohicans* (1757), Cora Munro identifies with Native Americans, drawing this parallel between her part–African American ancestry and that of the Native American, Tamenund. Their status is a result of "fate, the curse of my ancestors," as Cora calls it. Additionally, Cooper's work in *The American Democrat* (1838) clearly states the Euro American response to nineteenth-century conditioning: "All men are not 'created equal' in a physical, or even a moral sense, unless we limit the signification to one of political rights. This much is true, since human institutions are a human invention, with which nature has had no connection."[31]

Cooper prophesies with discomfiting honesty that "after slavery two races will exist in the same region, whose feelings will be embittered by inextinguishable hatred and who carry on their faces, the respective stamps of their factions."[32] Tocqueville concurs in *Democracy in America*:

> In that part of the Union where the Negroes are no longer slaves, have they come closer to the whites? Everyone who has lived in the United States will have noticed just the opposite. Race prejudice seems stronger in those states that have abolished slavery than in those where it still exists, and nowhere is it more intolerant than in those states where slavery was never known.[33]

Cooper has one redeeming excuse; Native Americans were as unfamiliar to him as to Europeans. Although some critics aver that Cooper's view of Native Americans was more complex, Roy Harvey Pearce contends, "We can observe how Cooper set the pattern for writers who would treat of the Indians, and how after him imaginative realization of the idea of savagism became a prime means to the understanding of American progress in the glories, tragedies, and risks."[34] For here in literature, as with the visual arts, the Native American/African American is given ultrahistorical status outside the Eurocentric world, thus replacing the concept of "men ... created equal." Reduced to brute level, stigmatized by color, caste, and slave/serf origin, they are sacrificed to the intellectual Euro American aristocratic ideal.

Melville's *Moby Dick* (1851) even extends the Native American/African American metaphor into the so-called Third World. Queequeg is Ishmael's early companion and a Polynesian prince; the crew of the *Pequod* includes Fedallah (a Parsee) and Asians, who are puzzling and mysterious. The Native American/African American aspect is seen in Tashtego, the Indian harpooner; Daggoo, a continental African, and Pip, the African American cabin boy. They introduce elements of some globalness into the Ahab/Ishmael search for world dominance; because Melville is American, he can attempt this rendering outside familiar Anglo European insular concepts. But alas, even he succumbs to stereotyping in the British manner. Pip (who ten years later Dickens would make into an "American" rags-to-riches hero) goes insane—or, at least, his vision of God makes him a social outcast. We are reliably informed by Melville that Pip "saw God's foot upon the treadle of the loom and spoke it," but this is not evident even in the novel's deepest textual meaning. What comes over is that Pip is a victim/object, Ahab's pet, and doomed to destruction.[35]

Only Ishmael outlives the world holocaust, certainly not because he is inherently good. Unlike Ahab (Arab?), who proves his own unworthiness, and the non-European/Third World characters (whose unworthiness is assumed), Ishmael is the embodiment of a super person, whose gender and ethnicity are contiguous with his autonomous and almost self-generating being. Because of a Eurocentric society-conferred power, Ishmael (from the Hebrew "God hears") is able to subjugate evil. His name-ancestry is interesting, for he represents both New World African European "outcast" and the son of Old World biblical archetypes, Abraham and Hagar. Ishmael's situation is further complicated because his descendant is the progenitor of Arabs (Ahab). Queequeg, despite his Polynesian aristocracy, has a difficult task as "pet." His coffin helps preserve Ishmael until he is rescued. Fedallah dies, before the *Pequod* is itself destroyed. Despite its color change, the *white* whale does triumph, as does the White Judaeo-Christian male Ishmael.

Seemingly, American writers remain trapped within a cycle of conflicting motifs, unable to posit a worldview at variance with perceived European belief. American literature does possess "idealized momentary associations,"[36] but that is indeed what they are—idealized. Of course, writers do go far beyond the limitations of English insularity (Conrad, no Englishman, excepted), but Natty Bumpo and his Indians, Huck Finn and his Nigger, Jim, as well as Ishmael and his crew, lead to an inevitable conclusion—another point of European and Euro American failed rapprochement. Even as the Anglo American male figure constantly prevents the restoration of order in the universe, the Native American and African make attempts, however inconsequential, at bringing back that sense of balance.

Schism with Europe principally came about because of this uncouth need to render Native American/African American humanity in nonpeople terms. Hiawatha became a national joke, parodied by successive generations of writers, because no "significant one" can accord to the "insignificant other" any claims to humanity, much less richness of spirit. Although Hiawatha is a "good Injun" and, before departing for the Isles of the Blest, warns his people to take up the new Christian religion with its Eurocentric appurtenances, readers are unwilling to accord him the position of epic hero and civilizer. Tarzan more easily does this later on, in a quaint role reversal, for Edgar Rice Burroughs cleverly appropriates the belief in "Indian Power" over landscape (Hiawatha's affinity with the natural world—the moon, Lake Superior, birds, and animals) and transfers them to Tarzan. Thus the Euro American myth of Native American power is placed, rightfully, in the context of the Eurocentric value system, within the province of the powerful White male. Tarzan (curiously only for those outside the orbit of American myth-making) takes on these accepted "Indian" powers to "civilize" Africans. As English aristocrat and inherent automatic decision maker, he can pass on his God-inherited order to the decision takers—mythical Africans in an equally mythical jungle.

American "rationalization" of their own reality therefore takes the European schema further. Noah Webster's 1828 *Dictionary* posits the dualism, as perceived by Euro Americans: On the one hand Native Americans possess "truth, fidelity and gratitude to their friends"; on the other, they are "implacably cruel and revengeful toward their enemies." Twain, Cooper, Webster, and the men of their time are trapped between a need to acknowledge European belief in Native American nobility, and a necessity to affirm a Euro American concept of Native Americanness. Kay Seymour Howe adds, "Since it was far easier to lament a race than preserve it, Americans accepted Indian extinction as inevitable and indulged themselves in sentimental nostalgia for a lost cause that was assuredly lost but that had never been a cause."[37] Consequently, a discrepancy exists between European "cause," located in fantasy, and American "effect," rooted in pragmatism. The "cause" paid lip service to European thought, but the "effect" acknowledged American racism.

Anglo American realistic dominance and hegemony established itself as the "positive," against which the Native American/African American stereotype would have to be adjusted as the "negative." In the process the latter would be defined as minor/minority, suggesting not merely a smaller numerical head count but also an irrelevant, contradictory culture, accorded an insignificant position in the cultural hierarchy. The result was the same for both Native

American and African American, as Tocqueville already recognized. John W. Blassingame equated it as follows:

> To argue, as some scholars have, that the first slaves suffered greatly from the enslavement process because it contradicted their "heroic" warrior tradition, or that it was easy for them because Africans were by nature docile and submissive, is to substitute mythology for history. The enslavement of Africans was intimately related to the history of Indian-white relations in the New World and certain historical and anthropological principles. . . . Neither group made effective slaves. On the other hand, in spite of the myths surrounding the "noble red man," when Europeans encountered Indians of a higher culture accustomed to systematic agricultural labor and sedentary habits (as did the Spaniards in Mexico and other parts of South America), the Indians were reduced to slavery or something closely akin to it.[38]

This inevitability of downgrading Native American/African American peoples arose not only out of historical necessity (although, obviously this played an important part) but also from the need to alter and change Euro American and European terms of agreement.

As Europe was globally dominant, items of its old cultural milieu had to be extrapolated and projected onto the American scenario. Such a transfer had to bring about a discontinuance, even a rupture in American values, since American-applied reality effectively altered the earlier arrangement.

In the nineteenth century, ancient subordination to land was replaced by dominance of the machine. In any case, in Europe, as older horizons closed, "nation" could be understood as lived reality, not necessarily connected with the claims of familiar terrain or traditional human ties. But as it took almost two weeks for communications to travel from England to America, it required almost a decade or two for European ideas to be transplanted. Thus the Industrial Revolution arrived in America when people were still intrinsically bound up with the land and when a non-urban mass (particularly in the South) would resist the invasion on aristocratic privilege.

Nineteenth-century history marks the collapse of an agreed order. At the center was the individual (European) in a group context, who was unable to prevent the change. In Europe, the Industrial Revolution disturbed the age-old position of landed gentry. By doing this, the easy ability of the "marching men" (the new mill owners and factory owners) to purchase social class upset the legendary status (and spiritual claims) of the "lords." Second, by the end of the century, Darwin's theories and those of earlier evolutionists confounded agreed theological reliance on accepted world order. In the same way that American folk society seemed to exist outside the construction of the older order, so it continued to remain apart from its destruction.

Similarly, the "landed gentry" in America should also have been outside strictures of change, for they were, in reality, large landowners who owed their estates to former colonial regal largesse. Their status contradicted the radical claims to an independent revolution, and it embarrassed others abroad with whom they sought alliance. For whereas in Europe peasants were becoming tenants, in America the slavocracy had to hold if the status quo were to be maintained. Thus, in an interesting manner, abolition became mandatory, as only in this way could Euro Americans once more gain full acceptance within the European family of nations.

A new situation called for the invention of new logic. At first, at the beginning of the Republic, there was little conflict. Just as individuals, at the personal level, were associated with the immediate extended family grouping, and coidentified with respective colonies, so, later on, as individual colonies merged into the proto-nation, individual consciousness altered and expanded into a new concept of nationhood. In Europe, the Industrial Revolution had helped ease this development, for it forcibly (through economic means) released humans from peasant status to worker status, from dependence on "farm" to reliance on "firm," in all instances away from the stability of the village church.

With the European dismantling of old theological foundations, the ex-colonial predicament of America is further stressed. No longer could common agreement be based on mutual acceptance of an old theology. Although, in the midpart of the nineteenth century, God still flourished in Britain, demise in Europe was imminent. As a European, Ibsen could demonstrate the utter futility of life, in, say, *Hedda Gabler*, or could mock death and the promise of an afterlife in *The Master Builder*. But there is little in English literature to mark this move away from faith in an old theocracy to new outright individual quest. Dostoyevsky, almost singlehandedly, propelled the novel into the twentieth century by taking away its raison d'être as man-in-society, substituting instead person-in-a-void. Yet Robert Browning could still claim that "God's in His Heaven/All's right with the World."

Browning, in time, would become odd man out in Europe, for in 1922 T. S. Eliot would correct the supposedly wrong assumption of composure with a new multilayered text that, at one stage, would state a personal and generational inability to connect. All around, Eliot argued in *The Waste Land* (1922) lay a Europe in need of redemption, of saving. Not only did it suffer from the wounds of the recent war, but the carnage wrought by moral bankruptcy was omnipresent. Despite appearances to the contrary, Eliot was an American; true, a Jamesian Anglophile, but an American none the less. As such he, like Ezra Pound and indeed the entire generation of the 1920s, takes on and takes over pan-European consciousness, which is German, French, Italian, and English but especially American, all at the same time.

American Europhiles can pretty well opt for any national space—clearly denied to the culturally contained British. But in the twenties this was not merely the province of the Euro American, as had hitherto been the case. African American males like Langston Hughes and Richard Wright, female African Americans like Josephine Baker, Jessie Fauset, and Nella Larsen, and the female Jewish American, Gertrude Stein, were all equally at home in Europe. Such considerations will come later on in this study, but they are mentioned here as logical extensions through which former colonized myth-takers themselves become myth-makers.

NOTES

1. Jan Read, *The Moors in Spain and Portugal* (London: Faber and Faber, 1974), 53–59, 71–85, 92–96, 147–151, 174–180, 212–219.

2. Max Lerner, *America as a Civilization* (New York: Henry Holt, 1987), 974.

3. Bernard Bailyn, *The Origins of American Politics* (New York: Knopf, 1968), 13.

4. Jennifer Monaghan, "Literary Search and Gender in Colonial New England," *American Quarterly* 40, no. 1 (March 1928): 22–23.

5. Joseph P. Callahan and Leonard H. Clark, *Introduction to American Education* (New York: Macmillan, 1977), 61.

6. See Hoxie Neale Fairchild, *The Noble Savage* (New York: Columbia University Press, 1928), for a thorough although somewhat pedantic study.

7. Jean Jacques Rousseau, *Émile* (Woodbury, N.Y.: Barron's Educational Series, 1964), 61.

8. Ibid., 92.

9. Ibid., 133.

10. Ibid., 162.

11. Benjamin Franklin, "Observation Concerning the Increase/Peopling of Mankind, of Countries, etc.," in *The Writings,* 10 vols., ed. Albert H. Smyth (New York: Macmillan, 1905), 3:72.

12. Franklin, *Writings*, 3:73. Emphasis added.

13. Thomas Jefferson, "Notes on the State of Virginia," in *The Portable Thomas Jefferson*, ed. Merrill D. Peterson (London: Penguin, 1975), 192.

14. Jefferson, "Notes," 192.

15. Ibid., 188–189.

16. Ibid., 188.

17. Recent scholarship has not sought to ignore the position of Sally Hemmings as mistress. See especially *Jeffersonian Legacies,* ed. Peter S. Onuf (Charlottesville: University Press of Virginia, 1993), which arose out of the October 1992 conference held at the University of Virginia. There the debate about Jefferson's "mongrel" family continued to rage.

18. Alexis de Tocqueville, *Democracy in America* [1899], ed. J. P. Mayer (New York: Harper and Row, 1969), 349.

19. Ibid., 355, 358.

20. Edward Long, *History of Jamaica* (London: Printed for T. Lowndes, 1774), 478.

21. Valaurez B. Spratlin, *Juan Latino: Slave and Humanist* (New York: Spinner Press, 1938), also has some fairly decent English translations of Latino's poetry, 90–202.

22. J. W. Schulte Nordholt, *Het Volk dat in duisternis Wandelt* (Arnhem, 1956), 17. I comment on Latino and his critics in my book *The Black Mind* (Minneapolis: University of Minnesota Press, 1974), 68–73.

23. James Boswell, *The Life of Samuel Johnson,* 2 vols. (London: Swan, Sennenschein, 1888 ed.), 1:145.

24. See *The Poems of Phillis Wheatley,* ed. Julian D. Mason (Chapel Hill: University of North Carolina Press, 1966). Also see *The Collected Works of Phillis Wheatley,* ed. John Shields (New York: Oxford University Press, 1988).

25. More recent scholarship has tended to stress a more politically oriented agenda on the part of some of these early African Brits. See Keith A. Sandiford, *Measuring the Moment* (Cranbury, N.J.: Susquehanna University Press, 1988); and Folarin Shyllon, *Black People in Britain* (London: Oxford University Press, 1977).

26. Jefferson, "Notes," 339.

27. Ibid., 7.

28. Reid Luhman and Stuart Gilman, *Race and Ethnic Relations: The Social and Political Experience of Minority Groups* (Belmont, Calif.: Wadsworth Publishing, 1980), 236–237.

29. James Fenimore Cooper, *The Pathfinder* [1840] (New York: G. P. Putnam's Sons, n.d.), 139.

30. James Fenimore Cooper, *The Redskins* [1846] (New York: G. P. Putnam's Sons, n.d.), 307.

31. James Fenimore Cooper, *The American Democrat* (Cooperstown: H & E Phinney, 1838), 4.

32. Cooper, *American Democrat,* 175.

33. Tocqueville, *Democracy,* 343.

34. Roy Harvey Pearce, *The Savages of America* (Baltimore: Johns Hopkins University, 1953), 197.

35. Toni Morrison comments that even in the distorted presence of African Americans or their absence, "the shadow hovers in implication, in sign, in line of demarcation." See Toni Morrison, *Playing in the Dark* (Cambridge, Mass.: Harvard University Press, 1992), 46–47.

36. Richard Chase, "Melville and Moby Dick," in *Melville: A Collection of Critical Essays,* ed. Richard Chase (Englewood Cliffs, N.J.: Prentice-Hall, 1962), 57.

37. Kay Seymour Howe, *Cooper's Americans* (Columbus: Ohio State University Press, 1963), 161.

38. John W. Blassingame, *The Slave Community* (Oxford: Oxford University Press, 1979), 4.

3

New Haven Africans and
New England Transcendentalists ──────────

Despite the manner in which Anglo orientation plagued American cultural development, there were always countermovements as sectors of American society continued to push for independent stances. One of these was evident during the trial of fifty-three Africans who had appeared off the coast of New England in 1839 and claimed to be free people. For almost two years they lived in the area and fought their case. One African American even returned to Africa with them after the Supreme Court had ruled in their favor.[1]

The Transcendentalists did not have this option of leaving. They had established Brook Farm, near West Roxbury, Massachusetts, between 1841 and 1847. They had also set up another cooperative community, Fruitlands, at Harvard, between June 1844 and January 1845. When their two settlements did not succeed, they were forced to close them down.[2]

There are some points of similarity between these two groups. Both were living as outsiders, apart from Euro American mainstream society. Both were seeking to establish group attitudes as a way of life. At Brook Farm, Fruitlands, and the African community in New Haven, the emphasis on community life meant that labor was a common endeavor that would benefit the welfare of all members. One major distinction existed: The New Haven African group had been forced into its position of isolation, although its community did remain a logical extension of African folkways. On the other hand, the Transcendentalists had freely opted for a lifestyle at variance with the prevailing Anglocentric one.

Neither of these two groups remained totally outside the control of Anglocentric America. To some extent, the New Haven Africans were prevented from this, owing to the constant vigilance of well-meaning members of various missionary societies, who saw in the Africans good fodder for their plans to evangelize Africa. The African group was forced to depend on the larger American community for support, whereas both Transcendentalist communities attempted to be self-sufficient, even if they did not succeed. New Haven Africans faced the task of converting a not-too-willing public into becoming ardent supporters of their cause and supplying them with money, food, clothing, and shelter. At one stage, the sum of four hundred dollars was raised in Philadelphia, mainly from African Americans; at another point, the New Haven group was entertained at one of the best area hotels free of charge; at Lowell, when they visited a rug factory, the employees gave them a donation. On still another occasion, some of the New Haven Africans performed acrobatics in public, much to the chagrin of their well-wishers and their own consternation. But this was their form of fund-raising.[3]

Nathaniel Hawthorne lived at Brook Farm and afterward wrote *The Blithedale Romance* (1852) about his experiences there. Louisa May Alcott was the daughter of Bronson Alcott, one of the major influences behind both communities. She related, a trifle satirically, in "Transcendental Wild Oats" (1876) her father's social experiments at Fruitlands. Both Hawthorne and Louisa May Alcott stress the way in which the outside world brought about the collapse of the communities. For the Africans, their community had a temporary nature to it, ending when their court battle was successful. Their account appears in the Supreme Court records, "United States v. the Libelants and Claimants of the Schooner Amistad," (1841), hereinafter termed *Amistad*.

The New Haven Africans were frequently subjected to racial insults, and there is no doubt that they became a type of sideshow. But they used the opportunity to show their benefactors that they had understood the concepts not only of the Christian God but also the conditions of their enslavement. Additionally, they sang songs and even delivered speeches in their own language, thus providing their hosts with the opportunity of learning about an African culture firsthand.[4] Of course, these Africans constituted a radical minority at that time, as they were anything but Eurocentric. Fogel and Engerman in *Time on the Cross* inform us about the Europeanizing of the African population in the Americas:

U.S. slaves were not only in closer contact with European culture, they were also more removed from their African origins than were slaves in the Caribbean. Down through the end of the eighteenth century and into the nineteenth century, the great majority of the slave populations of the British and French Caribbean islands were born in Africa. Indeed, as late as 1800, one quarter of the populations of Jamaica, Barbados, and Martinique consisted of Africans who had arrived in the New World within the previous decade. On the other hand, native-born Blacks made up the majority of the slave population in the U.S. colonies as early as 1680. By the end of the American Revolution, the African-born component of the black population had shrunk to 20 percent. It hovered at this share from 1780 to 1810 and then rapidly headed toward zero. By 1860 all but one percent of U.S. slaves were native-born, and most of them were second, third, fourth, or fifth generation Americans.[5]

African Americans, as early as the eighteenth century, had been almost completely cut off from an African frame of reference. Hence, it would be quite natural for them to see Euro America, Europe itself, and particularly England as the focal point of cultural reference. Later, this acculturation will become additionally important when we look at the revolutionary activities of African America leaders born outside the United States. Obviously, the African cultural continuum reinforced cultural apartness from Eurocentrism.[6]

There were some attempts at separatism on the American mainland. During the nineteenth century, slave revolts were led by Gabriel Prosser and Jack Bowler in 1800, Demark Vesey in 1822, and Nat Turner in 1831. But these insurrections were all crushed, unlike the successful slave uprisings in Brazil, Cuba, Jamaica, and, most notably, Haiti. There was no slave community in North America where African Americans exist outside the orbit of majority European control. Hence the New Haven community was unique.

At the time, even in the North, the atmosphere was rife with antagonism because, even as it prescribed a lower status for African Americans, it stressed a higher position for Euro Americans and thus their seeming equality with the British. Lynde Walker insisted in *The Boston Transcript* that "the Negro was unfit for citizenship"; and the editor of the *American Quarterly Observer* gave tacit approval to slavery, "for thus white labor could do more respectful and useful work and this prevented extreme class differences among whites."[7] Against this background of northern prejudice, the famous case was tried.

Most of the Africans on the *Amistad* were Mende people. They came from a rich cultural heritage, living in what is today's Sierra Leone. Their distinction lay in the fact that they had never really been Anglicized; their language, strict initiation rites for boys and girls, marriage customs, and naming-ceremonies marked them as distinct, apart from their neighbors, the Temne, Vai, and especially the anglicized coastal Krios, whom the British had been returning to Africa from Jamaica, Nova Scotia, and England itself. The Mende were, therefore, familiar with Anglo norms for, as an indigenous people, they had not taken kindly to an Afro European usurpation of their land.[8]

Two African historians, Ajayi and Espie, note that in the nineteenth century, the Mende first faced evangelization from the United Brethren in Christ (now the Evangelical United Brethren) through the Freetown-Liberia-United States connection. Second, they were threatened by the rise of their equally powerful Temne neighbors, as well as by Susu and Sherbro invaders. Third, they managed to penetrate into Sherbro areas "unobtrusively" and "by peaceful means," thus

gradually becoming independent of them [their Sherbro Rulers]."[9] Furthermore, they were well organized socially under subchiefs and chiefs. The
powerful Poro society of males and the Sande society of females passed on
Mende law, educated children, and officiated at ceremonies. P. C. Lloyd
enumerates the disciplined way in which the Poro Society functioned and still
functions today:

> Elders perform important political functions. Membership of the cult may
> be open to all adult men, and most will join its lowest ranks; then, through
> the payment of fees, the giving of feasts and the performance of rites, some
> will rise through a series of ranks to the most senior officers.[10]

These were then very sophisticated people that a Spanish galleon in 1839 took
from Sierra Leone to Cuba. They endured the usual rigors of bad food,
dehydration, brutality, and imminent death.

On June 17, 1839, in Havana, fifty-three were auctioned, purchased, and put
on "La Amistad," which set sail for the port of Puerto Principe in Cuba. Four
days out, the trouble began. With Sengbe (also called Cinque) as leader, they
attacked their captors; when the revolt was over, they had imprisoned their
former enslavers in the same chains previously used for them. Then the Mende
set out for home, but unable to navigate, they ended up on August 26 off Long
Island, where they were put in prison. Here the legal fracas began.

At the District Court level (September 1839), "all claims to salvage the
negroes were rejected" and "the court decreed that the negroes should be
delivered to the President of the United States, to be sent to Africa." At Circuit
Court level (from November 19, 1839, until early 1840), the decision was
exactly the same. Since the Spanish claimants, José Ruiz and Pedro Montez,
objected, another appeal brought the case before the U.S. Supreme Court.

The Mende were defended by John Quincy Adams. The Supreme Court
documentation makes delicious reading:

> The negroes ... filed an answer denying that they were slaves, or the
> property of Ruiz, or Montez; and denying the right of the court under the
> Constitution and laws of the United States to exercise any jurisdiction over
> their persons. They asserted that they were native free-born Africans and
> ought of right to be free.[11]

In March 1841 the Supreme Court freed the Africans, partly agreeing with a
lower court ruling that they had been "kidnapped," and should be returned to
Africa. Howard Jones concludes:

> On November 27, 1841, the thirty-five Black survivors of the initial
> fifty-three on the *Amistad*, including the three girls, along with James

Covey, departed New York for Africa on the barque *Gentleman*. Money to support the voyage had come from the private donations, public exhibitions, and from the Union Missionary Society, which blacks had formed in Hartford to oversee the five white missionaries and teachers who were sent with the Amistad captives to found a Christian mission in Africa. With assurances from the British minister Fox of the "good offices and protection" of British naval commanders along the African coast as well as the British governor of Sierra Leone, the American vessel reached its destination in mid-January 1842, after a fifty-day voyage—nearly three years after the blacks had left their homeland.[12]

The Africans were "kidnapped," the District Court had earlier contended, "in violation of their own rights, and the laws of Spain" despite "a law of Spain prohibiting such importations."[13] A deposition from a British subject, resident in Havana, testified to the fact that they were "very recently brought from Africa," citing their use of Arabic, as some were apparently Muslims.[14] The Spanish consul stated that there was no law forbidding the importation of slaves into Cuba. The Supreme Court's decision almost had the ring of Lord Mansfield's.

Interesting testimony was given by a fellow Mende, James Covey, then only twenty years old and resident in New Haven. According to John W. Barber, an enterprising contemporary who interviewed all the captives and wrote a book about them, Covey's Mende name was Kaw-we-li, "meaning a road dangerous to pass."[15] The Supreme Court record captures Covey's own words, conveying the burgeoning nature of an emerging language process and thus adding a little to our understanding of countercultural existence beyond Eurocentric control. Covey affirmed that he

was born at Berong-Mendi country; left there seven and a half years ago; was a slave, and carried to Lumboko. All these Africans were from Africa. Never saw them until now. I could talk with them. They appeared glad because they could speak the same language. I could understand all but two or three. They say they from Lumboke; three moons. They all have Mendi [Mende] names, and their names all mean something: Carle, means bone; Kimbo, means cricket. They speak of rivers which I know; said they sailed from Lumboko; two or three speak different language from the others; the Timone [Temne] language, Say-ang-wa rivers spoken of; these run through the Vi [Vai] country. I learned to speak English at Sierre Leone. Was put on board a man-of-war one year and a half. They all agree as to where they sailed from. I have no doubt they are Africans. I have been in this country six months; came in a British man-of-war; have been in this town [New Haven] four months with Mr. Bishop; he calls on me for no money, and [I] do not know who pays my board. I was stolen by a black man who stole ten of us. One man carried us two months' walk. Have conversed with Sinqua [Sengbe]; Barton has been in my town, Gorang. I was sailing for Havana when the British man-of-war captured us.[16]

Covey interests us because he is not an artistic creation and consequently does not pose any of the problems associated with filtering fact from fiction. His testimony reveals several interesting points. He hinted that, even if he were to be dubbed a "slave," his fellow Africans were "free." After seven and a half years abroad, he had still retained his ability to speak Mende. He could identify that "two or three" were Temne, and he knew enough of the geography of his country to identify towns, rivers, and even adjacent groups like the Vai, a people who had perfected their own alphabet as early as the fifteenth century. Covey was undoubtedly trying to tell the Supreme Court that he was an Afrocentric and multicultured person, had known the British, had traveled to Cuba, could speak his own language (Mende), and could understand Temne and probably some Spanish. In addition, he was probably lettered in Vai, for to the initiated his mention of Vai country would indicate his knowledge of the people and their indigenous script, newly "discovered" by Europeans in the 1840s.[17]

Covey presents living evidence that not all African Americans in the nineteenth century considered themselves part of a Europeanizing process. Unlike the "master," Mr. Bishop, Covey is not seeking to become part of the Eurocentric continuum. His brief description reveals a whole person, one who had been exposed to various aspects of Eurocentric civilization but nevertheless maintained a knowledge of and a liking for his own people and his country of origin. He pinpoints something of a contradiction, in that, whereas Euro Americans and African Americans seem insistent on establishing those firm associations with Europe, he opts for a difference, one in which the European and African worlds are securely synthesized.

Covey's African patriotism seems certain. He is at one with his Mende clan, and it need not surprise us as he speaks up candidly for them. His English is nearly perfect and indeed highly commendable, after only a limited stay on the African coast and only six months' residence in New Haven. Recall that Mende life in Africa had established rituals and power positions, such as accession to the upper echelons of the Poro Society, and that at this time the Mende were at the height of their power. No doubt Covey recognized Sengbe as being an upper-ranking member of his society, either because of facial markings or because Sengbe had access to certain secret rites and knowledge within the Poro hierarchy, which Covey probably recognized. For simplicity's sake, almost as if talking down to the Supreme Court, he alludes to Sengbe by his Spanish given name, Cinque, but he also lectures the Court on the meaning and significance of African names. Finally, he admonishes the interethnic nature of the slave trade: "I was stolen by a black man who stole ten of us."[18]

Covey pleads his own case against Britain, but this part of his argument is ignored, as it cuts too close to Euro American filial ties with Britain. He demonstrates the situation in which he was "stolen" and "the British man-of-war captured us." He had been forcibly taken away from his own people "seven and a half years ago." His testimony contains his clear charge of hypocrisy, in that he and others like him—he says ten—were actually in the same position as the Africans on the *Amistad*. Yet, although he works without pay for Mr. Bishop, the Supreme Court fails to hear his condemnation against American slavery.

What is interesting in the responses made by Attorney General Henry D. Gilpin, Roger S. Baldwin, and John Quincy Adams for the Africans and the summing-up by Mr. Justice Joseph Story was that they all sought to show that the Africans should be freed (or not) for reasons more to do with European precept than with American concept. For instance, Attorney General Gilpin used this argument: that the Africans "existed as property at the time of the treaty in perhaps every nation of the globe; they can be demanded as property in the States of this Union to which they fly."[19] "International" law must be respected, he says.

Similarly, Baldwin invokes the prestige of the nation in his rebuttal, arguing that "it involves considerations deeply affecting our national character *in the eyes of the whole civilized world*, as well as questions of the power in the part of the government of the United States."[20] He utilizes catchwords that hark back to primitivism and its European link—"men found in a State of Freedom,"[21] New England obligations (Connecticut had passed Gradual Emancipation Laws in 1784), and "the principles of the Revolution, proclaimed in the Declaration of Independence."[22]

Baldwin further affirms that "Neither the law of nature nor the law of nations authorizes the slave trade."[23] Here he echoes again the Declaration of Independence and its concern for "a decent Respect for the Opinions of Mankind," providing "among the Powers of the Earth, the separate and equal Station to which the Laws of Nature and of Nature's God entitle them." This "law of nations" has been defined by George Anastaplo as "general understanding in the civilized [European] world."[24]

In delivering the opinion of the court, Mr. Justice Story shows equal concern for European laws:

If these negroes were, at the time, lawfully held as slaves under the laws of Spain, and recognized by those laws as property capable of being lawfully bought and sold, we see no reason why they may not justly be deemed within the intent of the treaty to be included under the denomination of merchandise, and, as such, ought to be restored to the claimants; for, upon that point, the laws of Spain would seem to furnish the proper rule of interpretation.[25]

Any "conflict of rights," Mr. Justice Story continues, "must be decided upon the eternal principles of justice and international law."[26]

The "liberal" finding was not due to the composition of the Court. Of the nine judges, seven were Democrats—Chief Justice Taney, Justices McLean, Baldwin, Wayne, Cutron, McKinley, and Daniel. Only two were Democratic Republicans (Jeffersonians)—Justices Story and Thompson.[27] But the latter won the day because their views expressed the direction in which European thought had projected itself.

We read the charges, summaries, presentations, and the Court's opinion in a real-life setting, and it confirms our belief in some of the issues we seek to explore. Covey did not allow himself to be branded as the opposite of European man—irrational and inferior. He is not engaged in a mirror-image reflection through which he seeks Eurocentric validation of his worth. He is important because he stands outside any generalizations about Euro American myth and history, representing an ethos of his own, frozen in time. The American participants attempt to construct imaginary bridges (justifying or condemning slavery), between macro-European symbol and micro-American response. Covey represents the interconnectedness of various worlds, which seem to come together in him.

In a sense, the trial is not really about *Amistad* or its unhappy cargo. The conclusions anticipate a larger conflict, wherein there is the dispute between Eurocentrism (with its foisted image of the Anglophile) and non-Eurocentrism, which takes its outline and dimension from African, Asian, and Native American models. The trial demonstrates that not everything fits pat into the Anglo American model. As ex-President John Quincy Adams noted in his fierce defense, in words that linked America to England, American Constitution to British common law, and pantheism to Christianity: "I know of no other law that reaches the case of my clients, but the law of Nature and of Nature's God on which our fathers placed our national existence."[28]

He was responding to a passionate letter he had received from Kinna, one of the Africans: "We ask we beg you to tell court let Mende people be free."[29] As rights of Spanish Cuba, Spain, and Britain were all involved, the case is of interest in such a study. For it surely attempts to see, in real terms, the extent to which America and Europe continued to be bound. The Supreme Court found that "the treaty with Spain cannot be obligatory upon them [the Africans]," assuming they were not slaves, and, even more surprisingly, stated that "the United States are bound to respect their rights." Furthermore, the Court argued that "when the Amistad arrived she was in possession of the negroes, asserting their freedom; and in no sense could [they] possibly intend to import themselves into the United States as slaves, or for sale as slaves."[30] The real irony was that the Supreme Court, at the height of American slavery and two decades before Emancipation, stressed that these Africans had arrived in America as free people.

The case was viewed by abolitionists as setting a precedent, but in reality it merely affirmed that these particular Mende were not property. For when slavery was finally abolished in the United States in 1865, it was the fifth last country to do so, preceded by such giants of present-day democracy as Chile (1823), Mexico (1829), Bolivia (1831), Uruguay (1842), Ecuador (1851), Peru (1854), and Venezuela (1854). Slavery was abolished in all British colonies in 1834, in all French and Danish colonies in 1848, and all Dutch colonies in 1863. In 1841, the Quintuple Treaty was signed by which England, France, Russia, Prussia, and Austria agreed to "mutual search of each other's vessels to end the slave trade." As early as December 1819, Spanish law had prohibited the slave trade. The *Amistad* decision may also be viewed as an attempt by the Supreme Court to reassert European legal continuum. Despite the fact that slavery worked, and slave revolts could not end a profitable business, and the Civil War alone could not have terminated it, something else did—America's desire to remain part of the "civilized" European world.

Unlike Covey, Euro Americans did not object to the process that brought them closer to "civilization." After all, this was the intention from the very founding of the Republic. The *Amistad* affair had the effect of emphasizing that America was "civilized." The ruling went against local concepts but nevertheless placed the United States squarely in England's court. Even though the Supreme Court's findings conflicted with "international law," it would have been applauded by William Wilberforce, George Canning, and William Pitt the Younger, on the other side of the Atlantic, as upholding the moral tenets of English law. Recall that Lord Chief Justice Mansfield had ruled in 1772 that slavery was incompatible with English law. In this other sense, the *Amistad* findings go beyond the law, beyond the slave issue, and become part of what continued to associate the former American colony with an English homeland.

The *Amistad* incident and Covey's persona belie the belief that all America was totally committed to becoming anglicized. Indeed, Covey represents and articulates an Afrocentric reality that runs counter to everything that had been assumed thus far. Seemingly, therefore, there were Africans in mainstream society (yet apart from it) who could still recall their homeland, its geography, place names, and language. Obviously, they could even interact with others in a manner that was different from that mandated by Eurocentric custom. Covey is not a great writer, poet, or artist, yet he emerges from history's fringes in a distinct way, identifying for us the subterranean drifts of a counterculture, and thus putting the lie to total Anglo cultural dominance.

A minority impulse also helps explain Emerson and Thoreau and especially Transcendentalism. Strange though this might seem, we are equating Covey's Africanity—his language and sense of place—with those of other, better-known "outsiders" who, likewise, did not see themselves in terms of a set image-made pattern of the "majority." Emerson and Thoreau (like

Covey) were able to be persons of two cultures, to move comfortably in and
out of two value systems—one confirmed by the majority, the other acqui-
esced to by a small minority.

In the nineteenth century, Transcendentalism demonstrated the presence of
real persons who inhabited a subgroup, existing beneath the consciousness of
the larger group and flitting easily between what was and what ought to have
been. Thus, Emerson claims that the "seer is sayer" as he identifies with "priest
or poet."[31] This derives partly from Shelley's concept of the poet as unacknowl-
edged legislator, but, in addition, shows the inklings of nonconformity, which
afterwards become his accepted rationale. Emerson is partly arguing against
blind acceptance of Eurocentric Christian dogma, and in "Self-Reliance" the
point is made even more directly. "Insist on yourself; never imitate," Emerson
declares, anticipating Whitman in what is less a gospel of individualism and
more a creed of the minority.

Therefore, Emerson opts for a true independence of will that will negate the
commonly acceptable:

> It is for want of self-culture that the superstition of travelling, whose *idols
> are Italy, England, Egypt, retains its fascination for all educated Ameri-
> cans*. They who made England, Italy or Greece venerable to the imagina-
> tion, did so by sticking fast where they were, like an axis of the earth. In
> manly hours we feel that duty is our place. The soul is no traveller: the
> wise man stays at home, and when his necessities, his duties, on an
> occasion call him from his house or into foreign lands, he is at home still,
> and shall make men sensible by the expression of his countenance, that *he
> goes the missionary of wisdom and virtue, and visits cities and men like a
> sovereign, and not like an interloper or a valet.* [32]

Just as with Covey, the multicultural African, still very recognizably an African
to his fellow Mende and, at the same time, an expert international witness before
the Supreme Court. Although his outsider status is imposed on him, it differs
little from others like Emerson who willingly opt out of Eurocentric confine-
ment. For at this point Emerson and Covey come together, true enough, out of
differing motives and different viewpoints but yet displaying remarkable una-
nimity. The projection of Eurocentric ideas may be an acceptable myth to a
majority group still unsure of its cultural emancipation, but the countercultural
viewpoint, whether from an Afrocentric or America-centered locus, liberates it.
There occurs not so much "nonconformity," in keeping with the standard
interpretation of Emerson's beliefs, but an attempt to free the culture from
external and alien fixations.

Emerson's God-within is not only an American nation desperate for birth nor
merely the individual hacking away at group conformity but also a perception
of submerged truths that reveal and validate a different consensus—a "minor-

ity" precept that will later be quickly and ardently accepted as part of the "majority" value system.

Transcendentalists go beyond the images of their time.[33] They are not engaged in group acts that allow us to conscript them into specific stances, as Taylor Stoeht clearly shows. The movement itself is broad, encompassing what is later to be termed the "Transcendental Club," actually an almost casual body of outsiders who met in Emerson's Concord home. First, they gave themselves the name "Symposium" or, with a hint of self-deprecation, the "Hedge Club" after one of their members. Between 1840 and 1844, some of them produced *The Dial*, which ran contributions by Emerson and Thoreau. But behind the movement, the "club," and the quarterly was one of those delightful historical eccentrics—Bronson Alcott, who felt himself unable to belong to the "club," the quarterly, or the movement itself.[34] He, like the African Mende Covey, stood outside the outsiders.

Experiments like Brook Farm and Fruitlands tell us much about the felt need to be not merely intellectually but also physically apart. Because they are all "acceptable" in contemporary mainstream thought, both Euro American "Transcendentalism" and African American "Separatism" speak to a loftier American need for identification, justification, and re-vision beyond Europe. Brook Farm, Fruitlands, and the African community in New Haven all advocate similar ideals: Because society seemed headed in the wrong Eurocentric direction, the only recourse was to opt out. New ideals stressed a new education, religion, morality, and a return to rural life.[35] Bronson Alcott's work was rendered almost futile, since neither his *Record of a School, Exemplifying the General Principles of Spiritual Culture* (1835) nor the two-volume *Conversations with Children on the Gospels* (1836–1837) distanced him far enough from the culture he sought to repudiate. Too much the idealist, he was barely saved from penury by the generosity of his daughter, which the success of her *Little Women* (1868–1869) and *Little Men* (1871) made possible. But even she had to admit in "Transcendental Wild Oats" that the movement was impractical. Yet Lawrence Buell, Taylor Stoeht, Anne C. Rose, and Leo Marx all agree that Transcendentalism contradicted perceived American reality. Therefore, even though it exists now as antiquated belief, its origin was very much a shift away from Eurocentrism.

In *The Blithedale Romance* (1852), Hawthorne's fictional character Miles Coverdale, spends time on the farm, much as Hawthorne himself had done. Hawthorne had declared, after four months at Brook Farm, that "labor is the curse of the world." More interestingly, toward the end of his stay, he added in a letter to his future wife that "there will be no more very hard or constant labor during the one other week that *I shall remain as a slave*."[36] Where Coverdale is concerned, Hawthorne warns us quite early that the setting is anything but Utopian. He is a "melancholy Jacques" in Shakespeare's Arden, and a companion startles him, reminding him of "the savage man of antiquity." Coverdale, for one, strongly disapproves of any kind of synthesis, registering only total confusion as he observes the community at play: "Among them was an Indian chief, with blanket feathers and warpaint, and uplifted tomahawk; and near him, looking fit to be his woodland-bride, the goddess Diana. . . . Another group consisted of a Bavarian broom-girl, a negro of the Jim Crow order."[37] Put simply, for both Hawthorne and Coverdale, the proximity of the European world to the Native American and African American intrudes, jars, and startles, making the achievement of community less desirable and more impossible. Coverdale had sought, in Zenobia, "some nature, some passion, no matter whether right or wrong, provided it were real." Instead, Coverdale found an illusion, the transplanted images of Arcadian Europe ill at ease in America. Hawthorne himself opted for conventional Eurocentric individuality, writing to his future wife, "We must not lean upon the community . . . the real Me was never an associate of the community."[38]

Both Thoreau's *Walden* and Emerson's *Nature* are about this personal assertiveness in the face of "majority" imposition. One should never surrender, at least not in any total and outright recasting of the self, to fit society's mold. Leo Stoller finds that although Thoreau

> was forced to retreat from his experiment in the simple economy [at Walden] and *to live in the only social structure which history had made available to him*, Thoreau did not abandon the ideal which had originally led him to the pond. . . . Thoreau refused to make his peace with a society inimical to self-culture, and he continued to denounce the evil practices of his countrymen with passion.[39]

Stoller further contends that Thoreau "provided an adequate example of the kind of simplicity that was based on the divided life."[40]

Thoreau did not ever fully acquiesce even to an inevitable relationship with majority history or to subsequent acceptance of a divided life. Emerson's mouse-trap and Thoreau's ritualistic bath in Walden Pond are both relevant aspects of the blend of practicality and mysticism—there is no separation. Recall Emerson's injunction regarding the salubrious effects of staying in one place, yet being able to contain an inner globalism. Pond and mousetrap are symbols of the larger, purer life, beyond the pale of the immediate, and the misgivings of Eurocentric society gone awry, parodied by Hawthorne as "masqueraders."

One way out of the quandary was for the minority (Covey, Emerson, Thoreau) to look beyond Europe in order to comprehend fully the uniqueness of non-European life. As Thoreau enjoins:

> To an American reader, who, by the advantage of his position, can see over that strip of Atlantic coast to Asia and the Pacific, who, as it were, sees the

shore slope upward over the Alps to the Himmaleh [*sic*] Mountains, *the comparatively recent literature of Europe often appears partial and clannish, and, notwithstanding the limited range of his own sympathies and studies, the European writer who presumes that he is speaking for the world, is perceived by him to speak only for that corner of it which he inhabits.* One of the rarest of England's scholars and critics, in his classification of the worthies of the world, betrays the *narrowness of his European culture and the exclusiveness of his reading.* None of her children had done justice to the poets and philosophers of Persia or of India.[41]

This is Thoreau at his most relevant for the multicultural proponents of today.

First, therefore, the "minor voice" had to denounce the very values that the "major voice" assumed. Second, the "minor voice" must establish its own tonal validity, even in this most basic verbal sense. "It is a ridiculous demand," Thoreau contends, "which England and America make, that you shall speak so they understand you."[42] In *Maine Woods*, he admires Native Americans praying, working, speaking an "unaltered Indian language," which European Americans do not understand.[43] Third, the "minor voice" must recognize, in this disparity, possible extensions of the self longing to be free from the trammels of majority control.

Thoreau cites his own contemporaries like Emerson, Alcott, and European writers from Ovid to Shakespeare to Tennyson; his all-inclusiveness enlarges "universality." For Thoreau is equally at home with references to African "Yoloffs"— probably the Joloff, in Nigeria—or to Mourzouk, Libya, or to a Persian poet like Muslih-ud-Din, Confucius, or Hindu scripture, particularly the *Bhagavad-Gita* from Charles Wilkins's translation, published in 1785 in London. This wide-ranging global reach establishes a new "universalism," positioning Thoreau and Emerson as direct ancestors of T. S. Eliot and Ezra Pound.[44]

Both Emerson and Thoreau showed that America's search for identity had to reach out to hitherto unaccepted cultures of the non-European world. The reasoning had more to do with self-discovery of their own minority voices than with eclecticism. William Drake concludes an interesting essay on *Walden* by affirming that "self-discovery is thus linked with discovery outside one's self."[45] It reforms, or seeks to change, the larger society.

Seemingly, Eastern philosophy and thought could liberate European ethnocentrism in America from the consequences of being too earthbound. After all, the core of Hindu belief is to free the body from worldly demands, so that the soul can join in the eternal life cycle of nirvana. Once the human persona no longer depends on an immediate and recognizable environment, she or he has freedom in the truest sense, an ability to enter the cycle of rebirth to higher and higher planes.[46] African theology[47] posits an alternative just as compelling. As the gods are anthropomorphic, humans may achieve god status and indeed may communicate with the divinity, as Covey must have recognized. For, because death and life exist simultaneously, gods, ancestors, and the living constantly interact. The text of Emerson's Harvard address, "The American Scholar," given in 1839, explains how this occurs: First, the seeker acquires knowledge of the past; second, through a harmony with the world, his communication with the deity is achieved. Finally, after the spiritualization of personal life, the task of renewing the majority society itself must be undertaken. The sojourner, like Krishna in the famous battle scene in the *Bhagavad Gita*, becomes personally responsible for society's future and takes steps to halt its recidivism toward chaos.[48]

Emerson and Thoreau spoke as eloquently as did Covey's brief statement to the Supreme Court. David Walker's lesser-known *Appeal* (1830),[49] seriously misinterpreted as a call to African American slaves to riot, was really more evidence of disenchantment. Walker's concerns are certainly not personal—he was a "Free Negro"—but he stood outside his own condition. Instead of India and the Far East, Walker, like Covey, substituted "Africa," but as metaphor only, in a comprehensive ultracontinental sense, involving the continent of Africa, the African diaspora in the New World, and the multiracial New World itself. Walker was just as prepared for violent revolution as for New World settlement. His option could not have been Fruitlands or Brook Farm; instead, he sought to move further afield, putting forward detailed plans for migration and settlement to East Africa, Central America, and/or Haiti. The motivation may differ, but the result is the same. Walker, like the New Haven Africans and the Transcendentalists, makes even clearer the concept of minority-within-a-minority. Few agreed with him, for resettlement (of which both Jefferson and Lincoln heartily approved) was a touchy topic. Even Covey would have wanted to reserve that option and not have it as a compelling injunction.

Of course, enormous differences existed between the New Haven Africans and the Massachusetts Transcendentalists. The major similarities of commonly held conceptions were outweighed by skin color differences, which, at least for the Africans and the free Negro David Walker, were the controlling factors of their lives. But a closer look reveals that all these men shared a similar predicament, in that they were yoked by the majority society to a Europe that they abjured and thus found themselves at odds with the value systems of a society in which they lived. They all chose the same temporary solution, and most fail and return to the larger majority society. At the end of "Transcendental Wild Oats," Louisa May Alcott paints this touching, if slightly sentimental, half-mocking portrait of Sister Hope, her mother, and Abel Lamb, her father:

So one bleak December day, with their few possessions piled on an ox-sled, the rosy children perched atop, and the parents trudging arm in arm behind, the exiles left their Eden and faced the world again.

"Ah, me! my happy dream. How much I leave behind that never can be mine again," said Abel, looking back at the lost Paradise, lying white and chill in its shroud of snow.

"Yes, dear; but how much we bring away," answered brave-hearted Hope, glancing from husband to children.

"Poor Fruitlands! the name was as great a failure as the rest!" continued Abel, with a sigh, as a frostbitten apple fell from a leafless bough at his feet.[50]

The experiment at Fruitlands had ended. The land is dead, and the people who had hoped to live off it, who had sought a new Eden and Paradise, must return to the outside world that they had discarded. Even Covey, it is said, was never quite at peace.

Outside the prescribing mores of their larger societies, New Haven Africans and David Walker, Transcendentalists, and Bronson Alcott all desired a liberty not afforded by national westward "expansion" or "compromises" over "slave" and "free" status. They shared a common discomfort, as they sought some different place, secure and apart, to articulate a new revolution of the spirit. Above all, they intimately realized that Europe could provide few answers to their predicament. Therefore, although Emerson and Thoreau could each claim to be legally a "free man" and Covey and Walker only "three fifths of a man," they all commonly acknowledged an urgent need for reform at the individual and societal levels. All spoke of a revolution emanating from a "minority" that would bring about the desired change. When they talked "revolution," all used the metaphors of their respective situations, for neither group had heard of the other, although they lived only a few miles apart. Therefore, we see them not as individuals, although this they certainly were, but as persons who all attempted to show differing manifestations that would have enriched the American experience, had some of their options been accepted. Sadly, they represent more the byways of progressive thinking than the main thoroughfare of accepted opinion.

NOTES

1. For background information on the "Amistad Affair," the best source is the Supreme Court records. See "United States v the Libelants and Claimants of the Schooner Amistad" (1841), *United States Reports,* vol. 40. Collected by Richard Peters (Washington, D.C.: U.S. Government Printing Office, 1941), 518–596. Hereafter cited as "Amistad."

2. For background information on Transcendentalism, I used the following: Brian Barbour, *American Transcendentalism* (Notre Dame: University of Notre Dame Press, 1973); Phillip F. Gura and Joel Myerson, *Critical Essays on American Transcendentalism* (Boston: G. K. Hall, 1982); Donald N. Koster, *Transcendentalism in America* (Boston: G. K. Hall, 1975); and Perry Miller, *The Transcendentalists* (Cambridge, Mass.: Harvard University Press, 1950). For fictionalized treatment of the Brook Farm experiment, see Nathaniel Hawthorne's *The Blithedale Romance* [1852] (London: Penguin, 1983); and Louisa May Alcott's "Transcenden-

tal Wild Oats" [1876] which may be found in Clara Endicott Sears, *Bronson Alcott's Fruitlands* (Boston: Houghton Mifflin, 1915), 146–174.

3. Christopher Martin, *The Amistad Affair* (New York: Tower Publications, 1970), 230–233.

4. Mary Cable, *Black Odyssey* (New York: Viking Press, 1971), 118–119.

5. Robert William Fogel and Stanley L. Engerman, *Time on the Cross* (New York: Norton, 1989), 23–24.

6. Frank Tannenbaum in *Slave and Citizen* (New York: Knopf, 1946) makes the argument that slavery was less coercive outside the United States. Although he does not contend that this may have caused more fraternizing and hence bonding, it would seem that this point is worth making.

7. Lorman Ratner, *Powder Keg: Northern Opposition to the Anti-Slavery Movement* (New York: Basic Books, 1988).

8. Christopher Fyfe, *History of Sierra Leone* (London: Oxford University Press, 1962).

9. J. F. Ade Ajayi and Ian Espie, *A Thousand Years of West African History* (Ibadan, Nigeria: Ibadan University Press, 1965), 336.

10. P. C. Lloyd, *Africa in Social Change* (Harmondsworth, U.K.: Penguin, 1987), 37.

11. "Amistad," 37.

12. Howard Jones, *Mutiny on the Amistad* (Oxford: Oxford University Press, 1987), 205.

13. "Amistad," 527.

14. Ibid., 533.

15. John W. Barber, as quoted in Cable, *Black Odyssey.*

16. "Amistad," 534.

17. For details of European knowledge of the indigenous African script, see F. E. Forbes, *Despatch Communicating the Discovery of a Native Written Character at Bohmar on the West Coast of Africa near Liberia* (London: privately printed by William Clowes and Sons, n.d.); and S. W. Koëlle, *Narrative of an Expedition into the Vy Country of West Africa and the Discovery of a System of Syllabic Writing Invented by the Natives of the Vy Tribe* (London: Jeys, Hatchards, V. Nisbet, 1849).

18. "Amistad," 534.

19. Ibid., 541.

20. Ibid., 547. Emphasis added.

21. Ibid., 549.

22. Ibid., 553.

23. Ibid., 558.

24. George Anastaplo, *The Constitution of 1787* (Baltimore: Johns Hopkins University Press, 1989), 9.

25. "Amistad," 591.

26. Ibid., 593.

27. Henry Campbell Black, *Black's Law Dictionary* (St Paul, Minn.: West Publishing, 1979), 1505.

28. John Quincy Adams, *Argument of John Quincy Adams before the Supreme Court of the United States in the Case of the United States, Appellants, v Cinque and Other Africans, Captured on the Schooner Amistad* (New York: S. W. Benedict, 1841).

29. Cable, *Black Odyssey*, 119.

30. "Amistad," 519.

31. Ralph Waldo Emerson, *Collected Works*, ed. Robert Spiller, Joseph Slater, and Douglas Emory Wilson, 2 vols. (Cambridge, Mass.: Harvard University Press, 1971), 1:76–93.

32. Emerson, *Collected Works*, 2:25–27. Emphasis added.

33. See Anne C. Rose, *Transcendentalism as Social Movement* (New Haven: Yale University Press, 1981).

34. Taylor Stoeht, *Nay-Saying in Concord: Emerson, Alcott and Thoreau* (Hamden, Conn.: Archon Books, 1979).

35. See, in particular, studies by Lawrence Buell, *Literary Transcendentalism: Style and Vision in the American Renaissance* (Ithaca, N.Y.: Cornell University Press, 1975); and Leo Marx, *The Machine in the Garden: Technology and the Pastoral Ideal in America* (New York: Oxford University Press, 1964).

36. Newton Arvin, ed. *The Heart of Hawthorne's Journals* (New York: Barnes & Noble, 1967), 75. Emphasis added.

37. Hawthorne, *Blithedale Romance,* 209.

38. Louise Desalvo, *Nathaniel Hawthorne* (Atlantic Highlands, N.J.: Humanities Press International, 1987), 98–99.

39. Leo Stoller, "Thoreau's Doctrine of Simplicity" in *Thoreau: A Collection of Essays,* ed. Sherman Paul (Englewood Cliffs, N.J.: Prentice-Hall, 1962), 42. Emphasis added.

40. Ibid., 45.

41. Henry David Thoreau, *A Week on the Concord and Merrimack Rivers.* In *A Week on the Concord and Merrimack Rivers. Walden; or Life in the Woods. The Maine Woods. Cape Cod.* (New York: Library of America, 1985), 115.

42. Ibid., *Walden,* 580.

43. Ibid., *Maine Woods,* 696.

44. The extent to which these references constitute what Edward W. Said in *Orientalism* (New York: Vintage Books, 1979) denounces as the "orientalism" of the Orient should be mentioned in passing. See Said, 5–6, 65–67, 325.

45. William Drake, "Walden" in Sherman Paul, *Thoreau,* 90.

46. For basic treatment of ideas of Hinduism, see Houston Smith, *The Religions of Man* (New York: Perennial Library, 1965), 14–89; and K. M. Sen, *Hinduism* (New York: Viking Penguin, 1962) 17–31, 53–57, and 86–90. Also see *Hindu Myths,* trans. by Wendy O'Flaherty (London: Penguin, 1975).

47. A good introduction to African religious belief may be found in two books by John Mbiti, *African Religions and Philosophy* (Oxford: Heinemann, 1969) and *Introduction to African Religion* (Oxford: Heinemann, 1978).

48. See Juan Mascaró's translation of *The Bhagavad Gita* (London: Penguin Books, 1962).

49. For David Walker, see *Walker's Appeal in Four Articles with a Preamble to the Concerned Citizens of the World in One Continuous Cry,* ed. Herbert Aptheker (New York: Humanities Press, 1968).

50. Alcott, "Transcendental Wild Oats," 173.

4

Black Leadership
and Eurocentric Ideals ─────────────

Eurocentric racial stances received a popular stamp of approval with Thomas Dixon's *Clansman* (1905). This marks an interesting point at which one may note another development of the nation's image, particularly because D. W. Griffith's *Birth of a Nation*, released in 1915, further popularized it through the new medium of the cinema. Griffith utilized his unquestioned genius for moviemaking to place his particular viewpoint of Southern domination by heartless Yankees firmly in the national consciousness. For the first time, cinema techniques were used that conjured up symbols of reality in the manner of a documentary. For instance, use was made of a type of interrupted narrative style, which enabled the moviemaker to attain apparent objectivity by telling the same story from apparently differing standpoints and settings. The film's success helped to project the account of history retold as indelible truth. "Darkies," at times Whites in blackface, were portrayed through character defects of which the defeated Euro American audience heartily approved—African American cowardice and simpleminded bravery, animal loyalty and treachery, stupidity and limited intelligence, even when employed for the "right" cause.

Even before the movie, Dixon had established a touring company that popularized the major theme: the South was a defeated nation at the hands of Northern barbarians. Again and again, the correspondences are made between the South as a projector of light and civilization and the North as a harbinger of darkness and savagery. Families are torn apart and deprived of household heads, as the North imposed the ultimate disgrace—"darky" rule. We see "ignorant" Negroes attempting to debate in the legislature, sitting feet up and intellect down. The South, the message stated clearly, attempted to preserve English and European norms, but Northern carpetbaggers and Southern scalawags conspired against the restoration of this true order.

Again the Eurocentric ideal is invoked, particularly in the instance of the Ku Klux Klan, first started in 1865, the year of the Thirteenth Amendment, outlawing slavery, and fully established by 1867. The K.K.K. are "knights" in the tradition of King Arthur. They ride horses and swear allegiance to each other. They protect "honor," particularly that of Guinevere-type Southern maidens, when they ride into battle against any who would defame these women. Malory would not have recognized his Knights of the Round Table, but little matter. These latter-day Southern saviors were knights, with chivalric hoods and regalia, mounted on horses. Their white gowns further emphasized their supposed pristine goodness.

At the center of their ritual was, of course, the cross, a symbol of Christian belief, but interpreted anew. No longer does it represent crucifixion and death of the good, but its flames reveal its power to destroy all who would dare usurp the rightful authority of the Euro American southern males. As W. E. B. Du Bois and the "Niagara Movement" (later the NAACP) noted, the warriors of the Klan unleashed a degree of genocide unequaled until then in American history, apart from the wholesale destruction of Native Americans. Griffith documents, in terms that all can recognize, the "seen" images that would become inextricably bound up in the American psyche. He does not pretend that his work is fiction, but rather, particularly for the unsophisticated, it became the dramatization of a new historical truth.

However misguided this may all seem, it showed how new American variants of Eurocentricity blended Anglo French Arthurian myth with Christian symbols. One may perceive in this a scatterbrained ethnocentrism, especially as it later ferreted out Nazism as a current reference point. But both Griffiths and Dixon knew what by now should have been most evident—American Eurocentricity was so firmly in place that the idea of Europe (in whatever form) could be used to manipulate American images, however bizarre. The Klan represented an extreme true enough, but continues to indicate some of the absorptions that became part of mainstream American thought.

As the nation moved toward the end of the nineteenth century, it imitated the worst aspects of England's imperialism. If Queen Victoria could proclaim herself "Empress of India," Americans could look nearer home for justification of their own imperial destiny. This new fervor is accompanied by an exaggerated patriotism, from Francis Scott Key's composition of the "Star Spangled Banner" in 1814 through Julia Ward Howe's "Battle Hymn of the Republic" in 1862. This may have been acceptable in the public sphere, but when it invaded the more private nature of artistic input, there is cause for worry. At their worst, Twain, Whitman, and Crane, among others, insisted on a kind of sentimental reverence for country that seemed to derive itself from this spillover of patriotic fervor.

In an attempt at understanding the Klan, we must therefore see it, not as "southern" but as American. The six young ex-Confederate soldiers who originated it in Pulaski, Tennessee, sought authenticity for its name in the Greek word *kuklos*. At first, as David Chalmers shows in *Hooded Americanism*, the main purpose was "horseplay," then "terrorism," and only later "vigilantism." Their meeting in April 1867 in Nashville, which elected former Confederate general Bedford Forrest as head, had nationwide aims, with an "empire" divided into realms, dominions, provinces, and dens, each headed by a Grand Dragon, Titans, Giants, Cyclops, and Ghouls.[1] The curious admixture of the vocabulary of Grimm's fairytales, Greek epic, and the language of the British Empire was quite intentional in the attempt to provide legitimacy. They were then ready for warfare against their own "colonizers."[2]

European American racism and African American class consciousness addressed themselves to the same goal—a desire to be incorporated into the "civilized" European world. However, the Klan and the turn-of-the-century millionaires, the African American nationalist and the middle-class had to be rejected as irrelevant within the tight confines of European class structure.

In British and American literature, had anyone looked, there was ample precedent for finding the "nigger." Thomas Carlyle had given his full approval in *Occasional Discourse on the Nigger Question* (1853), arguing quite bluntly that a Black person was "useful in God's creation only as a servant."[3] Other British authors like Michael Scott felt that Blacks were fair game; in *Tom Cringle's Log* (1829–1833) and *The Cruise of the Midge* (1835), they are given names like Snowball and made to seem extremely foolish. For Henry W. Grady, "the negro stood in slavery days, open-hearted and sympathetic, full of gossip and comradeship . . . contented in the kindly dependence that has been a habit of his blood."[4] Bailey spoke of "a lazy, shiftless, irresponsible mass of [African American] laborers that require the closest supervision."[5] Thomas Page added quite bluntly:

> The intelligent negro may understand what social equality truly means, but to the ignorant and brutal young negro, it signifies but one thing: the opportunity to enjoy, equally with white men, the privilege of cohabiting with white women. This the whites of the South understand; and if it were understood abroad, it would serve to explain some things which have not been understood hitherto. It will explain, in part, the universal and furious hostility of the South to even the least suggestion of social equality.[6]

African Americans seem to exist by special political fiat. Constitutional amendments, by their very nature, represent a legislative afterthought. African American "rights" to be free, to become citizens, and to vote were of such a nature. The Thirteenth Amendment (1865) stated that "Neither slavery nor involuntary servitude, *except as punishment for crime whereof the party shall have been duly convicted*, shall exist within the United States" (emphasis added). This has been interpreted as "abolishing" slavery. But two points should be made. First, the modifying clause could well apply to both "slavery" and "involuntary servitude." Second, and this holds good for all amendments: They may be rescinded or ratified by three-fourths of the states.[7]

The Fifteenth Amendment (1870) stated that "The right of citizens of the United States to vote shall not be denied or abridged . . . on account of race, color, or previous condition of servitude." Such right to citizenry had been granted by the Fourteenth Amendment only in 1868, barely two years before. The Thirteenth, Fourteenth, and Fifteenth Amendments remain as constant reminders that real power lay with the Eurocentric majority. The most that could be hoped for was that these would be fair-minded persons of goodwill. Despite the frailty of these amendments, which suggest that African Americans live on tolerance in the United States, and despite the Civil Rights legislation in 1964 and a Voting Rights Act in 1965 (both subject to constant political tug-of-war), the K.K.K. and its supporters, to this day, have little cause for worry. Indeed, Benjamin Quarles has written that only after World War II did the Supreme Court begin

> to show an increased concern about civil rights and individual liberties. It began to go behind the formal law as stated in order to discover whether it was being fairly applied. It began to look beyond laws enforcing segregation to see whether the separate facilities provided for negroes were in fact equal to those of whites.[8]

This continues to exist at the heart of civil rights up until the present. Hence the dire need to have a Supreme Court that is not opposed to basic ideals.

The struggle through the courts was anything but easy but slowly seemed to indicate a direction in keeping with the famous *Amistad* case. In 1944 the Court ruled in *Smith v. Allright* that "a political party could not exclude a voter because of race"; in 1946, in *Morgan v. Virginia*, it concluded that an African American passenger did not have to conform to state laws of segregation; in 1948, in *Shelley v. Kraemer*, it decided that race or color could not exclude a person from ownership.[9] Despite *Plessy v. Ferguson* (1896), where separate but unequal had become national law, the Supreme Court had continued to make humanitarian decisions until the onset of the Reagan years. Long before *Brown v. the Board of Education* (1954), Supreme Court rulings had ordered the admission of an African American student to the University of Missouri in *Gaines v. Missouri* (1938) and likewise in 1948 and 1950 ruled that Oklahoma should provide two African American students with a truly "separate but equal" education. True enough, in the 1950 case of G. W. McLauhan, the Supreme Court was "requiring that he sit at a designated desk in an anteroom adjoining the classroom, apart from other students, to sit at a designated desk in the library, and to eat in the school cafeteria at a special time."[10] But a definite pattern was being set that would lead to the *Brown* decision.

Several cases had been brought by the NAACP, which W. E. B. Du Bois had launched in 1905. Even in the early days of the Niagara Movement, they were able to mount protests against Dixon's touring company at a Chicago theater. Bedford Forrest could have agreed with Du Bois that the main issue of the twentieth century would be the "color line." It was just this that marked out a new and different image for America—not necessarily one the country wanted, but nevertheless one that was imposed on it.

The struggle of the African American "minority" again ran counter to Euro American "majority" accepted opinion and belief. At the same time all America was being involved in a European perception of the New World as "object." For, although Europeans had contended within their own separate national spheres, they viewed others from a very monoethnic and monocultural perspective. Their ethnocentrism was rooted in separate national existences but combined power and common interests. Bismarck's Berlin Conference of 1884–1885 officially guaranteed a unified European hegemony on the African continent. The United States was present at the conference.

A significant irony is that even African American spokespersons tended to be involved in the Eurocentric ideal. Du Bois, himself a "mulatto," must have realized this when he felt compelled to state that his own racial makeup was Native American, French, Dutch, and African but, "Thank God, no Anglo Saxon." But because of his own initial Euro American background and schooling, the same type of Eurocentric ideas are observed as in the larger society. For instance, his Pan African Congresses were all held in America or Europe, never in Liberia or Africa. Even the one that brought together African leaders for the first time took place in 1945, in Manchester, England. Further, Du Bois advocated a strict hierarchy among African Americans, not unlike the elitist class system of Europe, in which a "talented tenth" would rule. Thus did the alleged spokesperson of African American rights contend:

It goes without saying that while *Negroes are thus manifestly of low average culture*, in no place nor at any time do they form a homogeneous group. Even in the country districts of the lower South, Allison Davis likens the group to a steeple with wide base tapering to a high pinnacle. This means that while *the poor, ignorant, sick and anti-social form a vast foundation, that upward from the base stretch classes whose highest members, although few in number, reach above the average not only of the Negroes but of the whites, and may justly be compared to the better-class white culture.* The class structure of the whites, on the other hand, resembles a tower bulging near the center with the lowest classes small in number as compared with the middle and lower middle classes; and the highest classes far more numerous in proportion than those among blacks.[11]

An invented "class" system for African Americans may be seen, in a way, as ridiculous. One could argue that the slave/ex-slave remains permanently outside the domain of his master/former master's societal parameters. Or, put differently, as skin color had clearly marked out African Americans, they could either opt for permanent "underclass" status or create new concepts of class, based on an independent and different culture. However, there's the rub: American culture was neither independent nor radically different, and early African American leaders were at pains to stress their own Eurocentric similarities in order to gain acceptance. Even a case as radical as Marcus Garvey's, who through his United Negro Improvement Association had advocated a "back to Africa" movement, may be seen in this light. Garvey imported the trappings of the British colonial governor—his plumes, helmet, uniform, dress, and parades—to his Harlem followers. They did not recognize the images, but clearly for Garvey, these were the symbols of real authority.

Downgrading African Americans was one way that Euro Americans sought to establish a class system, in keeping with Europe. Both North and South were in firm agreement; in fact, the acceptance begins to blur distinctions between a "liberal" North and a "conservative" South. In his important work, *An American Dilemma*, published in 1944, Gunnar Myrdal places the point in perspective:

> To the author it has become apparent that the Northern romanticism for the "Old South" has the same basic psychology. It is, likewise, only the other side of Yankee equalitarianism. The North has so few vestiges of feudalism and aristocracy of its own that, even though it dislikes them fundamentally and is happy not to have them, Yankees are thrilled by them. *Northerners apparently cherish the idea of having had an aristocracy and of still having a real class society—in the South. Some manufacture the myth of the "Old South" or have it manufactured by Southern writers working for the Northern market.*[12]

The romanticized past of America meant that the Euro American female had to be placed on an equal, distant, and romantic pedestal with her European counterpart, as Myrdal further explains, in keeping with our previous allusion to the obsessions of the K.K.K. with Euro American womanhood:

> The "woman on the pedestal" pattern is found outside the American South, of course. It is a general trait in Western civilization and had extreme expression among the feudal nobility of the Middle Ages and the court nobility of France after Louis XIV. It was given added impetus by the loss of the economic function of middle class women at the end of the 18th century. But nowhere did it appear in such extreme, sentimental, and humorless form and so far down in the social status scale as in the American South.[13]

This is a situation from which women are still attempting to free themselves, and feminists have contributed much to unraveling some of the misperceptions.

"Assimilation" for African Americans therefore meant the absorption and acceptance of all these beliefs. However, a turn-of-the-century African American faced a quandary, for how could she or he adopt a Europe, as realized in America, that had condemned her or him to a permanent underdog status and still reclaim Europe? The answer lay in shifting the emphasis from race to class, as Du Bois realized. By acknowledging that the "Talented Tenth" among African Americans was a new kind of aristocracy, a new super-Negro could be created. So Charles S. Johnson (cocomposer with his brother of that civil rights staple "Lift Every Voice and Sing," often called "The Negro National Anthem") had this to say:

> The greater sensitivity of the upper-class Negro to racial discrimination is attributable to two factors: (1) his greater familiarity with political and social thought, and (2) the contradiction between his personal achievements and his social position. The upper-class Negro is more aware of the regional variations in racial prejudice. He sees the race system of the South as a local phenomenon, while the less educated Negro is apt to regard white domination as part of the order of the universe. The upper-class Negro also feels himself entitled by training and ability to achieve a high social position in the community—a position denied by reason of race alone.[14]

Johnson estimated that the "lower class" amounted to 82 percent, the middle class to 12 percent, and the upper class to 6 percent, in which latter group he no doubt counted himself.[15] He himself argued that this "folk Negro" class had a set of values totally different from his:

> The "folk Negro" organization of life and of values has been essential to survival and to the most satisfying functioning of the members of the group in their setting. Many things for which the larger dominant society has one set of values, meanings, and acceptable behavior patterns—marriage, divorce, extra-marital relations, illegitimacy, religion, love, death, and so forth—may in this group have quite another set. This helps to explain types of personalities developed under the peculiar circumstances of life of the "folk Negro" and makes their behavior more intelligible. The increase of means of communication and the introduction of some education is breaking down the cultural isolation of this group.[16]

Such narrow-minded elitism may be understood only in the context of an ardent desire for Eurocentrism.

"Folk Negro" values were therefore to be actively shunned, for they seriously detracted from African American intellectuals ever becoming part of a Euro

American elite. Therefore, the Eurocentric thinking of African American leaders ran completely counter to opinion at the grassroots level. This is why Alain Locke had to oppose Melville Herskovits's theories in *The Myth of the Negro Past* (1941), which clearly demonstrated African presence in America. Locke opined that any alternative was dangerous propaganda, for if Euro Americans believed it, they would think African Americans unworthy of assimilation. Equally, E. Franklin Frazier would have no truck with such folly; in *The Negro in the United States* (1957) and *Black Bourgeoisie* (1957), among other works, Frazier is passionate and adamant about the absolute lack of African connections in African American life. He was not merely having a debate with Melville Herskovits, whose work in Dahomey (now Benin), Surinam, Haiti, and Trinidad had provided him with proof as to how African retentions provided a connectedness. Frazier was actually articulating the disparate viewpoint of the African American intelligentsia, who feared extinction or expulsion. The Japanese/African American genocide connection was made by Du Bois and others in the early part of the century. It continued to be articulated to this day, most notably in the 1987 Irangate-censored testimony of Oliver North, who admitted that the Reagan White House had a plan in force to detain and incarcerate large numbers of African American citizens, mainly in Japanese prisoner-of-war camps, in the event of civil disturbance.[17]

To return to the premise at the beginning of this chapter: The very fact of African American presence, made visible through enfranchisement, exists as amendments to the central legal document of the land. What was amended may be emended. Continued African American minority existence in the United States depends on Euro American majority goodwill. This is not a comforting thought, but it is the only way the relationship of the Constitution and the amendments involving African Americans may be understood.

If, at one end, Euro Americans sought to retain African Americans in a "caste" system, at the other, W. E. B. Du Bois, Charles S. Johnson, and others of their ilk wished virtually the same, except they wanted to substitute "class" for "caste." Gunnar Myrdal sums up the situation quite aptly:

> As had already been indicated, there are many upper class Negroes who try to escape from race and caste. *They have arranged a little isolated world for themselves and want to hear as little as possible about their being Negroes or the existence of a Negro problem.* They make it a point not to read Negro papers or Negro books; they keep themselves and their children apart from "common Negroes." *They try to share the conservative political opinions of the whites of similar class status; they often over-do this considerably.* They despise lower class Negroes, and they balance the account by despising lower class whites too.[18]

Du Bois had complained thus in 1899:

In general its members [the African American intelligentsia] are curiously hampered by the fact that, being shut off from the world about them, *they are the aristocracy of their own people, with all the responsibilities of an aristocracy, and yet they, on the one hand, are not prepared for this role, and their own masses are not used to looking to them for leadership.* As a class they feel strongly the centrifugal forces of class repulsion among their own people, and, indeed, are compelled to feel it in sheer self-defense. They do not relish being mistaken for servants; they shrink from the free and easy worship of most of the Negro churches, and they shrink from all such display and publicity as will expose them to the veiled insult and deprecation which the masses suffer. Consequently this class, which ought to lead, refuses to head any race movement on the plea that thus they draw the very color line against which they protest.[19]

Later on, opinions would change; indeed, Du Bois would be expelled from the NAACP in 1948. But, even as African Americans and European Americans were radicalized into new postures, they took even these new attitudes from France (e.g., André Gide and Jean-Paul Sartre) and Germany (e.g., Leo Frobenius). Gide in *Voyage au Congo*, Sartre in his introduction to Senghor's anthology, and Frobenius in his voluminous study of African folklore had given European respectability to Africa. Even Ezra Pound was won over, writing a most laudable appreciation of Frobenius in Nancy Cunard's anthology.[20]

This all points to two significant factors; first, that "upper class" African Americans tended to be as Eurocentric as Euro Americans and, second, that the "folk Negroes," effectively and mercifully cut off from Westernization, were able in no small way to preserve aspects of a culture different from Europe's and defined today as "African American," yet one that ought to have been articulated as indigenous to America. When the fad about things exotic had been sanctioned in the 1920s by Europe, some African American intellectuals could go slumming and find a reservoir of preserved folklore. This would last only until the stock market crash abruptly cut off their Euro American patronage.

Actually, this subterranean culture was a synthesis, utilizing the appurtenances of Europe and Africa to create a unique American blend. Jazz was one form which this took, as African music was played on European instruments. A second form existed in the "slave narrative"—oral literature that was written down, sometimes by a non-African American. A third form occurs in the attempt to set African "music" and European "words" into a new form—to create blues and rap, which come out of the church and the street respectively. In both instances, words are made to "sound" like a preacher's intonation, and music is made to be "spoken" like a layman's colloquialism. Put differently, "music" imitates "words," and these actual words take on a life of their own, producing the "dozens," "jive talk," and the sermon. At the "folk" level, jazzman, slave narrator, and rapper are all combiners of words and music derived from the despised African American folk experience, adding to a unique way in which Eurocentrism is rectified. This goes largely unheard by mainstream America.

At the more visible and audible levels, Griffith was able to popularize distorted versions of earlier writings by revered figures like Jefferson, Franklin, Washington, and Lincoln, employing film to validate myth as history; and his work was presented as history when *Birth of a Nation* was later taught in American schools. Today, this attitude has encouraged more hate leaders like David Duke, Lyndon H. Larouche, and Tom Metzger, leader of the White Aryan Resistance. At the same time, Afrocentric impulses move beyond religious eccentrics, like Father Divine and Daddy Grace, to the political antiestablishment views of Hon. Louis B. Farrakhan. Not surprisingly, extremism on both sides leads to a surprising degree of consensus. Duke and Farrakhan have more in common than is at first apparent. One opts for extreme Eurocentrism, the other for an equally extreme Afrocentrism to denounce the core of values of contemporary American society. Both would agree on separation.

"White ethnocentrism" and "Black integrationism," also possess the same goals. One sought to join a larger community of European nations by proffering an ideology that suggested that its proponents deserved special consideration out of an identification with European "class" interests. The other attempted to place African American integration into wider mainstream Europeanized America, often asserting that African Americans were, in reality, like European Americans, as they too understood "class" notions, and offered proof that their leaders were products of similar European American mores. When African American leaders proffered "class" for Euro American "caste" (which should have locked out the entire African American group), they sought to extricate the leaders but sacrificed the "folk Negro" populace on the altar of expediency.

More important, both the Garveyites and the Klan of yesteryear and the Black Nationalists and White Supremacists of today agree on the need for separation. Both fringe groups exist as "history-takers" rather than "history-makers," as they both look elsewhere for justification and legitimization to mythical deviant European thought and to invented radical African belief. Just as Europe seemed to sanction Euro American attitudes, so too does it legitimize Du Bois's Pan Africanism and Garvey's "Back to Africa." In the latter case, the most thriving branch was his London headquarters, at a time when few Blacks lived in England.

As Black separatists identify themselves with Africa, and White supremacists with Europe, both envision Europe as the locus of their ideology. Many prominent African Americans like Paul Robeson, Richard Wright, and Du Bois himself saw the new Europe of the Soviet Union as the ultimate hope for human salvation. At the extreme end, latter-day White supremacists see Nazi Germany as a natural spawning ground for their own activities, and some Black supremacists used to see European/Marxist models as justification for their own approach. Perhaps the reasons lie more in external structures, which have little to do with American aspirations and more to do with Europe's own concept of itself.

European/New World relationships may be seen in four distinct phases: First, Pope Alexander VI's Bull of 1492 effectively located controlling devices in Europe. The Bull had divided up the world into Spanish and Portuguese spheres of influence. Even though the Dutch, English, and French soon joined in, fighting their way toward the spoils of battle, the point is nevertheless evident. Rome had identified western Europe as cultural and spiritual intermediary, and this world doctrine would last until the end of the nineteenth century. As America was "discovered" and colonized, Eurocentrism acquired a new base.

Second, when Count Bismarck summoned European powers to the Berlin Conference between 1884 and 1885, this formalized a similar relationship with Europe. Even though America had long since formally declared itself independent, its own Eurocentric inclinations had this double effect: On the one hand, America sought to emulate Europe, as seen in its own "internal" expansionist tendencies of "Manifest Destiny" of the 1840s, which, ironically, brought the nation into conflict with England over Oregon and with France over Louisiana and Florida. On the other hand, America's "external" expansionism, first formulated in the Monroe Doctrine, was later modified in 1904 in Theodore Roosevelt's annual message to Congress. The United States, he said, would constitute itself as "an international police power," in today's jargon, a "superpower."

Under the guise of anti-imperialism, Secretary of State William Jennings Bryan and President Woodrow Wilson dispatched marines to Haiti (1915–1925), Santo Domingo in 1916, Nicaragua in 1916 and 1927–1933, and Mexico in 1917. Just as Europe had carved up an African empire, America had won itself one in the Caribbean and Central and South America. Eurocentric colonialism was also imitated and imported.

Third, the Paris Peace Conference of 1919 marked a new beginning in European/African and European/New World relations. As Germany and Italy had been removed as controlling forces, some African countries formerly under their authority obtained a degree of autonomy. Likewise, after entering World War I in 1917, the United States broadened its range into the European theater. Although the United States did not sign the Treaty of Versailles, in 1921 it made a separate peace with Germany. Although during *les ans entre les guerres*, America deluded itself into a false isolationism, it was soon shattered. The stock market crash of 1929 linked the United States with western Europe in economic collapse, and World War II brought the United States permanently onto the scene of Anglo European conflict and resolution. Not only did Winston Churchill give away large chunks of the empire for American bases, but also American generals and soldiers fought on the same Allied side, and against their distant European relations. Anglo Europeanism was validated as good public policy after two world wars.

Fourth, post-1945 marked a different arrangement. The United States, France, China, England, and the USSR made themselves "permanent members" of the United Nations Security Council with veto power. FDR, along with Churchill and Stalin, had met in Teheran in 1943 and in Yalta in 1945; the United States was one of the "Big Three." Eurocentrism was confirmed as inseparable from Americanism.

These four stages demarcate not just a growth from subject to peer, but a shift from colonial to emperor. NATO was its political expression; the International Monetary Fund (IMF) and the World Bank its economic force; and the "U-Bomb" (as the atomic bomb was then called) its physical repressant to keep everyone else (including Europe) in check. H. G. Nicholas in *The United States and Britain* characterizes this era as follows:

> The end of the war which the atomic bomb so signally accelerated created a new situation. In the U.S.A. there was a powerful conviction of possessing "the secrets" of the bomb. Opinion was divided as to whether these "secrets" should be preserved as an American monopoly or put under some form of international control. For Britain, anxious both to develop the peaceful potentialities of atomic energy and to have atomic weapons of her own, neither attitude was promising. *The monopolists were opposed to any sharing, the internationalists were opposed to singling out any one country for partnership.* Truman's announcement in October 1945 that the United States would not share the "know-how" of the bomb's manufacture with its allies precipitated a meeting in November at Washington (at which Mr. Mackenzie King was also present for Canada) from which emerged an "agreed declaration," which, *while advocating international control and inspection, provided for "full and effective cooperation" between the United States, the United Kingdom, and Canada.* But at the operational level this agreement went awry, British requests for information encountering a blank refusal. While Attlee was still trying to secure from Truman what he regarded as fair implementation of a tripartite agreement, Congress on 1 August 1946 passed the McMahon Act, which in effect slammed the door on the disclosure or exchange of information in the atomic field. There was thus no alternative for Britain but to go it alone.[21]

America had won the war but lost the cultural battle. But, if history teaches anything, it must surely be that the world is not a bystander. The nuclear club gave way to nuclear proliferation. By the end of the twentieth century, when Gorbachev's *perestroika* had ensured the economic and political collapse of the Soviet Union and the Soviet bloc, events had seemingly gone full circle. The United States assumed the former European monopoly on power, for it was now sole superpower.

A final irony occurs when America exported to the European mainland its own fears and mythologies, telling German innkeepers to establish bars for

"Amis" (Euro Americans) and "Schwarzen" or "Negerinnen" (African Americans). Germans may have been confused, but they complied with the reality that the Kerner Commission was later to state boldly: the acknowledgment of two Americas, one Black, one White. American Eurocentrism had been returned to Europe with a racial twist, one with which, at least historically speaking, Europe had at that time limited experience. Europe would soon catch up, as the more rightist movements against the *Ausländer* would demonstrate.

From the turn of the twentieth century, race began as a metaphor to define American reality and image. Earlier we had observed this particularly in the visual images of *The Clansman* and *Birth of a Nation* as they sought to represent history. In turn, we noted that the K.K.K. was only the bodily manifestation of a larger issue that continued to plague American society—a desire to remain a cultural extension of Europe. Klan regalia and paraphernalia made visual the concerns and symbolized the actions of some members of the larger majority Euro American society, not merely in terms of supposed racial superiority but also in its greater claims to European similarity. Also, we noted that, surprisingly, some members of African American society did not possess goals dissimilar to those of its Euro American counterpart, whatever the level or wording of rhetoric. African American consciousness, very much like Euro American consciousness, was directed toward one end: African Americans, at the micro level, wanted full assimilation into White Eurocentric America; Euro Americans, at the macro level, wanted complete integration into Europe. In fact, these tendencies could even lead toward identification of mutual interests.

So-called White racism and so-called Black nationalism thus find more common ground. Garvey and the K.K.K. could and did agree to work together, for their end was the same, removing African Americans from the country. At the other end of the scale, "moderate" African Americans and "liberal" Euro Americans could hark back to the old Noble Savage myth, although, of course, they would not have thus stated it. They could both concur on two points: African Americans possessed certain characteristics—dance, music, laughter (Du Bois and James Weldon Johnson both agreed); and when "educated" (actually "Euro Americanized"), they were capable of (a) becoming excellent, nonthreatening citizens and (b) keeping other African Americans in place. This is what the African American middle class had always cherished.

If our larger model remains true, then Alexander VI's Papal Bull, Bismarck's Berlin Conference, the Paris Peace Conference, and post-1945 events show the United States involved first as victim, later as victor, but always within the format of Europe. As the relationship vis-à-vis Europe altered even more, America transferred to its former mentor the trappings of its own culture, whether these were in the form of ground-to-air missiles, B-2 bombers, stealth aircraft, nuclear capability, computer technology, or its own version of Eurocentric reality.

Role reversal is not as sudden as it seems; to understand it, we must examine American trends that forcibly allowed the country to enter the European club and establish kinship. One easy way of seeing this from a single perspective is to examine the role of the new moneyed millionaires, for they are the first Atlanticists, moving beyond the parameters into which the colonists were forced to anchor themselves and taking on European garb, long before the American expatriates of the 1920s. They could claim an affinity with both shores, in some cases because they were European-born (like Andrew Carnegie) or, at most, a generation removed. They gained admittance to Europe because their wealth and the advent of the steamship afforded them easy access, and their new dollars signified a newer and different "aristocracy" from the Old South. Untainted by a slavocracy, they could present themselves as living proof that both Adam Smith and Ragged Dick coexisted; as firm believers, they declared that wealth was born out of a rags-to-riches concept.

It became necessary to invent a new image for the millionaire. Horatio Alger's books for boys (some of whom he has been accused of sexually molesting), served as models. From 1869 to his death in 1899, Alger's Ragged Dick, Luck and Pluck, and Tattered Tom expressed the bootstrap theory that, through much hard work, the poor boy could rise from poverty to wealth. Later on, Donald Trump would refer to his father's acquisition of wealth as "classic Horatio Alger,"[22] and Lee Iacocca would remember his own father's belief in the limitless possibilities of America—"the freedom to become anything you wanted to be."[23] All of this is, of course, before the sobering economic realities of the 1990s.

Before Horatio Alger, the belief could have been extrapolated from John Locke's "Original Contract," and particularly from his *Second Treatise of Civil Government* (1690), in which he argued that although the earth belongs to all men, personal labor decides what is owned by an individual. Adam Smith's *Wealth of Nations* (1776) likewise declared in Book 4 that Americans "will be one of the foremost nations of the world." Labor of the nation equates with its life and establishes value; and in more advanced societies, wages, profit, and rent determine price. The nature, accumulation, and employment of capital lead to increase in productive labor and to decrease in interest rates. The ardent pursuit of self-interest is tantamount to the public interest. Europe had so said.

Locke and Smith became part of the American myth. Not unnaturally, it led to a situation where a peculiar American combination of Locke's "personal labor" and Smith's "self-interest" combined into Horatio Algerism. However, the result is very different. By 1986, according to Thomas Dye in *Who's Running America*, a national elite amounting to 7,314 positions emerged that,

> taken collectively, control half of the nation's industrial assets; half of all assets in communication, transportation, and utilities; half of all banking assets; two-thirds of all insurance assets; and they direct Wall Street's

largest investment firms. They control the television net-works, the influential news agencies, and the major newspaper chains. They control nearly
40 percent of all the assets of private foundations and half of all private
university endowments. They direct the nation's largest and best-known
New York and Washington law firms as well as the nation's major civic
and cultural organizations. They occupy key federal governmental positions in the executive, legislative, and judicial branches. And they occupy
all the top command positions in the Army, Navy, Air Force, and Marines.[24]

The United States had not become a capitalistic society on the model of Adam
Smith but, instead, a monopolistic one.

Dye's analysis brings us to an interesting point. Just as at the local level
of political interaction, Europe remained the sounding board for Euro and
African American nationalists, so Europe equally became the reference
point for the "gospel of wealth," American ingenuity, and aristocratic
"borrowings" by America from the European aristocracy. This latter was
not new, for wealthy landowners in the colonial past had assumed that they
were entitled to some say in the governing of the territory. Before the
Industrial Revolution, wealthy agrarian landholders acquired homes in
London, Paris, Rome, and Madrid, vacationed at popular spas, resorts, and
hotels in Europe, and bought up the artifacts of European culture. At the
beginning of the present century, they could "purchase" European aristocratic titles and/or estates or, at the very least, European wives. Concerning
this, Ferdinand Lundberg makes the following point: "The chief assets of
Europeans have been hereditary titles, leisure-class manners, perhaps a
shabby estate or two, and passports into the world of snobbery."[25]

Andrew Mellon, like many another American magnates, married and "had
his children by a wealthy English woman [and] the McCormicks, Astors,
Fields, and others have contracted such unions with British commoners."[26]
Here the millionaires, were they so inclined, could have cited Edmund
Burke, who, knowing that people were not created equally, had championed
the American War of Independence but denounced the French Revolution.
There, he contended, the nobility had surrendered "regal authority" to
unskilled representatives, when they ought to have represented "the natural
landed interest of the country." Burke's *Present State of the Nation* (1769)
attacked George Grenville's decision to tax America, as did his *Letter to the
Sheriffs of Bristol* (1777); but his *Reflections on the Revolution in France*
(1790) supported aristocracy as essential to good government with its
"inherited rights." Thus the new American "aristocracy" could look toward
Burke and find, as Du Bois did, a pleasingly Platonic formula: the aristocratic Guardians, when well educated and cultured, could make decisions
for the general populace. Only such an elite could apparently rule, for their
wealth was stabilizing, productive, and creative.[27]

Humanitarianism as practiced by Cornelius Vanderbilt, Andrew Mellon, Henry Ford, Andrew Carnegie, and John D. Rockefeller was actually a way of creating and sustaining such an aristocracy, based not only on the benevolent manipulation of wealth but also on perpetuating Eurocentric values and beliefs. In reality, the millionaires were not aristocratic, but they relished the myth. Equally, their parade of superficial learning was a further extension of the rags-to-riches myth, as well as a wish to become a Burke-type aristocrat. Note J. H. Bridge on Carnegie:

> I have just glanced through his contribution to *Liber Scriptorum*, the first book of the Authors Club. It is entitled "Genius Illustrated from Burns." Here are references to the philosopher's stone, to Parnassus, Milton, Shakespeare (two), Goethe, President Arthur, Tennyson and to Walhalla. And there are quotations from Carlyle (two), Marcus Aurelius, St. Paul, Matthew Arnold (two), Shakespeare and Thompson—a good and creditable array for one without schooling![28]

The point unintentionally ridicules the rich as custodians of surplus wealth and knowledge that must be utilized for the glorification of the "race." Carnegie, who later retired to a Scottish castle, restated the credo in *The Gospel of Wealth*, almost echoing Du Bois:

> It is well, nay, essential for the progress of the race that the houses of some should be homes for all that is highest and best in literature and the arts, and for all the refinements of civilization, rather than that none should be so. Much better this great irregularity than universal squalor.[29]

Any conventional millionaire viewpoint sought to position America as part of Europe. The "home" to which Carnegie alludes is the basis for our understanding—it is male, American, and White. Often, it may be translated into European baronial terms like "Trump Castle," "Trump Tower," and "Trump Plaza," as the possession or home had to have a certain architectural sound that restored Europe and celebrated the norm.

Nick Caraway, the narrator of F. Scott Fitzgerald's *The Great Gatsby* (1925), comments on the link to the past and to Europe as he walks through Gatsby's house:

> And inside, as we wandered through Marie Antoinette music-rooms and Restoration salons, I felt that there were guests concealed behind every couch and table, under orders to be breathlessly silent until we had passed through. As Gatsby closed the door of "the Merton College Library" I could have sworn I heard the owl-eyed man break into ghostly laughter.[30]

The laughter arises because Gatsby's architectural monstrosity at West Egg, Long Island, exists as a symbol of futility, which the great, staring eyes on the occultist's billboard recognize. Daisy also sees the sham: "this unprecedented 'place' that Broadway had begotten upon a Long Island fishing village."[31] She is "appalled by its raw vigor that choked under the old euphemisms and by the too obtrusive fate that herded its inhabitants along a short-cut from nothing to nothing."[32] At the end of the novel, after Gatsby's death, Nick bemoans "that huge incoherent failure of a house."[33] The final rebuttal is that it stood for something that was clearly as relevant as Gatsby's pretensions to European culture.

Carnegie's castle, Gatsby's mansion, and earlier on Jefferson's Monticello were attempts at a false Eurocentric past in America. The millionaires sought this pretense in various ways, as their money became the means through which Europe could be acquired. It had to remain only a far-off vision for aspiring African American middle-class leaders. Robert Silverberg admits to a Jamesian negativism, claiming that "those who came to this green New World failed to find those traces of awesome antiquity on which romantic myths could be founded."[34] He means European antiquity, the absence of which Henry James bemoaned; the millionaires invented their own fanciful Europe.

This new model called for the construction of a missing history, both personal and national. Henry Ford, despite his well-known assertion that history was "more or less bunk,"

> collected on a titanic scale every jot and tittle of the American past that he and his emissaries could lay hands on—four poster beds, banjo clocks, cigar-store Indians, old boots, gas lamps, rusty old threshers, and wooden flails. . . . Thirty-four thousand Ford dealers, under instructions from the "Dictator of Dearborn" scoured the country side, unpaid, in search of Staffordshire china, antiquated stoves, and ante-bellum mousetraps. Old buildings, too, fell into the net and duly got shipped off to Dearborn: a Michigan log cabin, an 1850s firehouse, an old general store, an Illinois courthouse frequented by the young Lincoln.[35]

Likewise, Andrew Mellon (under whom it was once said, three presidents served), during the very depths of the Depression, flitted between Washington and London in his ceaseless search for European art treasures. He sought out the large collections held by the czars and, in 1928, proposed an art gallery for Washington modeled on England's National Gallery. From the impoverished Russian leadership under Stalin, Mellon procured the Hermitage Collection for six and a half million dollars, later acquiring Lord Devesne's collection of sculpture and paintings for twenty-one million. In 1936, Mellon offered his collection to what he saw as a culturally impoverished nation. When on March 17, 1941, President Roosevelt dedicated the National Gallery, he said that the collection represented the "living past" of Europe, which would now constitute the "living future" of America. His words are most significant, given the thrust of this argument.

European identification took still other forms, as the new millionaires in steel, automobiles, oil, and railroads distanced themselves from the old Cotton Kings. The latter had been haunted by the shadow of slavery, and their mansions had been erected as visible proof of the preservation of a feudal lifestyle long since discarded by Europe. The new Robber Barons (Carnegie hated the term) were nouveaux riches, but they were not haunted by any unfavorable past. Thus freed, from the 1870s onward, they gravitated to Newport, Rhode Island, erecting enormous and conspicuous palaces. Their summer cottages had neo-Greek facades, fountains, and statues. Tiffany's supplied a lineage and coat of arms. The Vanderbilts erected their own summer house in August 1892, complete with iron gates, porticos, balustrades, high ceilings, elaborate staircases, and a grand ballroom. There Cornelius Vanderbilt could live out his senile fantasy that he was the Prince of Wales; for one ball, his wife hired a group of actors, decked out as British marines. The act of playing British had reached a new level of absurdity.

The equally fictional Gatsby's life is similarly intertwined in legend. He is an Oxford man, a gambler, a bootlegger, a German spy, a war hero: "the vague contour of Jay Gatsby had filled out to the substantiality of the man."[36] The manipulation of the myth, intentionally vague, hinted at some dark secret, an origin that was never sure, a past that could be manipulated. It permitted a degree of self-inventiveness that spoke both to individual quirks (Gatsby's obsession with Daisy, Mellon's art collection, Ford's Motor Village), while still stressing an embodiment as Ragged Dick rising to wealth out of sheer personal determination. There is, therefore, a degree of "truth" in the assertions of Lee Iacocca and Donald Trump, for these speak to more contemporary aspects of the model. In a society that is supposedly egalitarian, wealth stands out only if it pretends to share a degree of commonality with nonwealth. Ordinary mortals thus become assured of their own possibilities. As J. Paul Getty put it, "It's more important for the man with The Millionaire Mentality to be able to think small than to think big."[37] This is the rhetoric of every presidential race, that to be really successful, one has to put forward the claim to be Ragged Dick; even Ross Perot stressed his humble origins.

A further aspect to the model of the millionaire is that money must largely be seen to be used as largesse. Therefore, the millionaire as benefactor is not merely an idealistic provider, but, in truth, a means of forging artificial links with the populace. Carnegie became very popular because his *Gospel of Wealth* provided this particular view of inherited wealth: The wife and daughters should be left "moderate sources of income," but "the thoughtful man must shortly say, 'I would as soon leave my son a curse as the almighty dollar.' "[38] He adds:

This, then, is held to be the duty of the man of wealth: To set an example of modest, unostentatious living, shunning display or extravagance; to provide moderately for the legitimate wants of those dependent upon him; and, after doing so, to consider all surplus revenues which come to him simply as trust funds which he is called upon to administer . . . —the man of wealth thus becoming the mere trustee and agent for his poorer brethren, bringing to their service his superior wisdom, experience, and ability to administer, doing for them better than they would or could do for themselves.[39]

The high-sounding, ever-conceding, certainly condescending argument really means that the man of wealth is able to propagate himself, in the manner of European royalty, through means other than his progeny. The Carnegie Church Peace Union, Carnegie Hall, the Carnegie Institute of Pittsburgh, the Carnegie Institute of Technology, and the Carnegie Institution of Washington established his name on the local front. But, especially for a Scotsman with obvious Eurocentric ties, the real task of this millionaire was to leave the American imprint writ large in Europe—hence, the Carnegie Dunferline Trust, the Carnegie Endowment for International Peace, the Carnegie Foundation for the Advancement of Teaching (with its Pension Fund), and the Carnegie Fund Trust for Great Britain, all ensuring the Europeanization of American wealth. Nor was he alone in these endeavors: Ford, Rockefeller, and Mellon also established name-bearing centers or universities at home and endowed foundations and fellowships that transported American wealth and attendant prestige back to Europe.

Not everything that flowed from America to Europe was free. At the national level, the new postwar image of America as material giver had a catch, as Robert Bremner points out in *American Philanthropy*:

Under the Marshall Plan, or European Recovery Program, which began in 1948 and continued until 1951, the United States helped nations of western Europe bolster their economies by means of grants and loans totaling $12.5 billion. *The Marshall Plan was a form of prudent investment rather than a display of loving kindness.*[40]

Such aid, approved by "influential citizens and interest groups,"[41] was only another way of giving taxpayers' approval to the millionaire's generosity. In both private and national philanthropy, the funding served to firm up Euro American relations, further emphasizing America's fascination with Europe. Not surprisingly, generosity on this scale did not extend to Japan, even after Hiroshima and Nagasaki.

As early as 1914, before active U.S. participation in European affairs, the Rockefeller Foundation had played an important role in assisting the Commission for Relief in Belgium (CRB) by buying food for its starving citizens. It "purchased almost a million dollars worth of food for the commission, chartered ships, and advanced funds for freight charges."[42] The economic linkage with Europe thus grew from individual to national focus. In both instances, the goal was to fortify the erection of bridges between America and Europe, from NATO through the G7 meetings, until the era of the 1990s when, in full control of the United Nations, the United States could manipulate the permanent European members to do its bidding, whether in the Gulf or in Somalia. The terms of the agreement have changed, but the close association remains.

At the domestic level, both Euro American donor and African American recipient are noted in Carnegie's interest in African Americans. In 1907, he delivered a lecture at the Edinburgh Philosophical Institution on "The Negro in America." Although he knew little about the subject, with the help of Booker T. Washington (to whose Tuskegee Institute he had given $600,000 in 1904), he drew a cheerful picture of African American progress. According to Joseph Frazier Wall, "The same hopeful note of progress as demonstrated by statistics ran throughout the address: illiteracy among Negroes cut mainly in half in thirty years, from 83.5 percent in 1870 to 47.4 percent in 1900; land ownership by Negroes in South Central States, 30 percent."[43]

Carnegie also noted "a surprisingly rapid rate of increase, one of the surest proofs of a virile race."[44] He pointed out that, from the Black race, millionaires, an astronomer, and a publisher had evolved. Above all, African Americans had given birth to Booker T. Washington, "the combined Moses and Joshua of his race."[45] His upbeat note, with which W. E. B. Du Bois could certainly have agreed, concluded on a most idealistic tone for his European audience:

> The advanced few are only the leaders of the vast multitude that are still to be stimulated to move forward. Nor are the leaders themselves, with certain exceptions, all that it is hoped they are yet to become. When you are told of the number owning land or attending schools, or of the millions of Church members, and the amount of wealth and of land possesst [*sic*] by the negro, pray remember that they number ten millions, scattered over an area nearly as great as Europe. The bright spots have been brought to your notice, but these are only small points surrounded by great areas of darkness. True, the stars are shining in the sky thru the darkness, but the sun spreading light over all has not yet arisen, altho there are not wanting convincing proofs that her morning beams begin to gild the mountain tops.[46]

Du Bois, for all the radicality of which Carnegie disapproved, would have identified himself as a member of the "advanced few" or, in his own words, "the Talented Tenth." Carnegie's lecture in Scotland had put the entire issue in focus. The millionaire chose his topic because racism was a part of the American lifestyle that he found embarrassing. His optimistic tone was an attempt at clarifying a situation, at making him and other millionaire seekers more palatable to Europeans. He could not have believed what he had uttered, but he said it because he felt the need to "correct" an image that his own countrymen had of America, and of him. After all, he was thinking of the British/U.S. political union that he devoutly desired.

Therefore, Carnegie sought to alleviate the race issue abroad by placing it in a comforting and acceptable role. This was perhaps an even larger attempt at myth-making than Gatsby's invented world with its multiple pasts. As we noted earlier, Carnegie's stance is very little different from that of African American and Euro American leadership, for they all sought to project themselves in the best possible European light. If race had become the central issue for America, the metaphor by which it defined itself and was defined by others, then for rich and poor, progressive and conservative, Euro Americans and African Americans, it had to be related in such a way that social admission into Europe's class and culture would not be impeded. Carnegie was really preparing the way for his own retirement to a Scottish castle, to assume the pretensions of baronial splendor.

Booker T. Washington also constantly stressed "acquiring the elements of civilization."[47] Although he eschewed the thought of a physical return to Africa, his book *The Story of the Negro* (1909) spoke of the way in which Africans had been intentionally distorted "in order to put the lofty position to which the white race has attained in sharper condition of a more primitive people."[48] This is pretty radical for Washington and for its time. Surprisingly strident though he could be, Washington still felt the need to play down the Klan: In *Up from Slavery* (1910) he comments, "Today there are no such organizations in the South. . . . There are few places in the South now where public sentiment would permit such organizations to exist."[49] For both Carnegie and Washington, admission to Europe meant pretending that the race issue in America was not threatening and indeed hardly ever existed.

Therefore the benign picture of race that emerges in *Up from Slavery* is, not surprisingly, like Carnegie's own in *The Negro in America*, precisely because Carnegie's source was Washington. They both dismissed race, but for slightly different reasons: Washington, of course, needed the financial support of Rockefeller and Carnegie in his fund-raising efforts, so that he could help African Americans enter the European American workforce, albeit at the lowliest level. Washington was gracious and grateful; for instance, speaking of Rockefeller, Washington declared with admiration:

> The more I come into contact with wealthy people, the more I believe that they are growing in the direction of looking upon their money simply as an instrument which God has placed in their hand for doing good with. I never go to the office of Mr. John D. Rockefeller, who more than once has

been generous to Tuskegee, without being reminded of this. The close, careful, and minute investigation that he always makes in order to be sure that every dollar that he gives will do the most good—an investigation that is just as searching as if he were investing money in a business enterprise—convinces me that the growth in this direction is most encouraging.[50]

Perhaps in these few lines lies the ultimate legend of the millionaires. They were servants of a Judaeo-Christian/European God, and their benevolence was divinely mandated. What Washington could only have guessed at was that their role as benefactors had set a new precedent for them and their nation as donors to postwar Europe.

Although Washington never exhibited the stridency that the popular view associates with Du Bois, he epitomizes the two major forces that define the country at the turn of the century—an emphasis on class and race. The millionaires had utilized their wealth to construct a most untypical Jeffersonian aristocracy, which Jefferson, despite his own "aristocratic" Eurocentrism, would nevertheless have been most surprised to see. Their money gave them access to Europe and allowed them, especially through their support of Washington, to attempt to deemphasize the Klan and what Carnegie had referred to as the more extreme elements among African American leadership, that is, people like Du Bois—although, as noted, he was hardly a threat. At the same time, conspicuous expenditure, particularly at Newport, allowed the wealthy to play at being Europeans.

One is reminded of an anonymous "Negro" in *The Great Gatsby*; he sees the accident in which Daisy kills Myrtle and knows the truth, which he, unspeaking shares with the narrator: "Only the Negro and I were near enough to hear what he [Tom] said."[51] The African American vanishes in the narration, but Gatsby's "Negro" is a little like Washington and Du Bois in seeking a type of presence, yet maintaining neutral anonymity.[52] What altered this occurred at a later stage of the European dominant model, particularly notable in the events between 1919 and 1945, which permitted the supposedly semiarticulate "Negro" access to Europe and allowed him or her to participate in the same kind of Eurocentric activity that had been part of the Euro American millionaire experience. The African American entered Europe accidentally as alien soldiers, demanding to fight for a country in which they played little part. They emerged later as artist, actor, and activist, defining with new music and new words more relevant and meaningful images of a multicultural America, still resisting its own possibilities.

To sum up: We noted how, in the eighteenth century, the importation of the Noble Savage was reordered, refashioned, and retained, thus marking an important linkage with but nevertheless a departure from European thought. In the nineteenth century, a mixture of Covey's Africanity blended with Emerson and Thoreau's global reach toward Indian mysticism to attempt to give the country a distinctiveness. At the beginning of the twentieth century, the situation is made clear for us: What is actually defining non-European American reality is not the stated promulgations of legislative bodies or opinion makers, who speak for a majority, while negatively reacting to any semblance of otherness. But in the twentieth century, the presence of the "Other," the African American, nevertheless points to preoccupations that would identify, single out, demarcate, and simultaneously express the cultural variety of the country. For three centuries the manifestation, mythic or real, of African Americans marks out a new cultural territory through which the United States could make its claim to global distinctiveness. Only this presence (given the "absence" of Native Americans) serves as a major factor that could pull the "civilizing" process away from overt Anglo Europeanization, if it were not constantly being resisted by large segments of the population.

NOTES

1. I am indebted to David M. Chalmers, *Hooded Americanism: The History of the Ku Klux Klan* (Durham, N.C.: Duke University Press, 1987), for background information.

2. National Association for the Advancement of Colored People, *Thirty Years of Lynching* (New York: NAACP, 1919).

3. Thomas Carlyle, *Occasional Discourse on the Nigger Question* (London: T. Bosworth, 1853), 28.

4. Henry W. Grady, *The New South* (New York: Robert Bonner's Sons, 1890), 152–153.

5. Thomas Pearce Bailey, *Race Orthodoxy in the South and Other Aspects of the Race Question* (New York: Neale Publishing Company, 1914), 342.

6. Thomas Nelson Page, *The Negro: The Southerner's Problem* (New York: Charles Scribner's Sons, 1904), 112–113.

7. "The tyranny of the majority" was a phrase coined in 1787 by James Winthrop, the antifederalist from Massachusetts. The problem was certainly recognized by James Madison and is an issue that we note continues to plague American administrations—even in 1993, in the ill-fated Clinton nomination of Lani Guinier.

8. Benjamin Quarles, *The Negro in the Making of America* (London: Collier-Macmillan, 1969), 236.

9. Ibid., 236.

10. Ibid., 237.

11. W. E .B. Du Bois, *Dusk of Dawn* (New York: Harcourt, Brace, 1940), 183. Emphasis added.

12. Gunnar Myrdal, *An American Dilemma* (New York: McGraw-Hill, 1964), 2:1223. Emphasis added.

13. Myrdal, *Dilemma*, 1:142. Also see 2:1204.

14. Charles S. Johnson, *Growing Up in the Black Belt* (Washington, D.C.: American Comment on Education, 1941), 312.

15. Ibid., 71.

16. Ibid., 75–76.

17. See Oliver North's testimony as reported in "Reagan Aides and the Secret Government," *Miami Herald*, July 5, 1987, 1 and 14a.

18. Myrdal, *Dilemma*, 2:764. Emphasis added.

19. W. E. B. Du Bois, *The Philadelphia Negro* (Philadelphia: University of Pennsylvania Press, 1899), 177. Emphasis added.

20. Nancy Cunard, *Negro: An Anthology* [1934], ed. and abridged by Hugh Ford (New York: Frederick Ungar Publishing, 1970). She stated, "I should also have more respect for the Afro-American intelligentzia and for the Negro millionaires, etc., that are rumoured to flourish in Harlem if they had shown more alacrity in hearing of an author who has shown their race its true charter of nobility and who has dug out of Africa tradition overlaid on tradition to set against the traditions of Europe and Asia," 393–394.

21. H. G. Nicholas, *The United States and Britain* (Chicago: University of Chicago Press, 1975), 130. Emphasis added.

22. Donald J. Trump (with Tony Schwartz), *Trump: The Art of the Deal* (New York: Warner Books, 1987), 66.

23. Lee Iacocca (with William Novak), *Iacocca: An Autobiography* (New York: Bantam Books, 1984), 7.

24. Thomas Dye, *Who's Running America?* 6th ed. (Englewood Cliffs, N.J.: Prentice Hall, 1986), 157.

25. Ferdinand Lundberg, *America's 60 Families* (New York: Vanguard Press, 1937), 9.

26. Ibid., 15.

27. Michael Freeman, *Edmund Burke and the Critique of Political Radicalism* (Chicago: University of Chicago Press, 1980), 21, 29–32.

28. J. H. Bridge, *Millionaire and Grub Street* (New York: Brentan's, 1931), 57.

29. Andrew Carnegie, *The Gospel of Wealth,* ed. Edward C. Kirkland (Cambridge, Mass.: Belknap Press of Harvard Press, 1962), 18.

30. F. Scott Fitzgerald, *The Great Gatsby* (New York: Charles Scribner's Sons, 1953), 82.

31. Ibid., 96.

32. Ibid., 96–97.

33. Ibid., 158.

34. Robert Silverberg, " . . . And the Mound Builders Vanished from the Earth," in *A Sense of History: The Best Writings from the Pages of the American Heritage* (New York: American Heritage, 1985), 46.

35. Walter Karp, "Henry Ford's Village," in *A Sense of History*, 658.

36. Fitzgerald, *Great Gatsby*, 91.

37. J. Paul Getty, *How to be Rich* (Chicago: Playboy Press, 1965), 43.

38. Carnegie, *Gospel of Wealth*, 21.

39. Ibid., 25.

40. Robert H. Bremmer, *American Philanthropy* (Chicago: University of Chicago Press, 1988), 163. Emphasis added.

41. Immanuel Wexler, *The Marshall Plan Revisited* (Westport, Conn.: Greenwood Press, 1983), 26.

42. Bremmer, *Philanthropy*, 122.

43. Joseph Frazier Wall, *Andrew Carnegie* (Pittsburgh: University of Pittsburgh Press, 1970), 973–974.

44. Andrew Carnegie, *The Negro in America* (Inverness, Scotland, 1907), 12.

45. Ibid., 40.

46. Ibid., 41–42.

47. Booker T. Washington, *The Booker T. Washington Papers,* ed. Louis H. Harlan, 9 vols. (Urbana, Ill.: University of Illinois Press), 3 (1974): 378.

48. Washington, *Papers*, 1 (1972): 402.

49. Ibid., 255.

50. Ibid., 373.

51. Fitzgerald, *Great Gatsby*, 125.

52. Toni Morrison has done an excellent task of highlighting these "absent" Blacks in Twain, Faulkner, and Hemingway. See Morrison, *Playing in the Dark*, 54–59, 66–69, and 70–90. She proposes four topics that need more investigation. She terms these "the Africanist character as surrogate and enabler" (51); how "Africanist idiom is used to establish difference" (52); how the Black character is "used to limn out and enforce the invention and implications of whiteness" (52); and "the manipulation of . . . the story of a black person, the experience of being bound and/or rejected" (53).

5
Imperialism and Immigration ───────────

Q ueen Victoria's death and Theodore Roosevelt's election to the presidency
are important events in 1901, as they indicate a course for the twentieth
century. The Roosevelt era (1901–1909) capped and sanctified the idea that
America, albeit secretly, could possess an empire. This period coincides with
similar European consolidation of empire, especially following Bismarck's
conference in Berlin. On the American home front, economic reasons could be
found in a booming internal economy, with a surplus to export.

By 1900, accumulated investment capital was in the region of $500m, and
new areas were sought for investment. As naval power increased, some capital
was utilized to found naval bases. In a way, without any attempt at politicizing
events, America's growth and conquest may be seen merely as one way capital
sought to find profit centers. This was also very much a turn-of-the-century
European practice, which treated colonies as a source of raw material.

Cuba was a case in point. Franklin Knight finds that even as early as 1878

> the United States had already replaced Spain as the dominant trading
> partner of Cuba, receiving 83 percent of all Cuban exports (compared with
> 6 percent that went to Spain), selling the Cubans about $1 million worth
> of goods per year, and investing more than $50 million in Cuba, mainly
> in the sugar industry.[1]

Not surprisingly, the effect of the 1894 U.S. tariff law, which imposed duty on
raw sugar, reduced Cuban sugar importation into the United States. The
Spanish-American War was in many respects brought on by the United States,

in the process of a hegemony, carefully detailed by Joseph Pulitzer's *World* and William Randolph Hearst's *Journal*. Undoubtedly, many Americans thought their country's intervention was desirable for humanitarian reasons; some, like Theodore Roosevelt and Henry Cabot Lodge, even viewed American intervention as part of a necessary, God-willed policy that America must pursue. Europe had the same view of empire, although it was less hypocritical.

American adventurism, as already noted, was part of its move toward acceptance of the western world. The parallels with Europe are clear, for European imperialism of the nineteenth century is the same as American expansionism. Such expansionism in America had been originally more "local" (which does not detract from it); it had pursued Indian conquest, conflict in Mexico, and the ill-fated 1812 war. After the Civil War, the course of American expansionism even more closely equals European imperialism, for purely "local" aggrandizement takes on larger continental, even extracontinental focus. Alaska was bought in 1867; under Grant's administration, attempts were made to annex Canada.

Most recent historians have tended to downplay expansionism as a reason for the political interest in Canada. Roger Brown, A. L. Burt, Reginald Horsman, Bradford Perkins, and others have claimed that Congress was interested in Canada more as a means of protracting war than as the spoils of settlement. Harry Coles, however, feels that Canada and Florida have to be seen as a joint European prize: "Certain members of Congress wanted both Canada and Florida, and it is possible that they voted for war hoping to get one or both."[2] Indeed, on September 27, 1813, William Henry Harrison landed troops in Canada and advanced to Amherstburg. Even when the conflict was officially over on December 24, 1814, Andrew Jackson still (granted the problem of trans-Atlantic communications) managed to engage his troops in the Battle of New Orleans. Both French and British were seemingly being destroyed by their kith and kin: Eurocentrism can follow very deviant paths.

"Twisting the lion's tail" became a favorite pastime for politicians as they sought to bait Europeans, the British especially, but Germans and Spaniards as well. The logic of Manifest Destiny seemed to have exhausted itself, as there were no more worlds to conquer on the home front. But it was revived in the latter part of the nineteenth century, backed by a new European model—the Malthusian/Darwinian "struggle for existence." The survival of the fittest meant that Europeans—and Americans, if they wanted to be seen in this new light— were duty bound to take on the world and to rule and subjugate others until they could force them into a true European-style "civilization." In America, the intellectual spokespersons for this new role were three academics at Columbia University—John W. Burgess, John Fiske, and Josiah Story.

At the more popular level, Captain Alfred T. Mahan published *The Influence of Sea Power upon History* in 1890. He urged the United States to emulate Britain and build a navy. The unspoken motive was that the United States would then become one of the "civilized" nations, and his words easily won over Theodore Roosevelt, Henry Cabot Lodge, Henry Adams, and John Hay, among others.[3] Christopher Hitchens shows similar notions of superiority are easily found in Cecil Rhodes, and his own claims for British ownership of Africa from Cairo to the Cape. Says Hitchens, about how all this led in 1899 to an easy American imperialism and thus to apparent oneness with Britain:

> It was the year of the consolidation of American power in the former Spanish possessions of Cuba and the Philippines, gained in a near-blood-less conflict. It was also the year of intense British difficulty with the Boer farmers in South Africa. Mahan was equal to both emergencies, since he saw in them the vindication of his theories of sea power, the common interest of the two countries, and the opportunity for American ascendancy.[4]

In 1895, the country from which I come played a major role in the American imitation of European adventurism. Even now, Guyana continues to dispute with Venezuela over their common boundary; I suppose they will continue to do this for quite some time. But in 1895 the Monroe Doctrine was invoked as Secretary of State Richard Olney insisted that the boundary dispute be subject to arbitration. Why? Because, he said, the United States was stated to be "practically sovereign" in this part of the world and "its fiat is law." The two parallel imperialist policies, one a copy of the other, and merely meant to give American sovereignty a leg-up, might have brought on a European-American conflict, had the British not backed down.

I don't know how the stories of Cuba, Hawaii, and the Philippines are told in those respective places, but I am certain that few Cubans, for instance, see Roosevelt and his Rough Riders as their true saviors. For my part, thoroughly schooled in British interpretation of world history, the Monroe Doctrine and its evocation were seen as mistaken ideals of a young America. It had failed, stated some simplistic historian of my grammar-school years, to understand the wonderful relationship between Britain and her colonies and the need for British power to be forever ready.

Yes, the times were jingoistic. At school we sang songs of dubious patriotism to a colonial enemy we did not recognize: "Rule Brittania! Brittania rule the waves / Britons never, never shall be slaves." America had many such songs to choose from: The 1893 Katharine Lee Bates "America the Beautiful," where

... pilgrim feet,
Whose stern, impassioned stress
A thoroughfare for freedom beat
Across the wilderness!

neatly summed up expropriation of Indian land at the continental level, and foreign territory at the extracontinental level, in one grand flourish. Julia Ward Howe's earlier composition, "The Battle Hymn of the Republic" (1862), gave conquest the flavor of religious exhortation—"As He died to make men holy, let us die to make men free." Even Francis Scott Key's words, composed in 1814 and published in 1857, expressed the clear injunction: "Then conquer we must, when our cause it is just, / And this be our motto,—'In God is our trust,' " God and patriotism went hand in hand. The European Crusades were fought all over again.

Of course the Twelfth, Thirteenth, and Fourteenth Amendments were a long way away, as was women's right to vote, but little matter. The more pertinent issue is that much of this posturing, which saw America as opposed to the "foul footsteps pollution" of the British, could be understood in Longfellow's "The Building of the Ship." In his *Seaside and the Fireside* (1849), the central symbol says all that could possibly be said about nationalism and its religious equation ("We know what Master laid thy bed. . . . "), expansionism ("Humanity . . . / Is hanging breathless on thy fate!"),[5] and Mahan's later call for sea power. Yet nationalism either did not or only seldom did clash with British aspirations, as both countries located a common and agreed target in the non-European person—an African (for the European) and Cuban, Puerto Rican, Nicaraguan, and African American (for the United States). This continued the link noted in mutual assumptions about the Noble Savage, fortified by the slave trade, and now again enshrined in outright racial dominance. Postslavery, pro-Darwinian intellectual revisionism by both Europe and America could agree on the concept of a civilizing mission.

On the West Coast, policy hysterically attempted to control any mistaken impression that American "immigrants" could be anything but Europeans. In 1882, immigration of Chinese labor was suspended; in 1908, the so-called Gentlemen's Agreement with Japan curtailed Japanese immigration. Contrast this to 1885 on the East Coast, when the Statue of Liberty was erected, and to 1886, when it was dedicated, or even to 1892 when Ellis Island officially became the stop for European immigrants. The Statue of Liberty was not erected in the South, Southeast, or West; the poor and wretched to whom it beckons are located to this day in the European homeland, and Lady Liberty looks that way.[6]

Geronimo's capture in 1886 placed internal struggle on the back burner. America was literally waiting for the *Maine* to blow up, as it accidentally did, in Havana harbor. By the end of the Spanish-American War, Hawaii is annexed, followed by Spain ceding the Philippines, Puerto Rico, and Guam to the United States. For all practical purposes, the Platt Amendment of 1901 made economic control of Cuba even more definite. This situation in Cuba lasted until 1959 and threatened in the 1990s to resume again.

America, however, at the beginning of the century had its empire, and John Phillip Sousa's "Stars and Stripes Forever" reflected this reality. Americans, like Europeans, could have it all ways: They could have nationalism (even with a shade of xenophobia) and patriotism (with more than a touch of ethnocentrism). The colonial experiences and ethnic prejudices common to both Atlantic continents served to associate them in a closer harmony.

Linkages with Europe were therefore reinforced, certainly never severed or even mildly strained. As noted before, Andrew Carnegie, as early as 1894, had begun to use his own wealth to propagate the idea of an Anglo American union. Concrete manifestations were seen in the first trans-Atlantic radio in 1901, the inception of Rhodes Scholarships in 1903, the former physically uniting and the latter academically linking, the two sides of the Euro-Atlantic. The Wright Brothers' success at flight in 1903 led inevitably to Lindbergh's New York to Paris flight, May 20–21, 1927. Lindbergh's feelings were very much in keeping with the time's fierce national identification (certainly surprising in his case) and the nonparadoxical European association (even more surprising in his case). Observe his contemptuousness and his joy as he gets ready to try to land. For example, the autobiographical *We* records: "When I saw this fisherman, I decided to try to get him to point towards land. I had no sooner made the decision than the futility of the effort became apparent. In all likelihood he could not speak English." Or, when he does see England, "The English farms were very impressive from the air in contrast to ours in America. They appeared extremely small and unusually neat and tidy with their stone and hedge fences." Or, even about Europe, he comments, "I had probably seen more of that part of Europe than many native Europeans." Finally, when he lands, Lindbergh comments on his welcome, "These situations were brought about by the whole-hearted welcome *to me—an American*—that touched me beyond any point that any words can express."[7] One could reasonably assert that the first man in the air looking down on poor mortals is entitled to feel a bit like this, but I would suggest, as Lindbergh makes clear, that this flight is really a symbolic early American conquest of Europe, which would be dramatized even more effectively less than two decades later on the Normandy beaches.

The *Spirit of St. Louis* initiated a series of goodwill flights across the Atlantic, but Lindbergh fled from the ill outcome of his own popularity, when his son was kidnapped in March 1932. He turned to Europe when the family sought a life away from the constant glare of publicity, and there he was decorated by the German government in 1938, an act that, along with his antiwar speeches, forced his resignation from the Air Corps Reserve. But Lindbergh represents the time: He is an American with strong European ties. He seeks to establish a link with Europe but wishes to define himself as an American, even if a Euro American. He is torn between his adopted country and a Europe that was home. Finally, he has to give in to the Anglo Europeans, whose new myth-making would soon make the "Hun" an outcast. No doubt there was more than a degree of personal confusion in this, for Lindbergh lived out his last days in Maui.

Other participants continued to explore their own dualism. Less well-known is Stephen Vincent Benét. His *John Brown's Body* won a Pulitzer Prize in 1928, and his *Western Star* won another in 1943. The latter saw the country as fit for epic poetry, delineated early settlements at Jamestown and Plymouth, and intended to portray the westward expansion in epic terms. The Council for Democracy published a piece by Benét, "A Creed for Americans," that seemed to sum it all up. "We believe," Benét wrote at some length, in "the dignity of man," "a free system of government," "free speech, free assembly, free elections," and "justice and law." Also Americans were "unalterably opposed to class hatred, race hatred, religious hatred" and supposed "economic responsibility" toward the poor. He adds:

> We know that our democratic system is not perfect.
>
> We know that it permits injustices and wrongs. But with our whole hearts we believe in its continuous power of self-remedy. . . . Through the years, democracy has given more people freedom, less persecution and a higher standard of living than any other system we know. Under it, evils have been abolished, injustices remedied, old wounds healed, not by terror and revolution but by the slow revolution of consent in the minds of all the people.[8]

By appropriating "democracy," the United States was seeking even closer links with Europe, particularly England.

Later on, Europe would be redefined. Mysteriously, there would be an "eastern" Europe, sinister, unreachable, and alien. But there would also be a "western" Europe, friendly, likeable, made in America's image, as near as Lindbergh's flight and yet still home.

Bifurcating Europe obviously made the country ready to listen to and act on Churchill's "Iron Curtain" speech at Fulton, Missouri, on March 5, 1946. There was something cozy about the mutually agreed characteristics of the new enemy without, now that the ancient warlord had safely done away with Hitler. Second, mutual responsibilities were also spelled out by Churchill, ones that could readily be undertaken by the United States, once appointed sole heir of "Great" Britain.[9] In a way, Churchill, the revered figure from the right part of Europe, was indicating clear approval for American imperialism in Cuba, Haiti, Puerto Rico, and Nicaragua. He was establishing a precedent that would mitigate against any pangs of conscience when in the 1970s and 1980s Grenada and then Panama were invaded and when the CIA would openly defy every written and unwritten international agreement by training and equipping a "contra" army to battle lawful governments.

Toward the end of the twentieth century, Manifest Destiny and the Monroe Doctrine had become tiresome clichés. Darwinian concepts of the struggle of the fittest had been expropriated into a totally different concept, Social Darwinism. Furthermore, patriotism had fallen on rough times, and only crackpots could talk of racial superiority or imperialism. Nowadays, there is a tacit understanding, and it is that the "Two plus Four" talks, or "Super Power" dialogue, meetings of the Big Seven, the permanent members of the UN Security Council, or the Conference on Cooperation and Security in Europe (CCSE) all refer to the same people. Georg Lukács has rightly stated that the accident of the first half of the twentieth century was that Britain and America both spoke English and so America automatically inherited the British mantle. Just before the oft-quoted bit about "speaking softly and carrying a big stick," Teddy Roosevelt said: "I believe in hitting the line hard when you are right." America was right, and it was hitting hard. It had willingly inherited the British mantle.

Twain's "Gilded Age" of 1874, in which individualism ran rampant, gave way to Henry James's *Awkward Age* (1899). In the James novel, both Nanda Brookenham (at her "awkward age" of the title) and her mother are in love with Vanderbank. She moves from childhood to endless flirtations in her mother's salon, opting at the end to live in the country and become his London mistress. Twain's Laura is as involved with the unscrupulous deals of Senator Dilworthy. At the end, Laura kills, whereas Nanda merely tries to find ways of surviving. Between the gilded age and the awkward age there seems little to choose, except that in both instances women are the victims. They do not obtain the vote until 1920, an ironic commentary on the contradictions of a society of freedoms and idealistic beliefs, but the most paradoxical of realities. However, both the "gilded" and "awkward" ages are myths: the United States is neither brash nor young. The earlier part of the twentieth century establishes dimensions within which its latter part may be understood. Lukács's prediction was correct in asserting that the latter part of the century may be noteworthy in that both the Russians and Americans happened to be White. We now know that they find rapprochement, as western Eurocentrism moves to eastern Europe.

As the twenty-first century approaches, one realizes that events take on the nature of a swan song. The British alliance gave Britain a half century of apparent dominance long after the country had been for all practical purposes "gone in the teeth," to use Pound's words. America bought the Churchill line, traded on the idea of legacy, and ended up by finding itself as a kind of imperialist latecomer in far-off regions of the world, shouldering the European legacy. Dien Bien Phu directly brought America into the terrible tragedy of Vietnam, which, from where I sit, was a colonial and nationalist struggle. The bombing of the King David Hotel and post-Auschwitz concerns directly involved America in the Middle East, after its own long period of anti-Jewish sentiment and neglect. Now even anti-Jewish immigration policies have been revived, for even when Gorbachev appeared willing to let the people go, America expressed its own unwillingness to accept them:

About 150,000 Soviet Jews have petitioned to come to the United States as refugees this year [1990], but the State Department has declared that only about 50,000 of these appeals will be granted, despite the upsurge in anti-Semitism in the Soviet Union. Those not granted refuge in the United States, of course, can go to Israel. So from a humanitarian point of view, the plight of the Soviet Jews is perhaps not as compelling as that of other refugee groups. Nevertheless, this decision has placed America in an embarrassing predicament after four decades of chastising the Soviets for imprisoning their own people.[10]

Despite America's negative encounters in the Far East, it still persists in supporting, but never articulating, the notion that it is a kind of heir apparent to European empire. At most, this is translated as "policeman for the world," but the link with Europe, never openly admitted, frequently has pernicious ramifications.

An examination of immigration policy in the late nineteenth and early twentieth centuries reveals the same ambiguous attitude toward western Europe. Immigration policy is certainly "White," but not yet unerringly "British." Before 1800, say, it seemed to have an ethnicity patterned on the inhabitants of the *Mayflower*. But the Homestead Act of 1862 had even encouraged Europeans to come to America, where horizons after all seemed endless. Yet if Stephen Crane's "Blue Hotel" can be utilized as more than fiction, it would seem that undesirable Europeans existed on the cultural fringes. In the short story, the Irish hotel owner, his son, and a mysterious Swede are seen as outsiders. Control of the continent itself seemed to lie with two native-born "Americans," a rationally minded "Easterner" and an impetuous "Westerner." Katherine Anne Porter's "Noon Wine" reinforces the point: Another Swedish stranger brings bad luck to the family farm.

If America were to be created in the image of Anglo-Europe (both Protestant and Anglo-Saxon), then Jews, Catholics, and others should be kept out. Although Woodrow Wilson attempted to veto this 1921 Congressional bill (he was less reluctant about banning Blacks from the White House and segregating the Administration), feelings were so strong that Congress limited the number of new immigrants to 3 percent: Each new arrival had to be drawn from Europeans who lived here before 1910. Of course, this tilted the matter in favor of Britain, which often did not use up its quota.

In 1907, Congress had set up the Dillingham Commission.[11] The commission identified two types of immigration: an "old" pattern that had come from northern and western Europe, which had assimilated well, and a "new" type from southern and eastern Europe, which had been slow to integrate. Obviously, "assimilation" meant the ability and ease of first-generation non-English to become anglicized. Indeed, this very process of anglicization (church, language, and light skin color) was deemed the desired goal. "Assimilation" was therefore the gap because of which dark-skinned Europeans and non–African American Blacks had failed to reach this goal of perfection.[12]

Of course the commission did not quite realize that, under the British quota, Black British "subjects" were able to slip in mainly from the Caribbean—Jamaica, Trinidad, and Guyana. However, when it became known in 1952, this oversight was quickly corrected. The McCarran-Walter Act put a virtual stop to legal non-White immigration from Central and South America and the Caribbean but left the door open for European and especially for British entrants.

When assessment of the Europe-America linkage is given, it must be stressed that from the early part of the century, the United States, quite intentionally through twin policies of overseas expansion and domestic restriction, tried to project itself in an Anglo image, even as it colonized people of color, refusing to let in even dark-skinned Europeans.

Why this fear of the same racial groups? Because, above all, America did not wish to promote itself in Europe as a mulatto culture. In *The Rising Tide of Color*, Lothrop Stoddard (writing in 1921) looks back favorably to the colonial past as "one continuous, drastic cycle of engemic selection."[13] His only solution: "Rigorous exclusion of colored immigrants is thus vitally necessary for the white people."[14]

Maldwyn Allen Jones concludes in *American Immigration* that "the last and greatest of the those waves, which brought to the United States a total of fifteen million immigrants between 1890 and 1914 were drawn largely from Austria-Hungary, Italy, Russia, Greece, Rumania, and Turkey."[15] Steamship companies had actively propositioned would-be immigrants in Austria-Hungary, Greece, and Russia. Agents used posters and circulars in order to encourage people to leave, and some steamship lines had even established local employment bureaus.[16]

Although Jones admits to these "pull" factors, he feels that the steamship itself, with its relative ease of crossing, was more instrumental. But in a sense this is a small, almost insignificant, matter. Actually, states vied with each other in order to attract cheap European labor, which would help bring about growth in relatively empty areas. Railroad expansion played no small role in providing jobs as well as settlements. But, more important were "push" factors, some of which were as dramatic as the Irish potato famine of 1845–1849, or local European issues that brought about a freer attitude toward emigration. Jones identifies the unification movement in Italy (1859–1860), reorganization of Austria-Hungary in 1867, and the freedom from Turkish rule of large Slavic areas after the Russo-Turkish War concluded in 1877. The end of official restraint meant that labor could follow jobs, much as the unfortunate Martin Chuzzlewit departs in the 1843–1844 Dickens novel of the same name for the Eden Land Corporation, a name that promises both a lost innocence and the possibility of renewal.

Ironically, Euro American former "refugees" sold their myth of life more abundant back to the European homeland. It was a myth that I knew, even though from the secondhand perspective of a colonial growing up in the 1940s and 1950s. I was aware of an important distinction that the British empire builders had erected. The successful people, later translated into those who occupied a certain class echelon in colonial society, either won scholarships or had their parents pay for them to go to England, not America. Going to America was actually a kind of last resort, usually attempted by the desperate souls who had failed to make it through the cruelly competitive educational tier system the British had devised. One had poor relations who had gone there—even some who had simply journeyed to a nearby island, yet returned complete with what we termed a "Yankee" accent. When they came back, they lavishly doled out dollars, at a time when dollars brought enormous rewards. Yet some of us diligently pursued our studies, hoping for the day when Mother England would take us into her kindly embrace.

In 1951 my father, a mechanic for seventeen years at the local Singer Sewing Machine Company, lost his job. The event was traumatic: He had six children, two about to "go England study." His Portuguese boss, my father said, had insulted him, asked him to lift a box when he (my father) was chief mechanic at the Singer Sewing Machine Company. The incident seems silly, a little humorous now, but then the grim reality of permanent unemployment faced my father. He didn't know of the imminent passage of the McCarran-Walter Act, but given his status, the United States was the logical place to go. One irony canceled all that: His passport had said, with typical British succinctness, "Mixed Native of British Guiana." The American embassy understood one thing by that and even encouraged his application for a visa. But, when the cold truth dawned that a "Mixed Native" was only the descendant of Indian and African parents, all bets were off. His application was rejected, and he had to go to England.

I tell this little story to illustrate an important point. Even if I personally had been dying to come, American immigration policy was not fashioned for Blacks and saw me as clearly irrelevant to the task of "Europeanizing" the nation. That events have gone full circle has more to do with the consequences of history than with any letup on the part of American immigration and foreign policy as directed toward its "backyard." In other words, the movement of people across the Rio Grande from Central America and across the Pacific from the Far East is the unfolding of the consequences of immigration and colonial policies gone askew. Nomads have ever sought to enter the settler's dwelling: hence, his moat, his drawbridge, his castle.

As the twentieth century comes to a close, so much of the late nineteenth-century (post-1865) and twentieth-century immigration law has remained merely as legal fiction. Immigrants have gone over the moat and drawbridge from the south and east, directly entering the castle. Blame America's wars and exploitation. The new immigration formula that seeks to distinguish between "economic" and "political" refugees went out the window, long before the Berlin Wall crashed. People will always try to come to America to find an audience or a market. This holds good for skilled and unskilled, for intellectual and peasant. Cubans and Haitians are in the same boat.

What is most evident is that America's Eurocentric preoccupations have had dangerous and deleterious consequences. Here one moves away from neat little arguments of how the European myth functions in art, architecture, poetry, and so on, to see it codified and inflexible, and how it affects real human beings. My father's story is one of many, illustrating the true human consequences that lie in grief and despair, when people are denied part of the very mythologies with which the country enshrines itself.

Yet the falsehoods persist that the country is open to all, that here lies the true realization of perfection. Afterall, Americans themselves came to believe this. The advent of the "dime novel," retelling history (especially the Revolution and Civil War) stressed the wonders of the land, much as the anthems had done. From 1860, when Ann Sophia Stephens wrote *Malaeska: The Indian Wife of the White Hunter*, popular works blended romance and adventure, feeding myth on myth. The works were read on all three sides of the Atlantic, supplanted at the turn of the century by popular magazines. Like the cinema that came after, they seemed to project an honest reality to America. Later heroes of the silver screen—such as Deadwood Dick, created by Edward L. Wheeler, and Nick Carter, created by J. R. Coryell—would all confirm its myth. Over and over again the desirability of America, the fortitude of its people, the beauty of the land, and above all its common accessibility are stressed.[17]

Of course, although propagandistic, even the heroes made an interesting point in our Anglo American equation. "Deadwood Dick," for instance, was the name used by the English-born frontiersman Richard W. Clark. As he battles Indians and guards gold shipments in the Black Hills of North Dakota, his Englishness (the novels were afterwards claimed to be almost autobiographical) gives the work its supposed authenticity for the American reader and its supposed legitimacy, from our vantage point, validating once more the Anglo American myth.

We begin to understand then why "pop" and Britishness go together; why, when we examine almost every facet of American life, the British presence obtrudes. Tarzan's origins are in Britain—he is the son of British aristocracy, as Edgar Rice Burroughs' *Tarzan of the Apes* (1914) makes clear. Succeeding Tarzans use the cinema to continue to project the image of the "civilized" wild man, who holds conversations with apes and speaks all known African languages. As previously contended, this could be a mere perversion of the Noble Savage, but its success speaks urgently to the Euro American need to be supreme, triumphant, and closely linked with their British cousins. If, in the process, African Americans made themselves look foolish as they skimmed through the movie lots of Florida, so be it. The message of the conquering White American male with British blood could not be missed.

Another instance from the movies will suffice. When *Gone with the Wind* premiered in 1939, the book by Margaret Mitchell had already won a Pulitzer Prize, in 1936. Like *Birth of a Nation*, the film dealt with the Civil War and Reconstruction, told from the viewpoint of the South. Like Thomas Dixon's *Clansman*, this book was also a best-seller and set up an all-time-high sales record of over a thousand copies in one day, not even equaled by the work of Salman Rushdie. The film ran for two hundred and twenty-two minutes. But its extra claim to authenticity lay in English actress Vivien Leigh's portrayal of Scarlett O'Hara. Although her then-husband, Laurence Olivier, has described this as her first major role, her Englishness was what the audience wanted, not her expertise. It gave a peculiar type of inconsistent yet legitimate authority to her role; she won an Oscar, and the film became an all-time "American" classic.

I will merely mention a few other aspects of Anglomania as seen in pop music: Elton John, the Beatles, the Rolling Stones, and other pop artists in America, a Black "Downtown" Julie Brown on MTV, perhaps even the constantly stressed Britishness of Bob Hope. Nor will I dwell on the popular success of something so English as the humor of "Monty Python's Flying Circus" and its insular references, which non-English people must have quite a hard time understanding. At least the English-born comedian Stan Laurel's slapstick was thoroughly localized from 1926, when the Laurel and Hardy team premiered. Nor should I linger too long over the impeccable "British" accents of the 1990s evening news anchormen, Peter Jennings (ABC), Tom Brokaw (NBC), and Robert MacNeil (PBS). Nor need I dwell on the manner in which what is "serious" is often equated with what is English—monologues from Alistair Cooke as he ponderously introduced us to "Masterpiece Theater" or even the voice of Sheila Walsh, a Scotswoman on Pat Robertson's "700 Club." Today's instances are legion: Lisa Stanfield, the "diminutive diva," is a pint-sized English singer who will bring soul back to the United States, now that we know for sure that Milli Vanilli lip-synch.

Every Christmas, Dickens's *A Christmas Carol* is revived. "Scrooge" has joined the American "language" as a pejorative noun. For New Year's Eve, "Auld Lang Syne" is required fare, even though the original had little to do with the time of the year and less to do with the United States. As Americans measure the year, so do they the day. Breakfast, lunch, and dinner contain the same staples as in Britain; people dress in almost the same manner and observe the same festivities in roughly the same way.

The persistence of European modes as the norm is all the more surprising here, because one finds in Germany, for instance, customs and observations that Americans have exported there. For instance, specific kinds of German food have been replaced by the omnipresent "burger"; Bavarian wearing apparel is today considered quaint and is worn only on ceremonial occasions. A "name's day" (*Namenstag*), when a person would normally observe the saint's birthday that coincides with his or her own, is slowly disappearing in Germany. But even as Germans, French, Italians, and Irish have dropped the hyphen from their ethnic nomenclature and become "American," they have become, in fact, "Anglo" Americans. As stated before, assimilation really means anglicization.

Because this is the "popular age," when the appurtenances of our culture seek to have us all involved in a common global experience (whether a film by John Houston or a piece of art by Andy Warhol), we note how we have taken on the prejudices and beliefs of the beginning of the century. Ethnic composition, made up of a silent disenfranchised minority, and gender composition, put together by females without a vote, counted for less then and does so now. The popular age was not the voice of the people, but the voice of organs of opinion wielded by millionaires, trans-Atlantic companies, and later global corporations and their interest groups.

Thorstein Veblen was way ahead of his time, but perceptive of its movements, when he observed in *The Theory of the Leisure Class* (1894):

> It is a matter of common notoriety that when individuals, or even considerable groups of men, are segregated from a higher industrial culture and exposed to a lower cultural environment, or to an economic situation of a more primitive character, they quickly show evidence of reversion toward the spiritual features which characterise the predicatory type; and it seems probable that the dolicho-blond type of European man is possessed of a greater facility for such reversion to barbarism than the other ethnic elements with which that type is associated in the Western culture.[18]

Veblen turns the tables and attacks the Vanderbilts, Carnegies, Morgans, and so on because they are barbaric social parasites, who "retard the adaptation of human nature to the exigencies of modern industrial life." However, they are not attacked as Europeans per se, but as belonging to an almost separate branch of evolutionary process. Veblen's societal analysis is ambiguous because, like the Robber Barons and Lindbergh, like Mahan and the confused immigration policy, there are three tendencies: First, there is the spoken, overly patriotic laudation of America, in keeping with popular literature and anthems. Second, there is the claim to communality with Europe in mutual social progress, which would supposedly prove the European intellect as superior, and therefore the Euro American. Third, there is Veblen's insightful thrust; he recognizes the sham and seeks genuine change.

Part of a movement running apparently counter to some of this lay in the origin of anthropology, as articulated by Margaret Mead and Zora Neale Hurston. A European voice, from Germany, that of Franz Boas, from 1899 a professor of anthropology at Columbia, underscored the need for science to be engaged. His *The Mind of Primitive Man* (1911) would be cited and often used by the opponents of the 1920 U.S. immigration policy. After Boas, people could no longer be classified as objects on an ascendancy ladder toward a European apex. He argued for the "civilization" of so-called primitive peoples, showing that culture was relative and that peoples had evolved in different ways. "Participant observation," now a sine qua non of anthropological study, was undertaken by both Mead, in Fiji, and Hurston, among southern Blacks. They proved beyond doubt that it would be possible to view another culture from within, in a dispassionate, uninvolved manner. Eurocentrism began to show its flimsy foundations, as a European pointed the way.

Yet the controversy that erupted over Mead and is still to occur over Hurston does not take into account the moral imperatives that caused these early pioneers to invent some of their material. Discussing Derek Freeman's attacks on Mead, Boyce Rensberger has put Mead in historical perspective:

> The issue for Freeman, as it happens, is not so much Margaret Mead herself as it is the controversy that launched Mead's career— the intellectual debate that sent Mead to Samoa. This was the question of whether the patterns of human social behavior are innate, fixed in the genes like bipedalism or speech, or whether these patterns are created anew in each generation, shaped into distinctive forms by local customs and teachings. This was the original nature-nurture debate, and Mead's book, her anthropological debut, would become one of the most powerful weapons used to silence the genetic determinists and inaugurate the long domination of cultural determinism in Western thought.[19]

The scholars are taking on the policy makers. They seem to be saying that you cannot justify inferior races, as Europeans do, by pointing to location and birth and either conquering them or refusing to admit them to live near you. Boas suggests grave doubts about Euro American absolutes: "Much of what we ascribe to human nature is no more than a reaction to the constraints put upon us by our civilisation."[20]

Both Mead's *Coming of Age in Samoa* (1928) and Hurston's *Mules and Men* (1935) and *Tell My Horse* (1938) deal with the important issue of justifying humanity in extra-European terms. Mead's book had, therefore, more to do with her own criticism of adolescence in Euro America, her aversion to its middle-class norms, and her support of the then-heretical view that American culture could possibly be heterogeneous. Equally, Hurston invented "legends" that Blacks supposedly told about their concept of God, stressing ethnic gender differences and so on. Hurston's sound was Boas's colored voice: "Nothing that God ever made is the same thing to more than one person. That is natural. There is no single face in nature, because every eye that looks upon it, sees it from its own angle. So every man's spice-box seasons his own food."[21] When Hurston was not being "factual" she factualized her fiction. For instance, near the beginning of *Their Eyes Were Watching God* (1937), a woman stands at the very beginning of creation, forming order from chaos: "So the beginning of this was a woman and she had come back from burying the dead."

Zora Neale Hurston writes epic-style, biblical, but seeking to invert European assumptions. Evolution is at the point of taking place, for a people who had been "tongueless, earless, eyeless," since "Mules and other brutes had occupied their skins."[22] At the end of the same novel, a Black woman is again one with her European counterpart—Eve-like, mysterious, with the power of resurrection, godlike: "She pulled in her horizon like a great fish net. Pulled it from around the waist of the world and draped it over her shoulder. So much of life in its meshes! She called in her soul to come and see."[23] Neither Blacks nor Samoans were factual, anymore than Eve. They were there to exert scientific or at least academic control.

Both writers were pamphleteers concerned more with debunking the increasing mythology of Anglo supremacy than with emphasizing any objective scientific approach. Always the stress is on common human attributes. Margaret Mead set her stage in this way:

In all of these comparisons between Samoan and American culture, many points are useful only in throwing a spotlight upon our own solutions, while in others it is possible to find suggestions for change. *Whether or not we envy other peoples one of their solutions, our attitude towards our own solutions must be greatly broadened and deepened by a consideration of the way in which other peoples have met the same problems.* Realising that our own ways are not humanly inevitable nor God-ordained, but are the fruit of a long and turbulent history, we may well examine in turn all of our institutions, thrown into a strong relief against *the history of other civilisations, and weighing them in the balance, be not afraid to find them wanting.*[24]

Zora Neale Hurston concludes her autobiography on a more direct personal note, but she also shies away from any absolute value judgment:

I have no race prejudice of any kind. My kinfolks and my "skinfolks" are clearly loved. My own circumference of everyday life is there. *But I see their same virtues and vices everywhere I look.* So I give you all my right hand of fellowship and love, and hope for the same from you. *In my eyesight, you lose nothing by not looking just like me.*[25]

The racial twist is even more interesting because as I have tried to show, Anglo America was not concerned with this, but with degrees of difference vis-à-vis Europe and Europeans. Before Zora Neale Hurston graduated from Barnard, "Papa Franz" (the name by which she affectionately called Boas) had obtained a fellowship for her to go South and collect folklore. Boas was also instrumental in assisting the twenty-four-year-old Mead to go to Samoa in 1925. The motives went beyond personal generosity—Mead and Hurston were expected to follow up on and correct the mistaken assumptions that had plunged the United States into cultural confusion.[26]

Later on, *The Report of the National Advisory Commission on Civil Disorders* (usually termed the "Kerner Commission" after its chairman, Otto Kerner, then governor of Illinois), after summing up the history of Black settlement and rejection in Chapter 5, stated, "Negro protest, for the most part, has been firmly rooted in the basic values of American society, seeking not their destruction but their fulfillment."[27] Hurston and Mead had tried unsuccessfully to use the Boas formula to suggest alternatives to Anglo assimilation. Yet I concede that the flip side of participant observation and the subsequent retreat from ethnocentrism affirmed a stale oneness that still looked as suspiciously male and European as Boas himself.

Few had paid attention to the real issue of the 1920s and 1930s. Because African Americans had felt themselves excluded and because Euro Americans were hell bent on establishing any link, no matter how, with the European mainland, the racial element was intensified. African American oral tales show their concerns. For instance, there is a folktale that Blacks tell of "Shine on the Titanic," which seems most appropriate here in this context. The account is collected by Roger Abrahams[28] among others[29] in various forms. The reference may be safely dated, as the *Titanic* sank on April 14–15, 1912, with a loss of 1,513 lives. Whatever may be the truth in African American belief that the *Titanic* had refused to carry Black passengers, newspapers of the day, like the *St. Louis Post-Dispatch* of April 16, 1912, seemed more concerned with information such as "Astor, Butt, Guggenheim and Many Other Famous Men Who Were on Board Not Mentioned Among Survivors" or "Money Loss is $20,000,000." Blacks recognized two factors: first, that the symbol of Euro American/European indestructability had perished and, second, that news accounts were more concerned with physical statistics and head counts than human misery.

Therefore, at the center of the African American account is a Black person, "Shine," then a derogatory name for "Negroes." He is a stoker on the ship, working in the hold. Thrice he warns the White captain of impending danger, only to be ordered back down to the hold of the ship in these words: "Shine, Shine get your black ass down / Got twenty nine pumps to pump the water down." Finally, Shine jumps overboard and begins swimming ashore. The White captain, naturally unable to swim (it is a Black folktale), offers Shine two symbolic bribes—money and his daughter. Shine's reply is a resounding negative. The account concludes by saying that, when news of the disaster of the *Titanic* reaches shore, Shine is in a bar, about to get drunk.

Within the concerns of our general thesis, the meaning of the account is clear. The story is in fact a dramatic restatement of African encounter in the Europeanizing of the New World, told from a Black perspective. When the story begins, Shine is clearly part of the historical process that has made him, in the legendary phrase, "separate but equal." From his lowly segregated position as stoker, he is clearly at the very bottom of the social structure. Indeed, to change status (and the action is peremptory, voluntary, and necessitated by the sinking ship of state), he *climbs up* to the Captain on three occasions to warn him of imminent danger. The Captain refuses Shine's attempt at accommodation, at altering his status from *segregated* to *integrated* person. Finally, Shine decides on the alternative posited by Garvey and advocated by the Klan—*separatism*; he jumps overboard. The ship is destroyed, but Shine survives; the Euro American/European alliance perishes, but the African American link endures.

Although Shine and the *Titanic* belong to legend, the tale nevertheless addresses the important issues of a people's concerns, stripped of the censorship of officialdom. Shine's attempts at "integration" may be observed in both the work of Mead and Hurston, as they attempt to rid America of its Eurocentric linkage and to establish more global ties. But, if imperialism and racism (with their attendant philosophies) were seen as ways of advancing internal economic growth and bolstering the continued Euro American alliance, then public moralist stances of the Boas/Mead/Hurston variety were bound to go nowhere. The public already believed its own mythology, its anthems, and its popular literature. The dominant nativism would and did triumph, as may be witnessed in the jingoistic zeal of the Reagan and post-Reagan years.

Randolph Bourne, as early as 1916, gave lie to the melting pot, "which never existed." He attacked one of the most cherished myths, which Euro Americans had conscripted—that of "freedom." Referring to the small-minded ethnocentricity that he found in WASP thinking, he contended, "We are all foreign-born," and roundly condemned as suspect even the motives of early colonists. Although Bourne's vision excludes Shine's world and mine, it is still one that attempts to turn history on its head, to prevent the constant feeding of the same misconceptions, as he notes:

The early colonists came over with motives no less colonial than the later. *They did not come to be assimilated in an American melting-pot. They did not come to adopt the culture of the American Indian.* They had not the smallest intention of "giving themselves without reservation" to the new country. They came to get freedom to live as they wanted to. They came to escape from the stifling air and chaos of the old world; they came to make their fortune in a new land. *They invented no new social framework. Rather they brought over bodily the old ways to which they had been accustomed.* Tightly concentrated on a hostile frontier, they are conservative beyond belief. Their pioneer daring was reserved for the objective conquest of material resources. In their folkways, in their social and political institutions, they were, like every colonial people, slavishly imitative of the mother-country. So that, in spite of the "Revolution," *our whole legal and political system remained more English than the English,* petrified and unchanging, while in England law developed to meet the needs of the changing times.[30]

For some reason, he was considered radical.

Part of the problem, as Bourne rightly sees it, was the refusal to develop a truly American "global" culture, relevant for every ethnic immigrant group. He continues:

> *The Anglo-Saxon was merely the first immigrant,* the first to found a colony. He has never really ceased to be the descendant of immigrants, nor has he ever succeeded in transforming that colony into a real nation, with a tenacious, richly woven fabric of native culture. *Colonials from the other nations have come and settled down beside him. They found no definite native culture which should startle them out of their colonialism,* and consequently they looked back to their mother-country, as the earlier Anglo-Saxon immigrant was looking back to his.[31]

But not for long, since Anglo-Saxons, now Anglo Americans, have been guilty "of just what every dominant race is guilty of in every European country: the imposition of its own culture upon the minority peoples."[32] They felt that America would be a new Europe, "deriving power from the deep cultural heart of Europe" and yet existing "freed from the age-long tangles of races, creeds and dynasties," for "America is transplanted Europe, but a Europe that has not been disintegrated."[33]

By the end of World War I, Bourne was dead. He had called for an end of Euroethnic conformism, which he rightly denounced as "hypocritical," as it worked only once the Other agreed to become the One. What he did not realize is that even African American leaders, as different as Washington and Du Bois and Garvey, found no fault with this and happily accepted the inbred notions of Euro American pretensions. Bourne's call was political, but he had the moral imperative of Boas, as both were saying that the dynamic intermingling of diverse peoples could result in a new world, a Europe refashioned, a synthesis only possible here.

Randolph Bourne's ideals of this new cosmopolitanism were a rallying cry for antiprovincialist advocates, for others who in succeeding decades continued to assail a society that did not seem to want to reach beyond its own parochialism. Along with Alfred Steiglitz and others of the so-called radical left, Bourne offered words of added importance because of their prophetic significance.

Now there are voices outside the sounds that the cliché-ridden anthems echoed. These lead us into the twenty-first century and the pragmatic realities of new demographic groupings—now Spanish Americans and Asian Americans, as David Rieff comments:

> This is all a far cry from the ways in which most Americans have traditionally imagined themselves or their country. *The "real" American, the "All-American boy" or the "girl next door," was supposed to be blond.* That may have been true once, but no longer. Whites comprised 90 per cent of the American population in 1920; a little under 80 per cent in 1985; and will likely constitute a little less than 50 per cent by the middle of the next century. In a society in which immigration has always played an essential role and in which race has always been the tragic, unresolved problem, these projections have the effect of unsettling nearly every traditional assumption. Moreover, the United States, as nearly every observer since Tocqueville has pointed out, is a country based on an idea of itself. *The question that now presents itself is how people will conceive of themselves as Americans if the image of a country made up of blacks and people of European ancestry is only part of the story.* The assimilationist model, "the melting-pot" that, mythically at least, served as a way of integrating the European immigrants who came at the turn of the last century, no longer works, but there is nothing to replace it. *No one seems even to know how to think about the question, much less answer it.*[34]

All the more surprising is it to note that the above response is made from England in 1990. Perhaps the agonies could have been avoided if more attention had been paid to the voices at the fringes of American society, for they had castigated the narrowness that resulted from a belief in European association (a thing in which American leaders so clearly believed) and proposed a new scope and vision in a global relationship (a thing that American leaders so adamantly opposed). Globalization, not Europeanization, could have changed the old myth and organized a new reality.

NOTES

1. Franklin W. Knight, "Cuba: Politics, Economics, and Society, 1898–1985," in *The Modern Caribbean,* ed. Franklin W.Knight and Colin Palmer (Chapel Hill: University of North Carolina Press, 1989), 169.

2. Harry L. Coles, *The War of 1812* (Chicago: University of Chicago Press, 1965), 34.

3. Alfred T. Mahan, *The Influence of Sea Power upon History* [1890] (New York: Dover Publications, 1987), was, supposedly, a historical survey, but stressed on the incipient U.S. nation the need to possess a large and powerful navy.

4. Christopher Hitchens, *Blood, Class and Nostalgia* (New York: Farrar, Strauss, and Giroux, 1990), 114–115.

5. Henry Wadsworth Longfellow, "The Building of the Ship," in *Seaside and the Fireside* (Boston: Ticknor, Reed and Fields, 1850). The poem was roundly denounced by abolitionists such as William Lloyd Garrison.

6. Two invaluable texts on American immigration compiled by Edith Abbott are *Immigration: Select Documents and Case Records* (Chicago: University of Chicago Press, 1924) and *Historical Aspects of the Immigration Problem* (Chicago: University of Chicago Press, 1926). See also the more recent study by Alejandro Portes and Rubén G. Rumbaut, *Immigrant America: A Portrait* (Berkeley: University of California Press, 1990).

7. Charles Lindbergh, *We* (New York: G. P. Putnam's Sons, 1927) as reprinted in *Great American Stories and Poems* [1919] compiled by Hugh Graham (New York: Gallahad Books, 1987 ed.), 314–315. Emphasis added.

8. Stephen Vincent Benét, "A Creed for Americans," in Graham, *Stories and Poems*, 347.

9. Hitchens, *Blood, Class*, 186–199, 240–243, 246–247, 249–251. Also see Amaury de Riencourt, *The American Empire* (New York: Dell Publishing, 1968), vi–vii, 4, 288–229, 43–47, 51–59, 71–74, 263.

10. Stephen Moore, "Flee Market: More Refugees at Lower Cost," *Policy Review*, No. 52 (Spring 1990), 65.

11. Dillingham Commission, *Report of the United States Immigration Commission*, 41 vols. 1911. 1st vol. (S. doc. 747, 61st Congress, 3d Sess.)–40th vol. (S. doc. 761, 61st Congress, 3d Session). In 1921, 1924, and 1929, Congress had enacted very restrictive immigration legislation. This legislation later became part of the McCarran-Walter Act, passed over Truman's veto on June 27, 1952.

12. See Jeremiah W. Jenks and W. Jett Lauck, "The Immigration Problem" in Funk and Wagnall's *Encyclopedia*, 6th ed., 1926. The authors summarize the findings of the Dillingham Commission.

13. Lothrop Stoddard, *The Rising Tide of Color against White World Supremacy* (New York: Charles Scribner's Sons, 1920. Reprinted, Miami: Mnemosyne Publishing Co., 1989), 262.

14. Ibid., 276.

15. Maldwyn Allen Jones, *American Immigration* (Chicago: University of Chicago Press, 1960), 179.

16. Ibid., 181.

17. I found the following works useful: Roger Dooley, *From Scarface to Scarlett: American Films in the 1930s* (New York: Harcourt Brace, 1984); Gerald Mast, *The Movies in Our Mist* (Chicago: University of Chicago Press, 1982); and Robert Sklar, *Movie-Made America* (New York: Vintage, 1975).

18. Thornstein Veblen, *The Theory of the Leisure Class* (New York: Mentor, 1953), 192.

19. Boyce Rensberger, "Margaret Mead: The Nature-Nurture Debate," reprinted from *Science 84 Magazine* (American Association for the Advancement of Science), 29.

20. See Margaret Mead, *Coming of Age in Samoa* [1928] (New York: American Museum of Natural History, 1973), iv.

21. Zora Neale Hurston, *Dust Tracks on a Road* (Philadelphia and New York: J. B. Lippincott, 1971), 61.

22. Zora Neale Hurston, *Their Eyes Were Watching God* (Greenwich, Conn.: Fawcett Publications, 1969), 5.

23. Hurston, *Their Eyes*, 159.

24. Mead, *Coming of Age*, 130. Emphasis added.

25. Hurston, *Dust Tracks*, 285–286. Emphasis added.

26. Several good studies exist on Zora Neale Hurston. I recommend *Zora in Florida*, ed. Steve Glassman and Kathryn Lee Seidel (Orlando: University of Central Florida Press, 1991);

and Robert Hemenway, *Zora Neale Hurston: A Literary Biography* (Chicago: University of Illinois Press, 1977), 35.

27. *The Report of the The National Advisory Commission on Civil Disorders* (New York: Bantam Books, 1988), 236.

28. Roger Abrahams, *Deep Down in the Jungle* (New York: Aldine Publishing, 1970). My quotations are from Abrahams, 120–129.

29. See Alan Dundes, ed. *Mother Wit from the Laughing Barrel* (Englewood Cliffs, N.J.: Prentice-Hall, 1973), especially 45–66 and 310–358; and Daryl Cumber Dance, *Shuckin' and Jivin'* (Bloomington: Indiana University Press, 1978).

30. Randolph Bourne, "Trans-National America," *Atlantic Monthly* 118 (July 1916): 87. Emphasis added.

31. Ibid., 89. Emphasis added.

32. Ibid.

33. Ibid., 91.

34. David Rieff, "The Transformation of America," *Times Literary Supplement*, No. 4547 (May 25–31, 1990), 543. Emphasis added.

6
Eurocentrism versus Ethnocentrism ──────────

S amuel F. B. Morse, inventor of the telegraph, tended not to be quite so global
in his domestic policy concerns for the United States. The *New York
Observer* published a series of his letters in 1834, which were later printed as
a pamphlet entitled *A Foreign Conspiracy against the Liberties of the United
States.*[1] The villain, Morse argued, was the Catholic Church, particularly the
"Leopold Association of Vienna," through whose founding of American Catholic bishops Morse detected the initial steps in a papal plot to take over the
country. Protestants did not lag too far behind: Rev. Lyman Beecher's *A Plea
for the West* (1835) saw an equally wicked pope and Holy Alliance at work
against the Mississippi Valley. As told by Beecher, Catholic immigrants were
being intentionally sent over in such numbers that they would eventually
overrun the region. Both Morse and Beecher used their own ethnocentric
concepts not merely to express a distasteful anti-Catholicism but also to state a
crude nativism, whose basic tenet was Anglo-Saxon dominance and sectional-
ism. Henry Ford's *Dearborn Independent* fulfilled its own part by scurrilously
attacking Jews. Also, even though it was a work of misguided fiction, Maria
Monk's *Awful Disclosures of the Hotel Dieu Nunnery of Montreal*, published
in 1836, claimed to be written from personal experience. Convents and mon-
asteries were places of sin, sexual immorality, and murder, proof positive of
papish immorality.

Xenophobia ran rampant in the name of patriotism. The Native American
Party, and secret societies such as the Order of United Americans and the Order
of the Star Spangled Banner were products of the late 1840s and 1850s. By
1854, the Know Nothing Party epitomized all their aspirations. The aims were

subtle, simply stated as "America for the Americans," by which they claimed that they wanted to keep out the criminal element. They gained a measure of success, electing governors, dominating some state legislatures, and even sending representatives to Congress. They fielded Millard Fillmore in 1856 as their presidential candidate. Both North and South were involved in Know Nothingism, and both knew the secret password, "I know nothing," and supported the protonativistic attitudes: Catholics were to be excluded from political and public office; foreigners could not be naturalized until after twenty-one years, and only American-born Protestants would receive official support at the booth. At its most basic level, America's Reformation movement sought to pit non-Anglo Europeans against the Irish, in particular, and all others, in general. At another level, the movement was an early indicator of the fierce and wrongheaded racism that manifested itself afterward in the Klan.[2]

The Civil War did not interrupt, but merely stalled the inherent animosities that Europeanization in its narrowest sense took. On the West Coast the Japanese were the enemies, which partly explains why it was relatively easy to incarcerate them after Pearl Harbor. General John L. De Witt, with the approval of military and political authorities, decided that the Japanese, citizens or not, had to be rounded up, evacuated from the West Coast, and placed in barbed-wire camps under armed guard. Despite the papish plots directed at the Irish or the fear of blood contamination directed at southern Europeans, no Italians or Germans were subjected to such humiliation. Japanese recompense was an empty apology from President Reagan and a promise, still only partly kept, to award them payment. The push toward association with Europe had led to this mindless assault upon America's own citizenry.

Some African Americans deeply believe that such incarceration and ill-treatment is not merely problematic but remains a feature of present-day government policy. After all, they argue, White American "racial purity" is threatened by the "yellow peril," as Homer Lea claimed in 1909 in California, and by the "mongrel bloods" coming from the wrong part of Europe, as Jack London stated in *The Call of the Wild* (1903) and *The Sea-Wolf* (1904). In much of London's work is his obsession with the "brute" (the non-Anglo, non-European) who will wreck society. Because the Nietzschean *Obermann* was quite definitely Caucasian, London, like others before him, again looked to Europe to justify Eurocentricity. Not unnaturally, African Americans were severely perplexed.

This passionate association with Europe, particularly England, has provided a degree of disquietude in the African American community. Sometimes it has taken the form of the need for urgent departure. For example, Garvey was anticipated by Paul Cuffe, a nineteenth-century New Bedfordshire shipowner who, on his own, took Blacks back to Liberia.[3] Often, the Eurocentric preoccupations of Euro Americans made African Americans more than a little queasy about their own place in the country. For instance, even though they were largely a non-issue in the pro- and anti-immigration debates of the nineteenth century, they did feature in public policy as differing regulations sought to restrict them from moving toward the Rockies. African Americans have historically felt threatened.

John Williams's work has been credited with a great deal of verisimilitude, especially as his access to FBI files helped him bring out his anti-Martin Luther King piece, *The King God Didn't Save* (1970). Williams' fourth novel, *The Man Who Cried I Am*, is a blunt eye-opener. Published in 1967, it concerns Max Reddick, a Black writer suspiciously like Richard Wright, dying of cancer and trying to piece together his life. He finds himself in possession of a classified government document, the "King Alfred Plan" (which Williams himself believes to be in existence). The plan, in effect, calls for the cooperation of the CIA, FBI, Department of Defense, National Guard, and police at the state and local levels in targeting Congress of Racial Equality (CORE), Student Non Violent Coordinating Committee (SNCC), the National Association for the Advancement of Colored People (NAACP), Southern Christian Leadership Conference (SCLC), and others. The King Alfred Plan describes in realistic detail how mass incarceration and destruction of African Americans is to be effected. Although the plan admits that some African American leaders had been bought out, still "there are always new and dissident elements joining those organizations, with the potential power to replace the old leaders."[4] The plan calls for twenty-four-hour surveillance of African American organizations. Max almost manages to forewarn Black-nationalist leader, Minister Q (Malcolm X?), but the leader is still murdered. Max himself is killed.

One may easily dismiss this as fiction, despite the author's denial, but it is not difficult to see how an inter-European hierarchical arrangement provoked, indeed even promulgated this fear. But our reference point does not end with John Williams and his demonstrated access to FBI files. Sam Yette's *The Choice* (1972), not a novel, reminded readers of the Japanese war camps and the relative ease with which Japanese were silently put away, with the approval of large segments of the Anglo American and African American population. *The Choice* takes over where fiction dared not venture. It detailed clear plans for removing African American leadership and people once the government deemed that a crisis was imminent.[5] Genocide was the ultimate weapon that would be utilized to promulgate the doctrine of Euro American superiority. If all this seems far-fetched, one should consider two points: first, that the central body politic in America had taught and continues to teach the devaluation of non-European cultural achievements and, second, that this cultural chauvinism was not suddenly invented to deal with African Americans, but had always been intrinsic to Anglo American and Euro American belief. This is the ugliest side to Eurocentrism, particularly virulent because it is practiced by a powerful majority against a powerless minority, in a country where numerical head-counting arbitrarily assigns absolute rights. Within the near future, when the minority becomes the majority, what will this suggest as a model?

All of this could have been dismissed as merely theoretical speculation from a novelist with a ripe imagination fed by his access to FBI files, and a political scientist with a fertile zeal. Yet many assert that the genocide theory accomplishes in a cruder fashion what assimilation attempted but did not achieve. Sam Yette's book is written against the background of urban conflagration, of civil rights gone wrong, with the still lingering question that Malcolm X asked on July 5, 1964, after the adoption of the Civil Rights Act about the need for such an act:

> Of the people who just got off the boat yesterday in this country, from the various so-called Iron Curtain countries, which are supposedly an enemy to this country, and no civil rights legislation is needed to bring them into the mainstream of the American way of life, then you and I should just stop and ask ourselves, why is it needed for us? They're actually slapping you and me in the face when they pass a civil rights bill. It's not an honor; it's a slap in the face. They're telling you that you don't have it, and at the same time they're telling you that they have to legislate before you can get it. Which in essence means they're telling you that since you don't have it and yet you're born here, there must be something about you that makes you different from everybody else who's born here; something about you that actually, though you have the right of birth in this land, you're still not qualified under their particular system to be recognized as a citizen.

> Yet the Germans, that they used to fight just a few years ago, can come here and get what you can't get. The Russians, whom they're supposedly fighting right now, can come here and get what you can't get without legislation; don't need legislation. The Polish don't need legislation. Nobody needs it but you. Why?—you should stop and ask yourself why. And when you find out why, then you'll change the direction you've been going in, and you'll change also the methods that you've been using trying to get in that direction.[6]

The basic outline "fictionalized" by Williams is "factualized" by Sam Yette. Yette cites recommendations of the House Un-American Activities Committee (HUAC) from Representative Edwin E. Willis to President Lyndon Johnson. After the "ghetto is sealed off from the rest of the city" by police, state troopers, the National Guard, and, if need be, the Army, seven further steps are advocated: (1) the imposition of a curfew; (2) the dispatch of foot patrols; (3) the suspension of civil liberties; (4) the proscription of movement through the issue of "census cards"; (5) encouragement by the "authorities . . . to report both on guerrillas and any suspicious activity"; (6) the declaration of a state of war and the imprisonment of dissenters under the McCarran Act; and (7) "the revolutionaries could be isolated and destroyed in a short period of time."[7]

Quotations are from "Guerrilla Warfare Advocates in the United States," a report by the Committee on Un-American Activities, dated May 6, 1968. African Americans see this as their "final solution," part of the ethnic hatred fostered by the Trail of Tears, Japanese imprisonment, the Tuskegee Experiment, and Edgar Hoover's Counter Intelligence Program (COINTELPRO).

The Tuskegee Experiment took place from 1932 through 1972 in the Tuskegee penitentiary. The U.S. government commissioned the Public Health Service to run "tests" on inmates on a "voluntary" basis. In reality, prisoners were injected with the syphilis virus, and their movements and contacts were studied and monitored over the next forty years. Only because of the Freedom of Information Act, passed in the early 1970s, is one even aware of these atrocities.[8]

Likewise, through COINTELPRO, J. Edgar Hoover's own misdirected racism caused many groups like the Black Panther Party, the Nation of Islam, and SNCC to be infiltrated and even destroyed. Leaders were either assassinated or made to appear to be informants. A columnist in the *Nation* sums up:

By 1967 J. Edgar Hoover had concluded that the Black Panther Party had replaced the Communist Party as the gravest threat to national security. In an August 25 memorandum to the F.B.I.'s Albany office the director confided his counter-intelligence program (COINTELPRO), whose purpose was "to expose, disrupt, misdirect, discredit, or otherwise neutralize the activities of black nationalist, hate-type organizations and groupings, their leadership, spokesmen, membership and supporters."[9]

Reality behind the first McCarran Act of 1950 is also frightening. Also termed the Internal Security Act, the act established and legalized various camps in the event of a state of emergency. Six detention centers—two in Arizona, and one each in Pennsylvania, Oklahoma, California, and Florida—were established and maintained by the Department of Justice. African Americans argue that these camps exist and were used to arrest and detain rioters in Washington, D.C. after Martin Luther King's death. H. Rap Brown, a cofounder of SNCC, relates such an experience in his book, *Die Nigger Die!*

Whether the pieces fit together or not, in the African American public mind there is a suspicion of Eurocentric hostility that might lead to what we now familiarly call "ethnic cleansing." Louis Farrakhan's appeal lies in just this direction, in that he openly accepts these as facts and speaks from this viewpoint. Most recently in 1989, even as conservative a television program as the "Tony Brown's Journal," sponsored by Pepsi-Cola, devoted a four-part series to the belief that AIDS is a man-made drug, intended for African and African American extinction.

As noted before, Oliver North did testify during the early Irangate hearings in July 1987 to the continued existence of such a plan during the Reagan White

House years. He spoke of "Rex 84" and the way in which it would be utilized to deal with African Americans in the event of civil disturbance. Familiar ground, already noted, was hinted at: the suspension of the Constitution, imprisonment without trial, and the use of permanent jail sentences. The entire Congressional response, lasting about five minutes, was abruptly cut off, and committee members were told that the matter could only be discussed in camera. Then Rep. William Gray tried to ask a question on the matter, and again the issue of national secrecy was invoked. Only one major newspaper (that I know of) carried even sparse details of the matter—the *Miami Herald*. Then the entire subject disappeared from public discussion. The *Miami Herald* buried most of the relevant part on page 14a of its Sunday, July 5, 1987, issue. It related that "Lt. Col. Oliver North, for example, helped draw up a controversial plan to suspend the Constitution in the event of national crisis, such as nuclear war, violent and widespread internal dissent or national opposition to a U.S. military invasion abroad."[10] Through the Federal Emergency Management Agency, military commanders would be appointed "to run state and local governments." An "official" was quoted as saying that "the contingency plan was written as part of an executive order or legislative package that Reagan would sign and hold within the NSC until a severe crisis arose."[11]

Martial law, especially as it affected African Americans, was outlined by John Brinkerhoff in a memo dated June 30, 1982. He was deputy for "national preparedness programs." The article continues:

> The scenario outlined in the Brinkerhoff memo resembled somewhat a paper Guiffrida had written in 1970 at the Army War College in Carlisle, Pa., in which he advocated martial law in case of a national uprising by black militants. The paper also advocated the roundup and transfer to "assembly centers or relocation camps" of at least 21 million "American Negroes."[12]

All of this is mentioned to indicate how, at a subterranean gut level, beyond spoken word or even gesture, the so-called minority population is tolerated. This persistent policy, at the highest level of government, maintains a stranglehold on African Americans, not deriving itself from any necessity, perceived or real.

We have noted that the loudest African American declaimers of Black rights, from the turn of the twentieth century, were seeking personal assimilation and acceptance into the Euro American power consortium. Repeatedly they stated that their intention was simply to have some African Americans included in the power bloc and the larger part totally excluded. Cynics would aver that now, at the end of the century, with the jails overflowing with African American males, their wishes have come true.

Super-ethnocentrism in America, therefore, logically ups the racial ante and takes on terrifying perspectives. For neat little narrow-minded beliefs held in monoethnic European countries really have no place in a grand experiment of globalizing the world in a given place—America. However, once the power structure maintains, however abjectly absurd, its ridiculous belief in a European diaspora, pluralism can have no meaning other than the allocation of half measures to even those willing to accept a tabula rasa. Yet the myth of European dominance persists. Witness Levine et al. in *Who Built North America?* published in 1989:

> *The settlement of British North America was part of a global process by which Europe established imperial dominance.* The driving force in the creation of new societies was *a series of national and social struggles in Europe* that, on the one hand, caused frustrated European rulers to look for new sources of wealth and, on the other, caused enough discontent among the common folk that many were willing to venture their all in a gamble of settling in a strange land.[13]

Partly true, but such an introduction omits particularly the indigenous American Indian, the African American, and the Asian and continues the propagation of the Eurocentric myth. In *Foreign Policy* (Summer 1990), Michael J. Brenner sees a unique role for the United States in Europe after 1992, as that "of honest broker and facilitator within the alliance and of underwriter for a Europe-wide settlement." He continues: "The United States is of Europe but not in Europe. Further, it retains a good measure of its moral authority—not only in the West as leader of the post war alliance, but *more broadly as the amalgam of European societies and the repository of common values* now in ascendance throughout the Continent."[14] Such a conclusion, at this stage of America's development, still ignores the history, ethnicity, and origins of half its people.

Racial considerations apart, the net result of avid Eurocentrism leads first to differentiations among Europeans regarding skin coloration and then to even more insidious distinctions, ironically within the framework of non-Europeans—color, lifestyle, habits, and mores. Indeed this is one of the major themes of Harlem Renaissance writers of the 1920s and 1930s, among male authors such as Wallace Thurman, Jean Toomer, and women writers such as Nella Larsen and Jessie Fauset. In the literature, degrees of skin coloration become the major dramatic reason why characters rise or fall, indeed survive or perish.

A dubious understanding of science was invoked in the European versus non-European contention. Madison Grant in the *Passing of the Great Race of America* (1916) bases his argument on biology and calls for aristocracy and racial purity as the pillars of any greatness. Hence inferior people hail from the Alps and the Mediterranean; Jews should be excluded, or the "great race" of Nordics that had made great soldiers, explorers, rulers, and aristocrats would be weakened by the "mentally crippled of all races."

Grant's writing was popularized by novelists, like Kenneth Roberts, in his "adventure" novels, *Arundel* (1930), *Rabble in Arms* (1933), and *Captain Caution* (1934), which told in sequence about Revolutionary War general Benedict Arnold, his march through the Maine woods, and his attempt to capture Quebec. In *Northwest Passage* (1937), Roberts also relates Indian campaigns; as late as 1940, *Oliver Wiswell* views the American Revolution from the English side. His novels advanced the view of Eurocentric superiority, as evidenced in a series of articles written in 1922 for the *Saturday Evening Post*.

Henry Ford used his millions to promulgate, in the *Dearborn Independent*, his anti-Jewish theories (no longer mentioned, since Ford is an "American" hero). The European versus non-European attacks shifted first to a search for an early pre-Hitler super race, found a butt in Jews, and later, as Roberts and Ford popularized Madison Grant's views, helped lead to a validation of the Klan. No wonder Jews and African Americans found common cause in the founding of the National Association for the Advancement of Colored People (NAACP). They had both been made irrelevant in the "national" preoccupation with Eurocentricity, and even those who wanted to join the club were prevented from so doing.

What is, indeed, ironical exists in the sure but steady manner in which the powerful Anglo ethnocentric nonmajority group renders, first, other Europeans (mainly Jews) and, second, Native Americans and African Americans as non-human objects. Malwyn Allen Jones shows how the myth of inferiority was first applied to darker-skinned Europeans in the 1920s:

> About the same time, publication of the results of the United States Army's wartime psychological tests on soldiers helped still further to condition the public to race thinking. The fact that soldiers from southern and eastern Europe had remarkably lower IQ scores than those from northern and western Europe and the United States was adduced as conclusive proof of Nordic intellectual superiority.[15]

By the late 1960s the victim had changed color, but the reasoning was the same as a new spokesperson, Arthur R. Jensen, was reported thus in the *Harvard Educational Review*:

> In a lengthy article, taking up most of the winter issue of the "Harvard Educational Review," one of the nation's leading educational psychologists, Dr. Arthur R. Jensen of the University of California at Berkeley, presents these major findings:
>
> —Negro scores averaging about 15 points below the white average on I.Q. tests must be taken seriously as evidence of genetic differences between the two races in learning patterns.

—Research suggests that such a difference would tend to work against Negroes and against the "disadvantaged" generally when it comes to "cognitive" learning—abstract reasoning—which forms the basis for intelligence measurements and for the higher mental skills.

—Conversely, Negroes and other "disadvantaged" children tend to do well in tasks involving rote learning—memorizing mainly through repetition—and some other skills, and these aptitudes can be used to help raise their scholastic achievement and job potential.

—Unfortunately, big programs of "compensatory" education, now costing taxpayers hundreds of millions of dollars a year, are doomed to failure as long as they pursue old approaches stressing "cognitive" learning.[16]

We should not find it particularly odd that, judging from his non-English name, the descendant of a former "victim" is quick to identify a newer victim. In a way it is almost a self-defensive posture, for it takes the heat off the informant and pinpoints the attributes of another nonperson in a different direction. Average people would not have been unaware of Dr. Jensen's pronouncements in the *Harvard Educational Review*, but as with Kenneth Roberts's racist articles in the *Saturday Evening Post*, this self-same ordinary reader was privy once more to the reawakening of racism. Today, despite the well-ordered rituals of interethnic socialization, the legacy of hostility is evident.

Apart from any queasy moral considerations one may have, the net effect of Eurocentrism totally involves the entire society in three major ways: politically, educationally, and economically. Since non-European Americans are treated as nonentities, they are denied an active role in the body politic. They must fight for what others take for granted and each human step, however ordinary, must be accompanied by hoopla. In other words, rights that are first refused, when "granted," are seen as coming from a "benevolent" giver. The African American "victims" are placed in a situation in which they are totally hopeless, as they may aspire to but cannot ever become Euro Americans. When "elevated," these individuals do not see themselves as being placed back where they ought to have been in the first place, but envision themselves either as deserving to be there because of some natural endowment (such as affinity with a European-type appearance) or as having aspired and succeeded in being there as a result of some herculean effort.

Indeed, I have often argued that even so-called radicals like Malcolm X and Louis B. Farrakhan are addressing not a Black audience but a White group, wishing to be heard, imploring that their status be changed. One thing stands out most clearly in my own meeting with Malcolm X in Africa: I felt he was merely trying to appeal to USAID and the expatriate American community. At the core of many of Spike Lee's movies lies a constant concern over the dormant tendency within many African American communities to engage in intraracial hostility. Another young movie producer, John Singleton, also sees the gang as a form of racial self-hatred, even ethnic denial. Both seek mainstream change.

At the educational level, the entire curriculum is geared up to serve the mythical whims of the Eurocentric fancifier. Hence, the debate, at times pretty bitter, over what constitutes the canon. Arthur Schlesinger in a recent *Wall Street Journal* article was quite passionate:

> Very little agitates academia more these days than the demands of passionate minorities for revision of the curriculum: in history, the denunciation of Western Civilization courses as cultural imperialism; in literature, the denunciation of the "canon," the list of essential books, as an instrumentality of the existing power structure.[17]

The canon is not reflective of endemic qualities of some absolute aesthetic that a given work possesses in itself and totally to itself. A nation's agreed-upon "reading list" is merely what the power brokers decide it has to be. Democratic principles do not prevail, and even if they did, so-called present-day minorities might find themselves as scarce as they are in the Senate. If those who control the country view themselves as the progeny of Europe and either do not see the others or view them merely as objects, then it follows that these "minor" people cannot usefully contribute to the "canon," the learning process of the "major" people.

This is the basis of the multicultural debate, for unless the validity of a people is accepted, their cultural values would seem to be of little consequence or relevance. However, the presence of new minorities is continuing to make different demands on the shaping of the curriculum. Original formats are calling for revision; despite the conservative battle for the retention of the "Great Books" as an essential part of the syllabus, women, homosexuals, and ethnic minorities demand change.

In a way the demand for multiculturalism derived from the rethinking that developed from the social and political unrest of the sixties. Progressives seek what they would term approaches to the curriculum that are free of traditional bias. Traditionalists assert that the basis of the culture of the United States is Graeco-Roman and Judaeo-Christian and that the curriculum must continue to reflect these approaches.

Because the aim is to free the society from the ethnocentrism in which it is embedded, it becomes necessary to make certain radical departures, for this is not a single culture but several; pedagogy must come to terms with the multifaceted world of the United States.[18] Once we recognize the uniqueness of each culture, without the need to have one dominate the other, then we can easily embark on a new curriculum, whose content reflects diversity.

Some critics of multiculturalism assert that there is something treacherous, unpatriotic, and certainly dysfunctional in attempting to move away from "national" preoccupations. For Arthur Schlesinger in *The Disuniting of Amer-*

ica, the United States has to set a monocultural example in a world rent by savage ethnic conflict; the United States must demonstrate "how a highly differentiated society holds itself together."[19] But the remedy is not to recognize diversity, to give equal time to disparate ethnic claimants, but to revert to the recognition of the officially approved Eurocentric curriculum.

Nor are the lines racially drawn, as might be expected. E. D. Hirsch cites Black sociologist Orlando Patterson with some relish, stating that "shared information is a necessary background to true literacy."[20] However, Hirsch's concept of cultural literacy is always grounded in tradition—"acquiring factual and traditional schemata"[21] or, elsewhere, "a much stronger base in factual information and traditional lore."[22] Clearly, by "tradition" Hirsch is referring to a Euro American concept of the world, replete with its values and belief systems, its mythologies, norms, and religion, what Hirsch readily admits is "cultural conservatism."[23]

The problem is that even though Hirsch pays lip service to minority cultures, again and again he harks back to a Eurocentric dominant focus—"Besides the English language and the natural legal codes, American culture possesses first of all a civil religion that underlies our civil ethos."[24] African American, Asian, Spanish-speaking, and Native American people are bound to question the "our"—what are the common themes, beliefs, ideas, agreed concepts that bind a multiethnic society into some specific cultural solidarity? Could this be enforced, would it be desirable?

Another "minority" voice that champions the cause of "traditional" canonical values is the Indian-born Dinesh D'Souza, whose *Illiberal Education* sounded a loud rallying cry that American academia was wrongly positioned. Under the banner of causes, he argues, such as racial and gay rights, proponents have demanded quotas. Not only have Euro Americans suffered in the process, but the very minorities themselves (the author, obviously, excepted) have been demeaned.

We read in D'Souza what few Euro American conservatives would openly espouse. White students, he tells us, who would normally "show sympathy and understanding for the difficulties endured by black and Hispanic students [do not] since they consider that affirmative action benefits are awarded at their expense."[25] His interpretation of what he terms Berkeley's "proportional representation" means "more blacks and Hispanics, fewer Jews and Asians."[26] D'Souza easily sorts out Euro American fears and anxieties and sides with the "winners," the majority, against the "losers," the minority. From here it is an easy step to the demolition of a multicultural curriculum.

He argues, for instance, that courses that promote multiculturalism do this based on "group representation" and suggests that creationism ought to have equal time. He is caustic against those who would lump "whiteness and maleness" as supposedly constituting the bulk of a curricular norm; for D'Souza "those are features, historically accidental, that happened to coincide with great minds who were working at particular times in particular environments."[27] Indeed, for D'Souza, "the Western tradition offers powerful and moving treatment of the issues of slavery and equality."[28] Yet he proceeds to denounce even relatively cautious scholars like Frank Snowden who sought to relate how the classics frequently included African figures, how indeed, as Snowden argues, the Greek world was relatively free from a preoccupation with color.

Against this viewpoint, Afrocentric scholars such as Molefi Asante argue that "without Afrocentricity, African Americans would not have a voice to add to multiculturalism."[29] Afrocentricity restores Africa as the pivot around which African Americans view their world. But the problem still remains—if we cannot accept D'Souza because of his fervent propounding of Eurocentrism, are we more easily able to relate to Afrocentric scholars as they "oppose the negation in Western culture"?[30]

The Eurocentric/ethnic-centered debate is the academic equivalent of the concerns expressed in this study. At the Eurocentric level, proponents advocate that the United States follow Europe and educate its young as future Europeans. At the ethnic-centered level, proponents seek to move away from overdue concerns with mainstream majority European bias toward new inputs. In part, the minority fear of total incorporation into the majority arises out of the same preoccupations expressed by John Williams, Malcolm X, and Sam Yette. Here the concern is as real, as now the issue is a little more subtle, but just as insidious—fear of cultural genocide.

Many of the criticisms leveled at the contemporary United States have arisen out of its close adherence to outworn and jaded European policy. At home, the result has been that the once supposedly "ideal" society has soured; it is now revealed as being clearly racist, sexist, elitist, and culturally impoverished. Not unnaturally, therefore, a great deal of the debate regarding education has tended to find ways by which this perverse cultural indoctrination can be further pushed. There is more resistance to this today because, given quicker and easier global communications and an ethnically changing population, people are no longer willing to buy into the European myth. However, a Eurocentric bias has engendered serious conflict, not least at the level of the curriculum, as noted.

Mortimer Adler is one of the major spokespersons on this. At the University of Chicago, the "Great Books" curriculum was adopted due to his influence. All undergraduates are expected to be inculcated with a thorough dose of western civilization—Archimedes, Planck, and Einstein; Herodotus, Hegel, and William James; Jane Austen, George Eliot, Conrad, and George Orwell; Ruth Benedict and Gunnar Myrdal. This was the holy "canon" and remains so for many other schools, often pitting them against Stanford, which radically altered its own curriculum.

In *Great Ideas from the Great Books* (1961), Mortimer Adler pontificated on the issues. A great man, he seriously asserted, "is a man who stands out, who towers above his fellows in some obvious way."[31] Herein lies the germ of the much-touted individualism, but a careful scrutiny reveals that this is actual advocacy of a familiar self-centered and rapacious philosophy. It shows little concern for a larger group, indeed even for the nation itself.

When any extra-self consideration is admitted into this sober reckoning, it is for the sacrosanct, conventional, nuclear family. The role of parents is literally purloined from the Bible: parents are warned not to spare the rod. Children must know that "all the great writers insist that parents should govern children firmly until they reach maturity."[32] A list of "great works" is appended. The solution, for Mortimer Adler, is secure, safe, pat, and unenterprising. The traditional European way is approved, and the more relevant American multiculturalism is rejected.

Recently, the Encyclopaedia Brittanica's *Great Books of the Western World* (1990), under editor-in-chief Mortimer Adler, endorsed this approach. One criterion specified that for inclusion a work "must deal with a large number of ideas that have concerned great Western writers for many centuries." This mandate, really a grandfather clause, was the major basis used to exclude minority and women writers. Editor Philip Goetz surmised that "probably in the next century there will be some Black that writes a great book."[33] Writing, like good wine, must age; writers must occupy tombstones before they speak.

This would be comical were it not for the fact that what is done at the University of Chicago and sanctioned by the Encyclopaedia Brittanica is taken as gospel truth purported to have academic credibility by the learned. A single act such as this sets back any real opportunity at a genuine pluralistic education because it refuses to face up to latter-day realities. The compilers of the volumes are still looking to Europe for assurance, which, when once located, continues to impose its distortions on a compliant American society. As a consequence of this, those who go through this system—of whatever color or social background—will continue to subscribe to its credos. Therein lies the real danger to the possibility of any true cultural independence for America.

At the larger level, the "Great Books" debate is actually a devious way through which European ideas continue to dominate American society. It imposes a rigid pattern on American thought, arguing that to create a true nation there must be a concept of "shared knowledge." The debate has spawned off other tomes that also attack any multicultural tilt in American society. Hence, Roger Kimball's *Tenured Radicals* (1990) locates the blame in legislation that has corrupted academia, giving "liberals" an excessive degree of control. Bloom's *The Closing of the American Mind* (1987) and Hirsch's *Cultural Literacy: What Every American Needs to Know* (1987) argue that the very beneficiaries of Western culture—minorities—ought not to be permitted to voice these concerns. Such minorities do not, they would contend, really exhibit diversity in American culture, but exhibit rather a conformity to radicalism. Naturally, with their viewpoint the then Reagan White House and its Secretary of Education, William Bennett, had no quarrel.

Adler, Kimball, Bloom, Hirsch et al. would expunge even the limited inklings of diversity in the society, as the smallest lack of European knowledge is equated with the absence of all true knowledge—indeed, the very advocacy of alternatives becomes a trivialization of all civilization itself. Thus these Eurocentrists denounce women's studies, African American studies, Latino studies, and Native American and Asian studies as fruitless lines of academic pursuit. Hirsch insists that such departures from formal Western thought have served only to introduce what he terms "the shopping mall school," which perverts "the whole system of widely shared information and associations."[34] Bloom sums it up: "History and the study of cultures [i.e., of the non-Western variety] do not teach or prove that values or cultures are relative."[35] African American scholars, like Martin Kilson, Thomas Sowell, and Shelby Steele, have obediently followed in their master's footsteps: the only road to the true emancipation of the spirit is a thorough whitewashing of the soul. One is almost back in a pre-Boas world before cultural relativism.

At the extreme end of the debate is Amaury de Reincourt who prophesied in *The American Empire* (1968) the only neat solution for Black refusal to allow White South African lordship: the United States would have to assume control and become "arbiter of the situation."[36] After all, if one is faced with a people unable to produce a culture, one is almost morally bound to take over. This much was already argued to justify incarceration and genocide of Native Americans, servitude of African Americans, and domination of all females.

De Reincourt dates the end of European empire, and the genesis of American empire in the postwar period. But the Monroe Doctrine of December 2, 1823, spelled out America as closet colonialist. Although it stated "the American continents . . . are henceforth not to be considered as subjects for future colonization by any European power," it continued to argue that "with the existing colonies or dependencies of any European power we have not interfered and shall not interfere." At this point the United States articulated fence-sitting as official policy. The United States was going colonial and would try its best to grab land and territory, but not from European powers. Such language, with that wonderful zest for ethical compromise, may also be noted in the Emancipation Proclamation of September 2, 1862: "all persons held as slaves within any state the people whereof shall then be in rebellion against the United States shall be then, thence forward, and forever free." Slaves became "free" in Confederate states, just as earlier on subjects had become "free" in European ex-colonies. Slaves were not free in Union states, nor were subjects "free" who were already dependents of Europe.

At the most hypocritical level, presidents Monroe and Lincoln could claim, respectively, "just principles" for the Monroe Doctrine and "the gracious favor of Almighty God" for the Emancipation Proclamation. Both had this in common: They assert the opposite of what they actually say, for in both instances the federal government established control over both sides of the debate. At another level, with both statements the Euro United States established itself as "lawgiver" on one hand but, on the other, retained Latin American peasants and African American slaves in a "subject/client" relationship. This has still not been appreciably altered.

From early on in the nation's history, these important pieces of legislation carry on the Eurocentric prerogative and effectively depersonalize African Americans and Latin Americans. Thus are the aspirations of a people denied, and the people become demonized and effectively rendered as the "Other" and the "Object."

Obviously, this is a sharp departure from the ideal principles that had spawned the American Revolution. Locke had held that authority derives only from the consent of the governed, and even if the Constitution were fuzzy on this, Locke's views were not. But Locke's ideas were imported by Europeanized Americans into the generalizations of the Constitution. Locke certainly did not express views that would have been compatible earlier with William Bradford's "just and equal Laws, Ordinances, Acts, Constitutions and Offices," which formed the Mayflower Compact of 1620. This rigidness soon led not only to the denunciation of Anne Hutchinson but also to the combined admonishment, by at least three of the sober-faced "founding fathers," of one of their most witty, fair-minded, and delightfully eccentric contemporaries, Thomas Morton, who dared to dance around a maypole with "Indian" women on a merry Mayday in 1627.

Perhaps it is because American history harks back constantly to the over-serious gravitas that the pronouncements of later interpreters like de Reincourt or Adler tend to be just so self-absorbed and oversolemn. True American culture, they would argue, emanates from the strict and joyless Eurocentric confines of William Bradford, Edward Johnson, and John Winthrop. Expelled is the humorous quaintness, even the very humanness, of Thomas Morton, as well as the sincere self-questioning of a mere woman, Anne Hutchinson.

As late as 1967, John Nef could still boldly argue: "The United States has open to it the possibility of leading the peoples of the world . . . into the Promised Land."[37] Therein lies the sanctimoniousness of the Puritans, without Morton or Hutchinson, without Native American or later African American or Latino presence. Leadership is unmistakably Anglo-Saxon.

Nor should one dismiss this type of discourse as silly patter, anymore than one can ignore Mortimer Adler. The apex of power-control in the society is quite definitely male and Euro American and very much committed to the propagation of its own belief system. The "special relationship" with Britain continues to manufacture newer and more fantastic myths that, however gross, engender in turn newer beliefs of their own.

There is a degree of irony in this mad rush to expunge the history of the non-Greek world from American culture. Scholars at the Afrocentric end of the debate have long asserted that the very Western culture in which direction eager advocates wish to direct American society owes much of its life to the fostering and nurturing forces of African, Arab, and other non-European peoples. Indeed, the origins of European culture cannot be understood in a vacuum but must, at the very least, be located in the Tigris-Euphrates valley. Even without the assistance of the Leakeys and Donald Johanson, the European past obviously shares with the world two commonalities.

First, both Frank Snowden, two decades ago, and Martin Bernal, more recently, have asserted that there exists what may be termed an "Ancient Model" of interaction between African, Asian, and European peoples. Such a paradigm, utilized by Snowden, identifies five areas of evidence: literary, epigraphical, papyrological, numismatic, and archaeological.[38] So far, Bernal has published only the first two volumes of a projected four, but the intention is to show that Greek culture existed only because of heavy borrowings from Egypt, as the Greeks themselves knew. Racial prescriptiveness in the more recent European period sought to ignore African-Egyptian influence and condemn them both to a backwater. Greece, like Topsy, apparently just growed.

Second, between 711 and 1492, the Moorish presence in Spain, southern France, and other parts of the Mediterranean, particularly with the advent of the Almoravids, brought the African and Arab world once more into contact with Europe. Not only was Andalusia an oasis of culture and refinement during the European Dark Ages but it also became a virtual treasure trove, as African, Arab, and Jewish scholars had managed to copy and translate, as well as to expand and develop, a great deal of Greek and Roman thought. This was how Europe knew its past. Without the library at the University of Toledo and the guardianship of European culture by these aliens, the present "Great Books" debate would be moot. Furthermore, aspects of the self-same modern Europe to which these neo-European Eurocentrics look were passed on via modern Spain and Portugal by Africans and Arabs, as may be witnessed, according to Jan Read, "in the arts, in the practicalities of life and in basic attitudes."[39]

Without my venturing into more detail, it becomes clear how the critical non-European dependency of Graeco-Roman culture asserts itself. The Greeks and Romans did not feel that their culture was tainted by the rest of the world. They took pleasure in the global relevance such an appeal would have; and they borrowed, inherited, appropriated, altered, or often simply stole aspects of these other cultures.

Any argument that seeks to assert Europeanness in America, even at this late stage, must fail because it lacks historical relevance here and because historical Europe, like latter-day America, obviously retained part of its world. Any proclamation of American triumphalism may declare superiority only in the martial arts, certainly not in cultural uniqueness or independence.

Eurocentrism would hardly have resulted in such vicious ramifications here were America only a single monocultural closed society, choosing to indulge in some harmless fantasy. But the extreme Eurocentric interpretations are particularly pernicious to persons of Latin American origin, who are quickly becoming the largest minority in the United States. Anglo Americanism is essentially a denial of their culture and values, especially those elements that could free and globalize American culture. Harking back to a mythic European past represents a contemptuous negation of their presence.

Latino victimization is particularly manifest at two levels: language and religion. The hysterical claims made for English as the sole American language are clearly race-based, ethnically promulgated, and historically unsound. The language dispute arises out of an Anglo concern for English as the sole vehicle of communication. Despite claims to the contrary, proponents are interested not merely in national unity but really in national conformity. The argument often made that earlier immigrants were forced to learn English is only a fatuous way of compounding the issue. For the earlier European immigrants had little choice; they were limited numerically, and in their pursuit of the "American Dream" they had been sold the idea that English was the only way of assimilating. They themselves bought into the view, as those who provided them with their livelihoods, demanded just this—a specific, precise monocultural attachment.

Today, Latinos often find that they can live, work, and entertain themselves outside the framework of majority Eurocentric cultural decisions. In California, Florida, and New York, they have established self-sustaining communities that, partake of American life, but on their own terms. At the second front, religion has become a burning issue, especially in Miami and New York. Cubans introduced santería, the synthesis of African Yoruba and European Catholic faiths. At first practiced underground, it later became more and more open. Botanicas now sell items for ritualistic usage; santéros and santéras openly advertise their services. One, in particular, Ernesto Pichardo, has gone public on various national talk shows, advocating santéria as a rich and viable alternative. Most recently, he has engaged a local city council in a lawsuit when it tried to prevent the establishment of his Church of the Lukumi in its territory. Rightly, he argued (and the ACLU supported him), that the Hialeah city council was contravening a basic principle of the Constitution by not permitting him to practice his religion. Pichardo won his case in a famous unanimous decision of the U.S. Supreme Court in 1993.[40]

These are not fringe issues, but ones that operate from a new and differing perception—the efforts on the part of a people to assert their distinctiveness, to protect themselves from the tyranny of majority Eurocentric culture. Indeed, the Bill of Rights anticipated their struggle. But, this is a new phenomenon in American history whereby immigrants only partly buy into the "dream." Those who thought up the covert Operation Peter Pan, by which, between November

1960 and October 1962, thousands of young Cubans were smuggled into the United States, must now be having second thoughts. For the children grew up concerned not with Mom and apple pie, but with Mama and congri.

Those who still advocate ethnic purity for a Euro America, uninfected by foreigners, find themselves in a quandary. America was never pure, and racial and cultural interaction was always a pragmatic reality, as Captain John Smith and Pocahontas, Jefferson and Sally Hemmings well knew. With the advent of Spanish-speaking immigrants, the situation is further complicated. Latinos, themselves the end process of synthesis at both racial and cultural levels, cannot fully comprehend crude classifications of Black and White. Therefore, they offer an interesting perspective for being neither poor nor rich, Black nor White, Catholic nor Protestant, existing as a bit of all of these. Their dualism sits comfortably with them, much to the alarm of both African and European Americans.

Here the United States has a final opportunity to stake out new cultural territory and, once and for all, to free itself from Eurocentric thralldom. Actually, this Latino presence can help return America to a past relatively free from European myth, for they represent, despite their own past problems at reconciliation, the synthesis of New World culture at its finest.

Even though the ancient forms of Graeco-Roman government represented ideals that the Founders wished to pursue, they were terribly ensnared in the admiration of the colonized for the colonizer. It was quite mistaken to see Rome, Sparta, and Carthage as embodiments of perfection. Perhaps the time has come to state quite categorically that the Founders were deluded and that John Adams was only articulating the received viewpoint of his time when he supported the establishment of America along the lines of ancient Greece and Rome. An ideal government surely depends on national character, not on semiaristocratic impositions from above. In any case, the agricultural and industrial revolutions changed, or ought to have changed, America's intoxication with Europe. The most that can be said for the ideas about the establishment of a classical republic in America is that it provided an idealized example from which to derive a reality.

America must now present itself as this reality. Crèvecoeur noted that farmers were much too busy for public issues, and even a neo-Classicist like Jefferson urged the nation not to look backward if it sought to achieve improvement of the human mind. For too long we have been trapped by European conceptions about the New World, varying from Plato's to Sir Thomas More's, Bacon's and Tomasso Campanella's. America can no longer survive as Europe's image of itself.

A refusal to move into new and differing non-Eurocentric viewpoints operates not only at the level of the idealized state but also from the aspect of a repressive church. Cain Felder has shown in *Troubling Biblical Waters* (1989) that the "underlying paradoxes" in Christian theology have produced racist tendencies. He attacks Eurocentric precepts and motifs, which have resulted in the denigration of African Americans and women. He blames the manner in which the interests of a particular group have mitigated against a thorough comprehension of the Bible. He does not reject Christianity; for him it is capable of an adaptation that can address the distortions of sex, class, and race in a contemporary non-Eurocentric but very Christian America.[41]

Alternative patterns to understanding American culture will help renew an awareness. New possibilities emerge, not least of which are those concerned with how well a relevant vision for this time may be implemented. Rethinking the past means a reversal through which present consequences may be visualized in a new perspective, not of "assimilation" or "integration" but of "cultural pluralism."

Of course, grave difficulties lie ahead. We have believed so long in an alien mythology that it becomes difficult to undermine it intentionally. But even as European culture speaks to a European environment, American culture must constantly rebel against it. Never mind the indwelling insecurity that ever seeks to drive individuals to copy past models that are powerful and close by. America's establishment and purpose represent a common endeavor to which all have contributed. American art and culture must be made in the image of just such a common interaction, through which a mini-world culture can be promulgated if we will only let it happen.

Nor should we advocate only the partial overthrow of a mistaken belief system, but a complete and total surrender to a more elevated and powerful conception. Officialdom preserves a sentimental view of the past, characterized by a toleration for sacrosanct but archaic models. Any new posture must call for a different degree of awareness, for a loss of compassion with familiar language and religious credos, and for the gain of new power alliances and cultural attachments.

Such an invitation is quite definitely a challenge, at the level of city, state, and country. It becomes more imperative now if America as a concept is to have any desirable meaning. Uncritical examination will only return us to the point of blind acceptance of what hitherto has always been taken for granted as national values. No longer can we claim a Jamesian innocence, since the world has grown older and many of our earlier illusions have been challenged, invalidated, and laid to rest.

Such critical change must acknowledge the inevitability of cultural disorganization, for few can justify the present state of affairs. Beneath the superficial vainglory and bombast, the trumpeteering and shameless display of what passes for patriotism, exists an ideal that speaks to an American social particularity. British imitation is stifling, and European mimicry is ill-becoming. Both are false and empty gestures from a bygone era. Today, there is a new burden that calls for national self-fulfillment.

Furthermore, America's own past should instruct it not to heed the conventions of Europe, because such models have failed, although they seemed at one time to define world history. American post-Revolutionary metamorphosis could have refused cultural subjugation and heeded the words and actions of "minority" voices, which warned against European effeteness. Writers and artists did, over time, call for the replacement of the staid Puritan image with one that graphically represented and emphasized a new thesis in social living— one that would span race, class, and gender. But it never happened.

America must chart its own separate course if it is to survive into the twenty-first century. Its major thrust must be to move away from the brutalization of victims to a significant elevation of their status as victors. Only then, truthfully, may one speak of a recognizable culture—not as an afterthought or a mere reworking of history, or even a rearrangement of political power. At its heart will exist the proclamation of a new convention, more precise and distinct, more conscious and total, and one that, through the exorcization of its unrelated past, reclaims the task of imaging the globe. This becomes the broad view that finally dismisses Eurocentrism as countercultural and exalts Americanism as globally representational. Only such a formula, out of its awesome and deep-seated truth, can achieve a decisive universal appeal. Only such a vision, with its distinguishing New World relativism and global consanguinity has the real distinction of universal claim.

NOTES

1. Samuel F. B. Morse, *A Foreign Conspiracy against the Liberties of the United States* (New York: Leavitt, Lord & Co., 1834).

2. For an update on Klan activities, see *Klanwatch* by Bill Stanton (New York: Grove Werdenfeld, 1991).

3. Paul Cuffe deserves to be better known, as an early African American entrepreneur and philanthropist who paid for and physically transported African Americans to Sierra Leone. See Lamont D. Thomas, *Paul Cuffe* (Urbana: University of Illinois Press, 1988), 65–71, 101–106.

4. See John Williams, *The Man Who Cried I Am* (Boston: Little, Brown, 1967), for the "King Alfred Plan" as detailed on 371–376.

5. Samuel F. Yette, *The Choice* (New York: Berkeley Medallion Books, 1972). See in particular 23–71 and 171–285. Some other sources deserve serious review: (1) CNN transcript, "The Doomsday Government," aired November 17, 1991; (2) *COINTELPRO: The FBI's Secret War on Political Freedom,* ed. Cathy Rerkus (New York: Monad Press, 1975); (3) the Martin Luther King FBI File, available through University Publications of America, Ann Arbor; and (4) *The Secret Life of J. Edgar Hoover,* by Anthony Summers (New York: G. P. Putnam's Sons, 1993). Also see Thomas Powers's review of sixteen related books in *The New York Review of Books*, May 13, 1993, 49–55.

6. Malcolm X, *By Any Means Necessary,* ed. George Brectman (New York: Pathfinder Press, 1970), 81.

7. Yette, *Choice*, 28–30.

8. See PBS documentary "The Deadly Deception," produced by Denise Dianni in the "Nova" series in 1993. Also see *Newsweek*, February 1, 1993, 66. Also consult Esmerald Barnes "Watched," concerning government spying on African American leaders in *Black Issues in Higher Education*, 10, No. 4 (April 22, 1993): 14, 16.

9. Alexander Cockburn, "Beat the Devil: Redwood Summer: Chico Mendez in the First World," *The Nation*, 2 July 1990, 6.

10. Oliver North as cited in "Reagan Aides and the Secret Government," *Miami Herald*, Sunday, July 5, 1987, 14a.

11. Ibid.

12. Ibid.

13. Bruce Levine, Stephen Brier, David Brundage et al., *Who Built North America?* (New York: Pantheon Books, 1989), 1:37. Emphasis added.

14. Michael J. Brenner, "Finding America's Place," *Foreign Policy* No. 19 (Summer 1990): 42. Emphasis added.

15. Maldwyn Allen Jones, *American Immigration* (Chicago: University of Chicago Press, 1960), 276.

16. Arthur R. Jensen's "Environment, Heredity and Intelligence" is here summed up in *U.S. News & World Report*, 10 March 1969, 48–49.

17. Arthur Schlesinger, "When Ethnic Studies Are Un-American," *Wall Street Journal*, 23 April 1990, 14A.

18. See a special issue of *Proteus* 10, No. 1 (Spring 1993) and the report of the New York State Social Studies Review and Development Committee entitled *One Nation, Many Peoples: A Declaration of Cultural Interdependence*, June 1991.

19. Arthur Schlesinger, *The Disuniting of America* (New York: Norton, 1992), 20.

20. E. D. Hirsch, Jr., *Cultural Literacy* (New York: Vintage Books, 1988), 10. Hirsch's quotations of Orlando Patterson do not support his argument. It is even more difficult to believe that Patterson (a British-educated Jamaican) would agree with Hirsch's listing of culturally literate requirements as in his Appendix, 152–215. Also see *The Dictionary of Cultural Literacy* by E. D. Hirsch, Joseph F. Kett, and James Trefil (Boston: Houghton Mifflin, 1988), which contains in 586 pages "what every American needs to know," as the subtitle confidentially informs us.

21. Hirsch, *Cultural Literacy*, 113.

22. Ibid., 140.

23. Ibid., xii.

24. Ibid., 98.

25. Dinesh D'Souza, *Illiberal Education* (New York: Free Press, 1991), 49.

26. Ibid., 31.

27. Ibid., 85.

28. Ibid., 90.

29. Molefi Asante, "Afrocentrism in a Multicultural Democracy," *American Visions* (August 1991), 21.

30. Molefi Asante, *The Afrocentric Idea* (Philadelphia: University of Pennsylvania Press, 1981), 170.

31. Mortimer Adler, *Great Ideas from the Great Books* (New York: Washington Square Press, 1961), 96.

32. Ibid., 193.

33. Philip Goetz as quoted in *Black Issues in Higher Education* 7, No. 23 (January 17, 1991): 18–20. "Great Books of the Western World" was published by Encyclopaedia Brittanica. In 1952, 54 volumes were published and 60 volumes in 1992. They represent the standard "Western" fare begin discussed here.

34. Hirsch, *Cultural Literacy*, 21.

35. Alan Bloom and Roger Kimball, *The Closing of the American Mind* (New York: Simon and Schuster, 1987), 30.

36. Amaury de Reincourt, *The American Empire* (New York: Dell, 1968), 254.

37. John Nef, *The United States and Civilization* (Chicago: University of Chicago Press, 1967), 256.

38. Frank Snowden, *Blacks in Antiquity* (Cambridge: Belknap Press of Harvard University Press, 1970).

39. Jan Read, *The Moors in Spain and Portugal* (London: Faber and Faber, 1974), 237.

40. The case was widely reported in the press. Supreme Court transcripts probably give the best account, as with the "Amistad" case. For background on *santería*, see Patrick Bellgarde Smith, ed., *Traditional Spirituality in the African Diaspora*, in the *Journal of Caribbean Studies*, 9, Nos. 1 & 2 (1993): 3–9.

41. Cain Felder, *Troubling Biblical Waters* (New York: Orbis Books, 1989).

7
European Visitors
to the United States ─────────────────

Early travel literature fixed the New World as an imaginative adjunct in European imagination. Columbus's task, as his journal testifies, was not so much that of "discoverer" but "namer." Columbus was an arrogant ethnocentric European, very much a part of his time, who forced a view of history that is very much how we still see the non-European world. It is an outlook that places Europe in the forefront and regards the Americas as mere backdrops, appendages to European reality. Therefore, the "New World" was novel, not merely because it provided an exotic appendage to Europe but particularly because it offered an imaginative and physical alternative. If one regards Columbus as a kind of archetypal voyager, several important points emerge from the *Journal* and other writings.

First, Columbus is himself symptomatic of the European quandary: There was no way left to go. Constantinople to the east had finally fallen, and with the Moorish expulsion a line had been drawn in the Mediterranean prohibiting further expansion or even cultural contact. Second, there was actually no Europe per se, but only warring factions of princedoms and fiefdoms in an eternal power conflict. Because of a population increase, expansion outward became the only plausible solution.

Clearly, West Africa was not a possibility; the so-called Guinea coast was inhospitable, not least for the important reason that indigenous Africans were averse to settlement, and the presence of yellow fever and malaria precluded large-scale permanent European settlement. Columbus's *Journal* speaks about the search for alternatives, one the mariner concedes had been virtually exhausted. He admits: "I have spent twenty-three years at sea, without coming off it for any length of time worth mentioning, and I have seen all the east and the west . . . and I have gone to Guinea, but in all those parts I have not found the perfection of these harbours."[1]

Quest for gold was subsumed within invented myths. Eurocentrism had to be pushed as an absolute, because it justified the capture of "Indians" as specimens on Columbus's proto-journey. In this context, God and Christianity, European languages, even Greek mythology, were all involved by Columbus as ways through which he was able to justify the demonization of indigenous New World peoples. Thus, his own ethnocentric fear of the Other gave rise to the belief that the inhabitants from the northern islands were indeed "cannibal," a term altered from "caribal," and then inflicted on the people who had overrun the Arawaks—hence the terms "Carib" and "Caribbean" in the New World. Columbus is therefore not merely a historical person; he is a myth-maker whose advent (unlike earlier contacts with Vikings, Africans, and Bretons) marks the beginning of the reduction of New World inhabitants to a subhuman scale.

Columbus's earliest letter, printed in Latin in May 1493, spells out some of the motives. God has directed his journey, and King Ferdinand and Queen Isabella deserve praise for following God's will. This is very much unlike the "pagans" of the land he wanted: "They do not hold any creed nor are they idolaters; but they all believe that power and good are in the heavens and were very firmly convinced that I, with these ships and men, came from the heavens."[2] As myth-maker, therefore, Columbus enunciates the new credo that European males are now gods, a viewpoint also advanced by Hernando Cortés, Francisco Pizzaro, and others. No doubt this was a heady acknowledgment that could scarcely be resisted. English literature would continue from *Robinson Crusoe*, through Conrad's *Heart of Darkness*, to writings by Somerset Maugham, Evelyn Waugh, and Ronald Firbank in constantly reiterating this absurdity.

As Richard Hakluyt's narratives testify, discovery was part economic boon (with the promise of gold) and part imaginative excess (with the lure of El Dorado). Early explorers had specific economic interests, for, after all, British and French firms had paid for their expeditions to America. But their journeys and settlement have also to do with expeditions of the mind, a very European mind, tethered to the bleak realities of the fifteenth century.[3]

Accordingly, Sir Walter Raleigh's *Discoverie of Guiana* (1595) was travel literature with license—special dispensation to alter the truth at will. Its purpose, after all, was to encourage Europeans to settle in the Americas. So Raleigh told of fabulous El Dorado, where the emperor bathed with gold dust; of a tribe of women whose right breasts were cut off to facilitate their use of the bow; of another group whose heads were between their shoulders. All of this was in the English-Indian South American empire of "Raleana." It was all make-believe but apparently substantive enough for Raleigh to be let out of the tower to make still another ill-fated expedition. Of course, the City of Gold, Amazon women, and monstrous humans were frequent fantasies of the medieval European mind. The distortions were merely implanted on the New World.[4]

What is recalled in the New World about Raleigh, as V. S. Naipaul (the *very* British Caribbean writer) notes, is that Raleigh is more myth than man. An informant tells Naipaul in Durham, North Carolina, "You must remember the majority of the Founding Fathers of this country were Southerners. The first English-speaking colony on these shores was founded in 1584 by Sir Walter Raleigh—not sixty miles from where we are—at Roanoke Island."[5] Raleigh, in other words, becomes the southern historical link to Britain, the South's claim to "civilization," much as Columbus and other conquistadors were for Spanish and Portuguese New World territories.

Drake had taken possession of New Albion as of 1577, Jamestown was settled in 1607 by a motley group that included English and Anglo Africans, and John Smith had explored New England and written about it long before the *Mayflower* arrived. Post-1620 settlement is well known and will not be documented here. What is more interesting for our purposes is that early settlement acts out the expected role of Noble Indian and Ignoble African. For example, Pocahontas's attempt to give her own life for John Smith's is recounted in his *Generall Historie of Virginia, New England, and the Sumner Isles* (1624). Strangely enough, the story of Smith's rescue belongs more to folklore than fact, for when he does mention the incident in works published before his *Historie*, it appears in totally different versions. Smith was like Raleigh, so the first account of Virginia settlement does not mention Pocahontas; but Smith seems to recall more as he becomes more expansive in later recountings.

The "saints" and "strangers" who came in the *Mayflower*—forty-one in all—had sampled the European experience. They had moved from Scrooby in England to Amsterdam and then to Leiden. Their early chronicler, William Bradford, records the origins of the Plymouth Brethren, their journey and settlement. *History of Plymouth Plantation* (circa 1630) is not like Raleigh's *Discoverie of Guiana* or Smith's *Generall Historie*. The reason is clear: Bradford is not a visitor but a permanent settler. Forced out of Europe, he and the *Mayflower* group epitomize the beginning of the immigrant pattern of European settlement in America.

These early settlers brought with them all the basic appurtenances of Anglo European civilization. This was a heritage that they would pass on to the benighted savages and the rest of the country. John Eliot converted Massachusetts Indians in 1640, preached to them in their own language, and compiled a complete Bible by 1683, making this the first one printed here. Religion, indeed, was the major linking influence with Europe. But post-Reformation Christianity suggested a degree of independence, manifesting itself in the new colonies by the kind of individual intuitiveness that Anne Hutchinson preached. Unstructured individualism could and did lead to the very intolerance from which the earlier settlers had fled, as witness Governor John Endicott's persecution of Quakers. The European religious war was fought just as fiercely west of Europe.

Therefore, battle over creed was waged here, much as it might have been in Europe. For instance, John Cotton, once in agreement with Anne Hutchinson's antinomianism, joined John Winthrop and others in denouncing her. Autocratic views on church matters spilled over to the state. Cotton and Winthrop made the Massachusetts Bay Company into a type of personal fiefdom, buffered by their own Eurocentric preoccupations with aristocracy and theocracy. For Winthrop, a democracy was "among the most civil nations, accounted the meanest and worst forms [sic] of government."[6]

Indeed the more one reads about early settlement of Europeans in the New World, the more one realizes how there exists a kind of proto-model that is altered only very slightly. Raleigh, for instance, had read Thomas Hariot in Hakluyt; William Hubbard's A General History of New England (1680) is utilized by Winthrop in his Journal (1790) as well as other works. Once the view is from without, the degree of replication depends more on what European readers had come to expect than on any mutually agreed-upon evidence locally observed.

Some cultured alteration, real and practical, did come about as a result of living within a new landscape. Nearly always, such change was focused on religion, but it was necessitated by new and vibrant urges arising out of a pragmatic rather than a spiritual necessity. Around 1734, the Great Awakening was led by, among others, Jonathan Edwards. Influenced both by Locke's Essay Concerning Human Understanding and Bishop George Berkeley's Alciphron (1732), Edwards sought to explore how the infinite will of God operated through the universe. He was drawn into a very European struggle against Arminianism, which had been developed by Dutch theologian Jacobus Arminus. His pro-Calvinist views are best epitomized in A Careful and Strict Enquiry into the Modern Prevailing Notions, of the Freedom of Will which is Supposed to be Essential to Moral Agency, Vertue and Vice, Reward and Punishment, Praise and Blame (1754). Individual choice cannot exist, as it consists only of ability to act arbitrarily on the basis of personal choice. The Arminian Liberty of Will is a fallacy, Jonathan Edwards advocates, as are other points of departure from Calvinist thought: notions of predestination, atonement, divine grace—indeed the entire apparatus of faith that posited a firm understanding of human will and freedom.

Calvinism was actually derived from Puritanism, itself an aspect of Anglicanism. Initially, Puritans had sought only to rid their church of excessive ceremony, but by the 1640–1660 Revolution, Puritanism became political rather than solely religious. Its opposition to authority, at the lay level, meant a strong advocacy of parliamentary power rather than divine right.

Local discussion and disputation freed the church, to some extent, from too close an alliance with its European counterpart. However, more often than not, responses arose out of a direct relationship among the various sects in Europe rather than America. Roman Catholicism made little impact in English-speaking North America, not because it was less powerful than in Europe but because, in America, serious forces were aligned against it. Attacks against nineteenth-century immigration from Ireland, Italy, and Germany were also church-directed as much as they were the result of Anglophobic settlers overly concerned with lighter skin coloration. There could be disputes among various sects in Protestant theology, but Roman Catholicism was viewed as a rank outsider despite its early start in 1565 at St. Augustine.

Americans seemed to want to return to essentials, hence, the constant appeal of fundamentalism until the present time. Its literal interpretation of the Bible, its adamant stance against Darwinian evolution (seen at its most bizarre in the Scopes Monkey Trial of 1925), and its attacks on the popular cinema, rock and roll, rap, and pornography are all ways of returning religion back to a simpler, uncorrupted origin. Out of the American, not European, experience were born the "come-outers" of Cape Cod, who saw truth as emanating only from their own hearts. Also, directly from American experience, came Richard Mather's Half-Way Covenant of 1642, which predicted full membership on the basis of the experience of a personal spiritual conversion. This should be balanced with Swedenborgianism, with its emphasis on God rather than the Trinity, appealing to Americans in the late eighteenth century, as well as Deism, emphasizing God's existence in the realm of nature, which is the cornerstone of Jeffersonian language and thought in the Declaration.

Indeed, William A. Clebsh has shown in *American Religious Thought* that the connection between politics and religion did alter the basic concept of God in America:

No longer did "the sovereign" signify a just Creator ruling a harmonious, dependent creation; it referred to an unjust British ruler lording over colonies obliged under God to establish their independence. In the age and spirit of the Revolution, traditional theologians struggled to show how the sovereign God could honorably forgive deliberately sinful man.[7]

There was a problem, though, with the idea of total political and theological independence. Ellis posits in *American Catholicism* that the political link with Europe forestalled a full attack against Catholicism during the Revolutionary War, "lest word of it reach Catholic countries like France and Spain which, as it was hoped, might be of service to their revolutionary cause."[8]

Undeniably, England, Germany, and Sweden influenced the growth and development of the church in America. But, perhaps more so than in any other institutions, we see early manifestations of a move toward an independent logic founded on pragmatism. Each person seeks to work out interpretations that seem more valid for America than Europe and more relevant in the new context of the New World.

As the arguments moved back and forth, they seem concerned with establishing a church free of the prejudices and assumptions of Europe. Undeniably, movements reach back to the European intellectual climate, but within the American context they assert a different kind of statement. Here, if a general point may be made, the emphasis is on faith by individual understanding of the Godhead, not through a state- or church-regulated hierarchical control. The solitary individual, in full control of his or her spiritual needs, may directly communicate with God. The religious debate is carried on by the New Humanism of Irving Babbitt and P. E. More (with its turning toward Hellenism), so that even Romanticism is visualized in place in America by Thoreau and Emerson; indeed, even when Cooper or Twain responds to Europe, there still exists an attempt to refashion America. The suggestion seemingly is that neither Europe nor America is what Europeans make of it, but what Americans, out of a pristine ability to instinctively tell truth, decide. This is the message that the televangelists carried back to Europe. As early as the fifties, Billy Graham pioneered this belief that a single human being, outside the context of the state church, could come to God. Although, with the downfall of Jimmy Swaggart and Jim Bakker, televangelism fell on rough times in the 1980s, its influence is still felt, particularly in Latin America, Africa, and China.

A pattern repeats itself. America first borrows models from Europe, alters and changes them into more pragmatic ones that serve its purpose at home, and then exports the new synthesis back to Europe and its former dominions. Surely it would not be too sacrilegious to assert that the fate of the frankfurter and the soul are almost the same. Their process of Americanization coupled with American marketability has given them both an interesting synthesis—one that has elements of the old and the new, the discarded and the redefined.

Bishop Berkeley's oft-quoted line "Westward the course of Empire takes its way" was applied not so much to Bermuda, as he had intended; Europe was heading west, and with it the entire assortment of western culture from Europe. By the time that Thackeray arrived, more than a century later, he was clearly impressed with what he saw. After his second visit to the United States, between October 1855 and April 1856, he completed the two-volume novel, *The Virginians* (1859). America, as Dickens later would also show, was indeed the land of possibility where a combination of sound common sense, luck, and hard work could bring about success. It was a variation of El Dorado, sorely needed by English Victorians.

Americans would have been very impressed with Thackeray's 1852 *The History of Henry Esmond*, the forerunner to *The Virginians*, 1857–1859, for it is to Virginia that the disillusioned Esmond emigrates with his new bride. A generation later, one of their grandsons would fight against the British. The year 1857 was the year of Dred Scott, and 1859 of Brown's raid on

Harper's Ferry. By 1861 the Gatling machine gun was invented, even as the attack on Fort Sumter initiated Civil War. From the British standpoint, however, if one were to judge from Thackeray, the myth of America as haven was still secure.

British intellect ever sought to find more wholesome and desirable living in America. Frances Wright, after two years in the United States, returned in 1824 to form the Nashoba Community in Tennessee. Robert Owens, an early British socialist, founded New Harmony in 1825, an agricultural settlement with a socialist base.

About a century separates two Frenchmen, J. Hector St. John de Crève-coeur, who came to New York in 1759, and Alexis de Tocqueville, who visited between May 1831 and February 1832. Crèvecoeur had the misfortune to ally himself with the Loyalists, but his *Letters from an American Farmer* (1782) describes his idyllic life on a New York farm. Tocqueville is not quite as ecstatic, but he was sufficiently impressed by America to compile his seminal work. Neither one sees nor wants to see Europe in America. Both attempt to chart new directions for political institutions. Their impediments are obvious; for Crèvecoeur, America is the realization of Rousseau; for Tocqueville, the plague of racism and the absence of aristocratic leverage spoil an otherwise utopian possibility. For still another Frenchman, Charles Fourier, America could be the location of his phalansteries, where human beings would interact with each other and God, free to pursue work as enjoyment and liberated from the tedium of the civilized world. At the North American Phalanx at Red Bank, New Jersey, an experiment in European utopian adventurism was founded in 1843. Europeans sought out America as part of a gigantic wish fulfillment.

Even as late as 1915, D. H. Lawrence looked toward the United States as the location for "Rananim." Taos, New Mexico, was to be an ideal place, where communal work and life would be accompanied with a natural lifestyle. Perhaps Lawrence, Frieda, and Mabel Dodge Luhan found Rananim at the New Mexico ranch near Taos. In any event Rananim, like the North American Phalanx, its Nashoba Community, and New Harmony were bound to fail. Their promise was in the trial, not the fulfillment. They were all legacies from Europe's own failed idealism and became continuous efforts to reconstruct More's Utopia. They point to European notions that America was still the stuff of dreams and to American idealistic beliefs that this was indeed the case.

This, of course, falls within the larger concern that Peter Conrad details in *Imagining America*. If indeed America was "imagined" even before Columbus, then obviously it was prone to become victim to its own myth. In turn, the new belief not only would be accepted within America, but would be exported back to Europe with suitable American blandishments. Europeans, especially the nineteenth-century British, came looking for the very thing they set out to see. When they found it (or at least thought they did), they were exultant; when they did not, they blamed America. For as Peter Conrad said, "The reality of America is selective, optional, fantastic: there is an America for each of us."[9]

British presence in North America has been presented as if it were monolithic. But this pattern of immigration varied, and with each new variation came differing attitudes and perceptions. As such, in order to fully comprehend British interaction and influence, an attempt must be made to look at the nature of settlement.

Such an examination places the researcher close to a question often asked but never satisfactorily answered. Where can one, with reasonable assurance, locate Euro American origins? The question, however, does presuppose a number of qualifications: first, that a definition of "America" is to be found outside its immediate geographical area; second, that the experience of "America" is a denial of cultural linkage with indigenous peoples; and, third, that the search for "America" must ignore persons of Asian and African origins and focus on Europe.

Of course, the question and the usual answers are absurd. The idea of "America" could not have existed in an environment depending solely on a British past. Nor could it have been solely British, as it is most unlikely that differing peoples would live close to each other, in a landscape alien to them all, and not draw on one another's mores.

One must assert that the concept of "America" is neither the traditional melting-pot nor Jesse Jackson's quilt. It is surely a bit of both of these: melting-pot, in that, in some instances, differing societal mores have merged together and quilt in the sense that ethnicity has been preserved for a number of reasons. Yet beyond all this is one major and insistent fact, that language—English—is the common factor that unites Britain and the United States. Put simply, British and American English "both come from the same source—the seventeenth-century English that British settlers brought to the east coast of North America."[10]

How did a handful of English-speaking settlers establish domain over language, institutionalize custom and belief, and convince later settlers that this was the most assured, appropriate, or even correct approach? The answer is found partly in something that is anathema to the idea of America itself—British sovereign power. Through this, Britain was able to establish colonial rule and thus to convince its fledglings that metropolitan mores were the desirable ones.

According to David Hackett Fischer, four British folkways may be identified. Between 1629 and 1775, Fischer shows that first the Puritans, then the Royalist Cavaliers, the Quakers, and finally, the border country English and Scots helped define regional cultures in the United States. He points out, "American ideas of freedom developed from indigenous folkways which were deeply rooted in the inherited culture of the English-speaking world."[11] But there are serious distortions:

The Puritan idea of ordered freedom was no sooner brought to Massachusetts than it became an instrument of savage persecution. The cavalier
conception of hegemonic freedom, when carried to Virginia, permitted and
even required the growth of race slavery for its support. The Quaker
version of reciprocal freedom was a sectarian impulse which could be
sustained only by withdrawal from the world. The back country belief in
cultural freedom sometimes dissolved into cultural anarchy.[12]

Therefore, when the British come over as visitors, it is of particular interest for
us to see what they see. Anthony Trollope's mother, Frances Trollope, lived in the
United States between 1827 and 1830. Her book on *Domestic Manners of the
Americans* (1832) was quite a point of contention in its day. Mrs. Trollope was
impressed with American standards of living, but she deplored slavery, what she
saw as the affected attitude of American women, and certain unsavory types of
business practice. Her major point, much as with Tocqueville, was that American
democracy had a tendency to provide an overall lowering of standards.[13]

Two of her sons visited the United States. The better-known, Anthony
Trollope, published *North America* in 1862. He felt that his mother's book was
"unjust" and set about the task of rectifying the situation. To a large extent,
unburdened by previous European accounts, he tried to present an honest
picture of pre-Civil War America. He must have been familiar with works such
as Basil Hall's *Travels in North America* (1829), Harriet Martineau's *A Retro-
spect of Western Travel* (1836), and Alexander Mackay's *The Western World*
(1850) as well as Olmsted, Dickens, and Tocqueville. But he writes about what
he observes, although he does continue to look at America from a solid British
viewpoint.

Trollope seems much more sympathetic to the kindred souls of the East coast
than toward those who live in the West. He, unlike the contemporary British
aristocracy, favored the North rather than the South. His prejudices are very
often on the surface: Westerners "are essentially a dirty people"; Washington,
D.C., was "a ragged, unfinished collection of unbuilt broad streets," and he
confessed to hating "Americans of the lower orders."[14]

Yet, what interests us particularly is that Trollope, country squire, does not
see any reflection of his England in America, not in New York, where he visited
in 1859, nor in San Francisco, where he came in 1873. His view is certainly not
Twain's in *Roughing It* (1872) which praises individuality and ruggedness.
About San Francisco, Trollope says this:

> I do not know that in all my travels I ever visited a city less interesting to
> the normal tourist, who, as a rule, does not care to investigate the ways of
> trade, or to employ himself in ascertaining how the people around him
> earn their bread. There is almost nothing to see in San Francisco that is
> worth seeing.[15]

British travelers brought obvious prejudices with them, but what is really fascinating is that, try as it might (and Trollope did), Euro America could not give back to them what they had expected. They had come to a country several times larger and with a greater ethnic mix than theirs, and yet they expected to find a faithful reproduction of their own reality.

Trollope was constantly trying to find a personal version of Europe in America. When he recognizes Europe, he applauds; when he does not, he denounces. Yet like his mother, he hated slavish imitation. For instance, in discussing precocious children in Newport, he found that their mothers often taught young girls to walk in a manner that resembled a gait "seen more often in second rate French towns, and among fourth rate French women."[16] This may not necessarily have been true—simply some rash judgment based on his own life in France.

Although the scenery could be quite beautiful, it is ideal only by comparison with Europe. He comments: "I know nothing, for instance, on the Rhone equal to the view from Mount Willard." And he is quick to realize that at the center of American life is a longing to be part of Europe: "An American whether he be embarked in politics, in literature, or in commerce, desires English admiration, English appreciation of his energy, and English encouragement." Trollope also notes that Anglophobia affects literature. He concedes that American readers like Cooper and Irving, but "English books are, I think, the better loved." Also, he attacks a great many of the newspapers of his day. They lack honesty and are "ill-written, ill-printed, ill-arranged, and in fact are not readable."[17]

With his wife, Trollope saw much of the United States. Always, however, despite some praise that he lavishes on the railroads, the post office, and the sheer vastness of the country, Americans have seemingly failed to live up to a European ideal. Often they are downright contemptible, like New York women, who are "more odious than those of any other human beings I ever met elsewhere."[18] In Boston, although he seemed to like a lecture by Emerson, he does not approve of Wendell Phillips, a prominent Boston abolitionist, because Phillips saw the English as enemies.

Even on the question of slavery, comparisons with England are made. He refers to 1834, when Britain took that "bold leap in the dark" and abolished slavery. Trollope suggests that America, and particularly the South, is backward, not merely because it did not abolish slavery but particularly because it did not recognize Britain's example and do likewise. Thus, even though Trollope declares that he abhors slavery and would never own a slave, his views of African Americans border closely on being racist. "They are like children" he informs us,

In many cases, practically, they cannot be enfranchised. Give them their liberty, starting them well in the world at what expense you please, and at the end of six months they will come back upon your hands for the means of support. Everything must be done for them.[19]

Of course, his view is that of his time, and in this way he exhibits no difference from Thomas Carlyle, for instance, who in *Occasional Discourse upon the Nigger Question* (1849) found that Blacks seemed much more agreeable to alcoholic sprees than to serious pastimes.

I have already suggested that in America the African American became a metaphor for defining super-Eurocentricity. As slave, and later as recently emancipated, she or he represented a way of helping to define class and social structure. By becoming the buffer, the African American served to define the difference between caste and class, and his degree of nonacceptance was in direct proportion to Eurocentric hierarchy. Put differently, as Trollope recognized, the further the distance between African American and Euro American, the greater the degree of the latter's conformity with Europe.

Hence, Trollope was quick to point out the very stereotypes previously identified by Jefferson:

> The abolitionists hold that the negro is the white man's equal. I do not. I see, or think that I see, that the negro is the white man's inferior through laws of nature. That he is not mentally fit to cope with white men,—I speak of the full-blooded negro,—and that he must fill a position simply servile.

Even so, despite Trollope's obvious prejudices, British custom is still triumphant. A Black person, he tells us, is not allowed to sit at the same table with one of his abolitionist benefactors, but he "might do so in England at the house of an English duchess."[20] Obviously, the British are even better at the fine elements of discrimination.

Charles Dickens's *American Notes* (1842) describes the first of his two tours to the United States, when between January and May 1842, he also recorded his impressions. Unlike Trollope he described American character as "chivalrous" but admitted in *First Impressions* (1841), "I don't like the country. I would not live here, on any consideration. It goes against the grain with me. I think it impossible, utterly impossible, for any Englishman to live here, and be happy."[21] He, too, despite comments relatively more objective than Trollope's, looks for and does not find any image of England in America.

For Dickens, the railroads are sheer pandemonium and Washington, on the eve of civil unrest, disgusts him; but he was on the "friendliest relations" with contemporaries like John Quincy Adams. He deplores Jefferson's abolishment of the cap and gown and longs for a more traditional British-type system that would emphasize the role of a judge:

> I cannot help doubting whether America, in her desire to shake off the absurdities and abuses of the old system, may not have gone too far into the opposite extreme, and whether it is not desirable, especially in a small

community of a city like this, where each man knows the other, to surround the administration of justice with some artificial barriers against the "Hail fellow, well met" department of everyday life.[22]

Both Trollope and Dickens constantly fault America, because in their eyes it lacks the trappings of a European hierarchy.

Because Dickens anticipated attacks, he tried to soft-peddle *American Notes*. For instance, the 1842 and 1850 editions had the following dedication:

> I dedicate THIS BOOK to those friends of mine IN AMERICA, who, giving me a welcome I must ever gratefully and proudly remember, left my judgement FREE; and who, loving their country, can bear the truth, when it is told good humouredly and in a kind spirit.[23]

He dropped it from the 1868 edition, after his second visit between November 1867 and April 1868. By then the preface of 1850 had been modified to include Dickens's view that the country had moved away from its ideals; but, as he adds, "the truth is the truth, and neither childish absurdities, nor unscrupulous contradictions, can make it otherwise." Dickens had also written an "Introductory, and Necessary to be Read" section, which he withdrew ten days before the first publication. There the cold rejection of America is present: "In spite of the advantage she has over all other nations in the elastic freshness and vigor of her youth, she is far from being a model for the earth to copy."[24]

Dickens describes a society that is neither European nor idyllic. He visited an asylum on Long Island and notes that party politics superseded the welfare of the inhabitants. In an 1844 letter, he condemns the press, as Trollope later did, for "that extraordinary disregard of Truth"; he finds that American society is violent, and attacks "the readiness of the people to take the law into their own hands."[25]

Comparisons with England always exist, and America often falls short. A hotel in St. Louis is "built like an English hospital"; a planter's house in Baltimore "brought Defoe's descriptions of such places" to mind; the steamboat Dickens sees in New York "to an English eye, . . . was infinitely less like a steamboat than a huge floating bath"; and a band of Wyandot Indians looks like English gypsies.[26]

With slavery and the condition of African Americans, he is harshest. Yet, despite Dickens's crusade on behalf of the English poor, his efforts strike us as hypocritical. The book appeared only eight years after Britain had abolished slavery, yet Dickens cites advertisements for runaway slaves as an American novelty, arguing that slavery had pernicious effects on the larger American society, serving to brutalize the populace. The tone of *American Notes* at this point is a trifle melodramatic, as Dickens enjoins against "triumph in the white enjoyment of their broad possessions."[27]

This is the second aspect to the Black as metaphor in American society. In the first instance, the need for repression was observed as a means through which Eurocentric class ties could be maintained. Now, as Dickens argues (not very convincingly), the same repression would be the way of reducing Euro Americans to what he terms "brutality." Hence, they would no longer be part of the Eurocentric continuum. Yet, as noted, the argument is false, as Britain had only recently repealed its own slave trade.

On March 11, 1841, Dickens wrote a letter from Washington after he had visited Richmond. Here he graphically describes a slave market, adding that: "My heart is lightened . . . when I think we are turning our backs on this accursed and detested system." Britain, Dickens suggests, had established a pattern that America should follow; Trollope makes the same point, although the reasoning is a little different. A slave-owner tells Dickens, "It's not [in] . . . the interest of a man to use his slaves ill. It's damned nonsense that you hear in England." Dickens then sermonizes: "That cruelty, and the abuse of irresponsible power, were two of the bad passions of human nature, with the gratification of which, considerations of interest or of ruin had nothing whatever to do."[28]

What neither Trollope nor Dickens was prepared to state was the simple fact that slavery represented a major aspect of the Europeanizing of America. In one fell swoop, slavery demarcated a lower feudal peasant class of permanent serfs and created a group of aspiring White elites. The problem was that, after 1834, the British felt that they could afford to glance disparagingly at a country where slavery was yet to be abolished, claiming a moral superiority to which they were not entitled.

The British saw little resemblance between moneyed Americans and their own upper class. Indeed many of the visitors (in Tocqueville's vein), deplored the absence of a real upper class. Mrs. Trollope could not conceive of a society that truly rejected a hereditary hierarchy:

> "I wonder you are not sick of kings, chancellors, and archbishops, and all your fustian of wigs and gowns," said a very clever gentleman to me once, with an affected yawn, "I protest the very sound almost sets me to sleep." It is amusing to observe how soothing the idea seems, that they are more modern, more advanced than England. Our classic literature, our princely dignities, our noble institutions are all gone-by relics of the dark ages.[29]

Her swipe at American slavery is based on their lack of class, as she sees it. She denounces some types of slavery but is easiest on the life of the "domestic slave in a gentleman's family," for it is "not among the higher classes that the possession of slaves produces the worst effects."[30] For Mrs. Trollope, Peter Conrad declares, travel is "the fortification of prejudice. She goes abroad to justify her preference for staying at home."[31] For her, slavery is endearing and very British.

Matthew Arnold paid two visits: the first was between October and March of 1884, publishing his *Discourses in America* in June of the following year. He paid his second visit between May and August 1886, two years before he died. He published "Civilization in the United States" in April of 1888; the work, directed at a British readership, delighted them but quite annoyed Americans.

Arnold found the United States "singularly free from the distinction of class" and concluded that for the ordinary person "things are favourable for them in America." But regarding its civilization, Arnold found America wanting: It lacked a sense of beauty in literature and the arts. Indeed, Arnold blames the very "democratization" of values for the glorification of the common man and for the "poverty in serious interest." America, he concludes, lacks "the great elements of the interesting, which are elevation and beauty."[32]

Dickens's Martin Chuzzlewit came to America to make a fortune, not to find culture, much as many real-life and other imaginary characters did. But he returns to Europe, to the familiar, because America is the fantastic, one that has to be conquered and suppressed. Waugh utilized these familiar images of a benighted America to describe a decadent Hollywood in *The Loved One* (1948). Columbus is back in the form of the young English poet, Dennis Barlow. Americans are comical because they are Americans and brutish because they are Americans, both so very unlike the English. When Barlow tries to arrange the burial of a friend this dialogue takes place:

" . . . I presume the Loved One was Caucasian?"

"No, why did you think that? He was purely English."[33]

Even though part of the satire is directed at the fatuous Barlow, the immediate implication is the over-concern of Americans with racial matters. The larger insinuation showed that Waugh viewed post–World War II America as inimical to the culture of *Brideshead Revisited* (1945). There all that is good is English: Homosexuality is English and German, not Latin; disparaging references are made to a "Jew boy," "a half caste choir," a Greek "smelling of hot oil and garlic and stale wine and old clothes."[34] If even a European connection for England is rejected by Waugh, is it any wonder that he should visualize America as a colonial outpost equally obsessed with ethnic matters?

Between the sixteenth and twentieth centuries, although the image of America moved through different phases, Europeans insisted on seeing it as a rigid formula. In all instances, it is imaged as strange, exotic, and bewildering. In all cases, it is the object either of scorn and derision or of surprise, acclamation, and Romantic exuberance. As European writers seem sure of their own superior vision, they merely stake further claims that America possesses some kind of protean form, to be constantly shaped and reshaped, not out of its own needs, but out of European expectations. America becomes for Europe, in a politically real and spiritually imaginative sense, Europe's chance for survival. The monster that Europe created outmastered its maker, yet the new master was unaware of his revised status.

With the relative ease of today's communications, due to Concordes, faxes, and fiber-optics, the Atlantic has shrunk. The ethnic composition of America's ruling class makes it even more prone to Daniel Boorstin's conclusion in *America in the Image of Europe*:

> At different periods and in several parts of the United States (especially on the Pacific coast and in the South) non-European notions have entered our thinking about ourselves. But all these variants have been transient, local and insignificant, compared with our tendency to discover ourselves as a kind of non-Europe.[35]

But "non-Europe" is not what the United States is but, indeed, what it must be, not merely in the narrow meaning of "transplanted Englishmen" who rejected Europe, but in a new liberating sense of what it means to claim a non-European global identity.

NOTES

1. Christopher Columbus, *The Journal of Christopher Columbus*, trans. by Cecil Jane (New York: Bonanza Press, 1960), 110.

2. Ibid., 196.

3. See Richard Hakluyt, *Voyages and Discoveries,* ed. Jack Beeching (Harmondsworth, UK: Penguin Books, 1972).

4. For an excellent discussion of medieval monsters, see John Block Friedman, especially the concluding chapter where he discusses the origins of the "Wild Man," *The Monstrous Races in Medieval Art and Thought* (Cambridge, Mass.: Harvard University Press, 1981).

5. V. S. Naipaul, *A Turn in the South* (New York: Alfred A. Knopf, 1989), 257.

6. John Winthrop, *Winthrop's Journal: "History of New England" 1630–1649*, 2 vols., ed. James Kendall Hosmer (New York: C. Scribner's Sons, 1908). Part of Winthrop's *History* appeared in the *Journal*, first published in 1790.

7. William A. Clebsch, *American Religious Thought: A History* (Chicago: University of Chicago Press, 1973), 220.

8. John Tracy Ellis, *American Catholicism* (Chicago: University of Chicago Press, 1956), 36.

9. Peter Conrad, *Imagining America* (New York: Oxford University Press, 1980), 4.

10. Robert Claiborne, *The Roots of English* (New York: Times Books, 1989), 5.

11. David Hackett Fischer, *Albion's Seed: Four British Folkways in America* (New York: Oxford University Press, 1989), 897.

12. Ibid., 897–898.

13. Frances Trollope, *Domestic Manners of the Americans* [1832] (New York: Alfred A. Knopf, 1949), 157–162, 292–293, 317–322, 354, 365. For further information, see Helen K. Heineman, *Three Victorians in the New World* (New York: Peter Lang, 1992), for an intense

study of Frances Trollope, Anthony Trollope, and Charles Dickens, particularly their view of the New World.

14. Anthony Trollope, *North America* [1862] (New York: Alfred A. Knopf, 1951).

15. Ibid., 541.

16. Ibid., 27.

17. Ibid., 39, 44, 503.

18. Ibid., 198.

19. Ibid., 359.

20. Ibid., 361.

21. Charles Dickens, *American Notes* [1842] (New York: St. Martin's Press, 1985), 86.

22. Ibid., 147.

23. Dickens, a "Dedication" to *American Notes*, 1842 and 1850 editions.

24. Dickens, *American Notes*, xi.

25. Ibid., 209–210.

26. Ibid., 179.

27. Ibid., 222.

28. Ibid.

29. Frances Trollope, *Domestic Manners*, 161.

30. Ibid.

31. Peter Conrad, *Imagining America*, 32.

32. Matthew Arnold, "Civilisation in the United States," in *Matthew Arnold,* ed. Miriam Alcott and Robert H. Super (Oxford: Oxford University Press, 1986), 489–504.

33. Evelyn Waugh, *The Loved One* (Boston: Little, Brown and Company, 1977).

34. Ibid., 304. It should be mentioned in passing that Waugh was himself quite infatuated with race, as noted in *Black Mischief* (1932), *A Handful of Dust* (1934), and *Scoop* (1938). The African is funny simply because he is alive.

35. Daniel Boorstin, *America and the Image of Europe* (Cleveland, Ohio: World Publishing, 1960), 20.

8
American Writers in Europe ──────────

In John Nef's conclusion to his important study *The United States and Civilization*, he writes a trifle optimistically, yet with a touch of nostalgia:

> For good or ill, the United States emerged out of the civilization it originally shared with western Europe, whence came most of the ancestors of those persons who now populate it. There was a time when Americans thought of themselves as a new people, free from the trials and strains of the Old World, free to ignore European experience. *These were not views which most of the founding fathers shared.*[1]

But, one should stress, these were opinions shared by the vast majority of Euro Americans, as we have noted. In the various fields of human endeavor—art, architecture, law, literature, music—the United States was never severed from its umbilical ties with Europe, and particularly Britain. Today, of course, such an influence exerts itself most obviously in matters pertaining to haute culture and, more obviously, the daily reality of global political alliances and control.

Naturally the cultural invasion of the 1920s did not happen without precedent. The country was predisposed to Europe—to visualizing and mythifying Europe and to rendering it as part of an experience termed "American." William Dean Howells's body of work charts this direction of American letters. Self-taught because of the migratory pattern of his early family life, he specialized in Latin, French, and Italian. In one of his novels this dialogue reinforces the importance of European languages. Bellingham asks Lemuel, "You don't happen to read French?" Lemuel shakes his head hopelessly, "I studied Latin some at school." Later on, another character "justified himself to his wife with an Italian proverb."[2] In most of Howells's works, either the characters occupy a Europe of the mind or Europe is physically there with them—they travel to and from Europe, they interact with Europeans, and most important, they often (as Howells himself did) return to the eastern American seaboard to best locate themselves and their class in a Eurocentric setting.

No where is this more apparent than in what Howells writes about the Pasmers in *April Hopes* (1888):

> Soon after their marriage the Pasmers *had gone to live in Paris*, where they remained faithful to the fortunes of the Second Empire till its fall, with intervals of return to their own country of a year or two years at a time. After the fall of the empire *they made their sojourn in England*, where they lived upon the edges and surfaces of things, as Americans must in Europe everywhere, but had more permanency of feeling than they had known in France, and something like a real social status. At one time it seemed as if they might end their days there; but that which makes Americans different from all other peoples, and which finally claims their allegiance for their own land, made them wish to come back to America, and to come back to Boston. *After all, their place in England was strictly inferior, and must be.* They knew titles and consorted with them, but they had none themselves, and the English constancy which kept their friends faithful to them after they had become an old story, was correlated with the English honesty which never permitted them to mistake themselves for even the lowest of the nobility. *They went out last, and they did not come in first, ever.*[3]

As far as Howells is concerned, Americans are drawn back to their country not out of the overzealous zeal of the anthem-makers but from a negative experience, one that not merely suggests but, more important, confirms their own alienation. *April Hopes* has its farcical side, but this idea of Europe as a false notion seems to derive from Howells's own experiences—he had been American consul to Venice, and observations of Italian life and translation of Italian poetry had featured in much of his early work. Later, his cultural intoxication with Europe was almost gone. Howells's 1899 publication of *Ragged Lady* continued to debate the twin but conflicting postures in his work—rustic American charm opposed to sophisticated European guile. The return to America was necessary, because Europe had corrosive and corrupting influences. Since the journey was postponed too long, the idea of America remained unfulfilled, as Annie realized: "After the death of Judge Kilburn his daughter came back to America. They had been *eleven winters in Rome, always meaning to return, but staying on from year to year, as people do who have nothing definite to call them home.*[4] Indeed, the general meaning of the work shows Howells's new interests in Machine Age industrialism and social reformation as an American reality.

Earlier on, between 1866 and 1870, as assistant editor of the *Atlantic*, he was able to enter "the 'old Cambridge' of Longfellow and C. F. Norton, the 'proper Boston' of Holmes and Lowell, and the international literary set of Fields."[5] Furthermore, lifelong friendships were made with William and Henry James and Mark Twain. He was influenced by and in turn influenced the major writers of his time. Under his editorship of the *Atlantic*, fiction by James and Twain was serialized. His time spans a period when he, in turn influenced by his reading of Tolstoy, Turgenev, and Ibsen, befriended realists like Stephen Crane and African American writers such as Paul Laurence Dunbar and Charles Chesnutt. As late as 1916, he can still praise the "new poetry" of Frost, Lindsay, and Edgar Lee Masters.[6]

Howells's travels to Europe and his admiration for some things European never made him completely Eurocentric. Unlike the inveterately Europhilic Henry James, Howells maintained a sense of balance. One would have wished for some Whitmanesque proclamations, but the sense of direction lay in the doing, in the construction of the novels that moved beyond say Bartley Hubbard's philanderings in *Modern Instances* (1882), to a true masterpiece of realism, *The Rise of Silas Lapham* (1885). In the latter instance, the young lovers are able to defy the Brahmin society of Boston and marry, just as Colonel Lapham is forced to take stock of his nouveau riche pretensions. Even during his socialist period, Howells shows the same rigid moralism. But class is not inherently evil; in *A Hazard of New Fortunes* (1890), Dryfoos, the ruthless millionaire, was once a farmer. Social conditioning, not genetic programming, accounts for the state in which human beings often find themselves.

At the heart of American letters lay a tradition that, without fanfare, was beginning to assert a new independence. Howells was at the center of this and is the most representative writer with a large body of work, clearly indicating an independent direction into which America should go. But perhaps one of the many reasons why Howells is not credited with the undoubted influence he had is that (to use Nef's words) he felt he was "free to ignore the European experience."[7]

Despite the undoubted accomplishments of the "expatriates" who went to London and Paris, the true fact, unlike the popular view, is that America was not a wasteland. Howells was ahead of his time, in that he sought to balance Boston with Paris and Rome. There is no Jamesian conflict; instead he opts for the real and the realistic—home. There one must come to terms with a new reality, represented by women's rights, class distinctions, social unrest, and so on. I suspect that an important reason why we read so little in the popular media about, say, either Thorstein Veblen or Howells is that they focused on social inequities, even finding a degree of understanding derived from their social concerns.

Henry James was a different writer, for he attacked without disturbing the basic Eurocentric arrangement. Matthiessen and Murdock claim that James often "reveals *the kind of American innocence* that he never lost. This *may have prevented him from becoming anything like as searching a critic of social corruption* as the French and Russian masters of the novel had already shown themselves."[8]

The *Notebooks* are indeed full of the beliefs that Howells had discarded. For instance, an entry for January 18, 1881, states this about a projected short story: "Mrs. T., living in America (say at Newport), has a son, young, unmarried, clever and selfish, who persists in living in Europe, and whom she therefore sees only at long intervals. *He prefers European life*" (my emphasis). Or, for another story, James recalls:

> I had preserved for long years an impression of an early time, a visit, in a
> sedate American city—for there were such cities then— to an ancient lady
> whose talk, whose allusions and relics and spoils and mementoes and
> credentials, so to call them, bore upon a triumphant sojourn in Europe,
> long years before, in the hey-day of the high scholarly reputation of her
> husband, a dim, displaced superseded celebrity.[9]

Probably this is the germination of James's "The Jolly Corner." Europe is America's glorious memory of itself.

Interestingly enough, American characters are laughed at for aspiring to a Europe that they cannot comprehend. In "Europe," Becky and her sisters are all mocked; the "limit of adventure . . . consisted only of her having been twice to Philadelphia. The others hadn't been to Philadelphia."[10] In a way she helps us understand "Daisy Miller," perhaps after all no rebel but merely an awkward American in the sedate world of Europe. Both Becky and Daisy must die at the end, for they are not equipped to deal with the larger reality of a Europe to which they nevertheless aspire.

James had moved to Paris in 1875, then permanently to London the next year. From the beginning, the differences between James and Howells may be noted: James's Americans nearly always come off second rate, unable to compete with their European peers. James operates from an eagerness to accommodate himself to the English and a wish to discard or dismiss anything seemingly American. In *Roderick Hudson* (1876), the American sculptor of the story fails to achieve discipline in Rome; in *The American* (1877) and *The Europeans* (1878), American and European standards of conduct are observed. Even if French royalty in *The American* is corrupt, perhaps murderous, it is up to Christopher Newman to conceal this. And although German Baroness Eugenia does not land a rich Bostonian, she almost brings it off with Acton. Therefore, James and Howells (to a lesser extent) are loyal extensions of Eurocentricity in American arts. Theirs is a logical pursuit that will be undertaken by American writers two decades later.

By 1918, Euro Americans and African Americans had been part of the political process set in motion by the new political rejection of neutrality.

Submarine maneuvers by Germany had brought U.S. merchant ships directly into the line of fire. President Wilson was forced to move from his stated position of "peace and neutrality with dignity and honor" to a declaration of war on April 2, 1918, for "the world must be made safe for democracy." On the home front, Charlie Chaplin joined with Mary Pickford to urge patriotism— "Buy Liberty Bonds." At the war front, as the bands played "Over There," some four million doughboys tilted the war in favor of Britain and France. Under the French High Commission, as legal segregation was still a fact of life, were the 369th, 370th, 371st, and 372nd African American regiments. They returned to a heroes' welcome in Harlem on February 17, 1919.

Euro American doughboys and the African American regiments had helped bolster a new assertive image of America in Europe. Added to this was the presence of Woodrow Wilson as ultimate peacemaker. In France, Italy, and England, he received a tumultuous welcome. Later the Senate rejected both the League of Nations and the Treaty of Versailles. But Wilson, with David Lloyd George of Britain, Georges Clemenceau of France, and Vittorio Orlando of Italy working out details of a future for Europe on January 8, 1918, put forward the single most pointed symbol of America's new role of leader in Europe.

Wilson's "Program for the Peace of the World" was clearly intended to move America to the European continent. Point 14, which argued for a League of Nations, pledged, "We stand together until the end." The message was clear: Wilson's America would side with the British and the French against the rest of Europe. The Senate's refusal to acquiesce merely prolonged the inevitability of this same cooperation in World War II. A sorry footnote to the consequences of America's intervention in World War I was the incarceration without trial of numerous non–Anglo European Germans whose loyalty, it was felt, could not be relied upon. With their rights suspended, they were condemned to forced labor.[11]

No wonder then that there was an artistic brain drain from the United States to Europe in the 1920s. Not only was there in the United States a sterile background, informed by old arguments about ethnicity, but also few intellectuals could envision America as a place of stimulation. Added to this there were severe problems: America's neutral posture outside the theater of European events seemed to many Euro Americans to be a way of opting out of history; second, the "small wars" at home over immigration (and its nasty accompaniment of loudly proclaimed nationalism) made many writers feel trapped within a type of closed-minded debate. Third, the entire educational process and ethnic focus of the nation had beckoned the writers, artists, and musicians to Europe. For Europe was the seeming reality against which America played out its trivia. Paris was now the mythical playground, as George Wiekes shows:

Paris attracted more Americans in the twenties than at any time before or since. The war was partly responsible, as the American Legion demonstrated by choosing Paris as the place to celebrate the tenth anniversary of American intervention. Prohibition also had its influence, for the younger generation wanted to get away from the whole repressive temper of American mores. But it was not so much the fleshpots as the freedom of Paris that attracted the young, not Babylon but Bohemia. . . . The Bohemia discovered by the Americans of the twenties was even more unreal, a Land of Cockaigne in which one could play at starving in a garret for art's sake without being either poor or creative. Paris was a place that evoked all the sentimentality of the nineteenth-century Bohemia, that permitted the young to lead the artist's life with none of its disadvantage, that tolerated or ignored Americans and allowed them to be as carefree and unconventional as they wished without the disapproval of society.[12]

Many of the important literary figures, Black and White, well into the end of World War II chose Europe as home: Ezra Pound, T. S. Eliot, Gertrude Stein, and Ernest Hemingway. Richard Wright, Langston Hughes, Claude McKay, E. E. Cummings, Archibald MacLeish, and others went for varying periods, often for the greater part of their lives, to live and work in Europe. Yet "Europe" was an idea, for American artists were not bound to any one place, as a national would have been. They could opt just as easily for England or France, Italy or Spain, or even Moscow, depending on whim and fancy. In a way, this gave American writers new kinds of possibilities denied to residents of European nation-states.

Confined and hampered by their respective cultures and languages, Europeans themselves (scarcely that, for they thought of themselves as nationals of specific states) did not travel easily. Nor did they possess the alacrity that would allow for leaping backward and forward across cultures and time in attempting to understand what it meant to be "European" in the early years of the twentieth century. American artists and writers had no such qualms, for as outsiders they could visualize Europe in a much larger sense and could embrace its history and traditions as rightfully theirs, as they saw it.

European myth had gone askew in America; the writers needed to restore it. This is surely part of what Eliot means in "Tradition and the Individual Talent," and just as surely what Pound suggests in "Hugh Selwyn Mauberly." From there, they could say, with James McNeil Whistler, "Why should paintings be looked at?" Or more bluntly, with Pound, "Damn their eyes. No art ever grew by looking into the eyes of the public."[13]

Gertrude Stein arrived in 1902, and by 1909, she had set up house with Alice B. Toklas at 22 rue de Fleurus. Pound went to Italy in 1908, London 1908–1920, Paris 1920–1924, and back to Rapallo, Italy, until the end of the war. Eliot lived largely in England between 1914 and 1932, and Hemingway, Malcolm Cowley, E. E. Cummings, and others took varying roles in World War I. Fitzgerald and his exotic wife, Zelda, lived from 1924 for two and half years in Paris, Sherwood

Anderson came to Paris in 1921, and John Dos Passos, after living in Spain in 1916, joined the Morton-Harjes Volunteer Ambulance Corps and was in France and Italy, staying on as a journalist until 1926. Between 1923 and 1924, Langston Hughes worked in a Spanish nightclub, and Claude McKay, in England since 1919, also lived in Spain and France. Some, like Henry Miller, Richard Wright, and James Baldwin, went to Paris after World War II. By then the initiative had virtually expended itself, but the idea of Europe, especially as concretized in Paris and, to a lesser extent, in London, retained its flavor as artistic capital of American culture.[14]

Most of the writers had come from the East coast, graduating from Radcliffe, Harvard, Yale, Princeton, or Columbia. They published poems, short stories, and novels; they wrote essays and started or helped to start new journals. For example, Ezra Pound and Wyndham Lewis edited *Blast* between 1914 and 1915; *The Dial* was revived and, although published in New York, printed many of the new writers living abroad, including Eliot, and awarded its "Dial Awards" to Sherwood Anderson, Pound, Cummings, and Eliot. Eliot himself edited the quarterly review *Criterion* from 1923 until 1929. Ford Maddox Hueffer (later Ford, as German surnames were none too fashionable), along with Pound and Hemingway, edited the *transatlantic review*. Ezra Pound was "foreign" editor of *The Little Review* (1914–1929) out of Chicago, which serialized James Joyce's *Ulysses*. Edited between 1924 and 1929 in Paris, *The Little Review* published Cowley, Eliot, Sherwood Anderson, as well as Amy Lowell and Carl Sandburg. Between 1925 and 1932, *This Quarter* was published, and *Transition* was published between 1927 and 1938 (except for 1930–1932), whose contributors included Hemingway, Stein, and Hart Crane. Sylvia Beach ran the small bookstore "Shakespeare and Company" and became the first publisher of Joyce's *Ulysses*.[15]

Part of the answer as to why Euro Americans came to Europe is found in the response to this:

"Why Do Americans Live in Europe?" [which] was the title of a symposium that appeared in *Transition* in Fall 1928. . . . Their answers vary considerably, but they share a common outlook: they do not generally think of themselves as exiles, however strong their objections to the intellectual, artistic, or "spiritual" (a word *Transition* used in its questionnaire) shortcomings of their native land. Furthermore, they do not take themselves too seriously. The answers consider various advantages to living in Europe. Not only is life cheaper, but the compulsion to make money is not so all-consuming. Europe allows leisure and reflection. "What America needs is a gospel of laziness." Europe values the arts and confers self-respect on the artist, while America has no use for him, leaving him with a guilty need to justify himself. Europe is tolerant, takes a more realistic view of human nature, and leaves a man freer to lead his private life. In short, artists as a group find in Europe the kind of life that is most conducive to creation.

And by Europe they usually meant Paris, where most if not all of them were living at the time and where the overwhelming majority of Americans in the twenties preferred to stay.[16]

There American writers came into contact with their European counterparts. For although Americans squabbled endlessly among themselves, they did not seem to regard Europeans as rivals. Whether they coedited journals or collaborated with each other, Eurocentric feelings on the part of American writers conditioned them to accept a secondary role, as culture vultures. Gertrude Stein bought up Picassos and Matisses, like a latter-day Mellon, as did Hemingway and Sherwood Anderson. Pound had lived with Yeats, and later both he and Eliot shared a keen understanding of what Joyce was attempting to do in his new work, which delved beneath the conscious actions and speech of people. Also, they knew and helped each other. Perhaps Pound remains the most generous, in that he not only assisted in getting Joyce and Stein published, but also performed his remarkable task in editing Eliot's *Waste Land* (1922). Edmund Wilson's *Axel's Castle* (1931) gave critical approval to Eliot, Joyce, and Stein, placing them within a European tradition that included Yeats, Valery, Proust, Rimbaud, and Villier de l'Isle-Adam.

There was neither a preplanning of the exodus nor even a definite "expatriate" movement. For my purpose here, I wish merely to show that the best and most representative American writers from the 1920s to the late 1940s saw themselves as fulfilled only if they could live within and write from a European setting. This was a major aspect to the continued Europeanizing of the American mind.

As already noted, the truism does not hold good merely for writers of a Euroethnic background. Langston Hughes, Countee Cullen, Claude McKay, and later Richard Wright and James Baldwin saw Europe, particularly Paris, as offering them an outlet that they did not have at home. Motives were different; Euro Americans were fleeing from the constricting atmosphere of a nation turned inward toward isolationism, whereas African Americans had cause to be concerned with more basic issues of true freedom and liberty, as well as the ability to interact across racial lines. Despite the lull of the Harlem Renaissance, when Harlem had become intoxicatingly beautiful, with its jazz, its poets and novelists, its actors, and its exotic setting, reality came with the stock market crash of 1929.[17]

African American writers were, therefore, equally lured by their own Eurocentricity. However, in Paris, although Wright did meet Stein, the world of Wright himself as well as earlier sojourners like McKay, Hughes, and poet Countee Cullen, existed apart from the Europeanized American salons of Ford Maddox Ford and Gertrude Stein. These African American writers also contributed to a plethora of newspapers at home, and some few journals, like *Opportunity* (founded by Charles S. Johnson) and *Crisis* (founded by W. E. B. Du

Bois). But in Paris, they interacted with a new breed of English-speaking ex-French colonials, the future leaders of the *négritude* movement. They knew and met Léon Damas, poet and essayist from French Guiana, Aimé Césaire, poet and playwright from Martinique, and Léopold Sédar Senghor, poet and essayist from Senegal.

France's *évolués* from its colonies were beginning to turn the tables on the metropole and defining themselves anew with an urgent persistence. Damas comments that in a February1934 article of a journal, *L'étudiant noir*, which they launched, Césaire had coined the word "négritude," or Blackness, itself a revolutionary concept at the time. In an interview with me, Damas spoke about "the relationship which existed between the New Negro, the Negristo of Cuba, and the Indigenism of Haiti. I remember at the same time we were receiving *Crisis* and *Opportunity*, we were also in contact with Countee Cullen, and Alain Locke."[18] Damas added that Alain Locke frequently came to Paris and that they all knew Du Bois. Damas also stated that he had read Langston Hughes's poetry and had even published Wright in translation.

Ironically, though, if African American writers sought to escape the racial entrapments of the United States, they failed. For, despite the apparently easier integration of Euro Americans into European society, African Americans still had to come to terms with their race as a basic issue even in Europe and its prevailing and indisputable commonality for the African, African Caribbean, and African American. Europe was not, for African Americans, an untrammeled, free, and liberating environment, although admittedly it helped many of these writers see the wider world ramifications of their status.

Still their own Eurocentric belief persisted. As late as 1954, Richard Wright, a specially invited guest of President Kwame Nkrumah, treated with all the awe, reverence, and dignity that hitherto he had never been accorded, still thought back, from the newly independent Ghana, on the beauty of the thoroughfares of Paris, constantly harping on the stupidity of his generous African hosts. Still later, Baldwin, radical though he projected himself, reflected on his contacts with Africans, noting that their terms of reference were so different that, as he once said, "we almost needed a dictionary to talk."

Embedded in those statements lies a patent reality—both Euro Americans and African Americans had been duped into a belief that they were all somehow logical extensions of Europe. Both flirted with a vague idea of Europe as central to their unfulfilled quest; although at times African American writers were drawn back on themselves to their role as *functional* writers, more often than not they merely played with the themes. What is even more significant for both ethnic groups from America is that Europe had begun to have an early love affair with Blackness as an exotic thing. Both American ethnic groups accepted this as true.

As early as 1889, the Universal Exposition of Paris had brought a new and differing world to Europe. Along with descriptions of French colonies in the

Pacific, Indo-China, the Indian Ocean, and the Caribbean, Parisians saw and observed the arts and culture of Africa. The exhibition was conceived on a grand scale, occupying about 200 acres on both banks of the Seine, and attracted 32 million visitors. Above all, the American presence was there: 336 paintings by 189 artists were featured, among them James McNeill Whistler. Several paintings won medals, and others were bought by the government of France. The 1889 Paris Exposition blended art and architecture, culture and technology. Its symbolic point of the promised grandeur of the twentieth century was the Eiffel Tower, specially built for the exposition.[19] Above all, it introduced the "other" to Paris.

France seemed to epitomize Europe, in that it had actively sought to import even what seems now like the exotic. For culture-starved Americans, having painfully gone through Reconstruction and post-Reconstruction, the retreat to empire and the isolationism of pre–World War I, the movement of its writers, painters, entertainers, and artists can be understood, especially in the larger context of seeking to be a part of a new type of Eurocentric culture.

On June 4, 1910 the Ballets Russes produced "Shéhérezade." The ballet brought together a number of distinguished people who managed to alter ballet into a completely different form. Michel Fokine sought a new realism, and with Sergei Diaghilev he assembled a choreography that was different from classical ballet. More dancers were reintroduced to ballet, as well as new music, experimental designs, and, above all, the use of a wide range of color. Through the use of the whole body, the directors and performers sought to render their new fascination with non-European art forms. Of course, it was an enormous success.[20]

What was probably more interesting for the French spectators, apart from the technical innovations, was the exotic glimpse it gave to non-European lifestyles. Unfortunately, such a retrospection merely conjures up the making of new stereotypes. The ballet introduced the Shah, his court, and his wife and concubines to the European stage. Eroticism became truly credible when, on the Shah's hunting expedition, the women bribe the eunuch and engage in an orgy. "Shéhérezade" introduced, or rather reinforced, certain stereotypes associated with non-Europeans: their rhythm, love of colors, and sexuality.

Into this pattern of stereotype, Josephine Baker promenaded her leopard, doing her famous entertainment act. She gave Europe what it had expected: a "harem dance," to drums, with Josephine Baker in a skimpy outfit—all against a backdrop of palm trees. America could offer her only bit parts in the Plantation Club at Harlem. By 1925, she was the star feature of "La Revue Nègre," and later performed at the Théâtre des Champs-Élysées. As seen with the release of the HBO movie, the fascination with Le Baker is still not yet over; she is still being adored for the wrong reasons, and few are daring to question either French attitudes at the time or her own willing compliance in easily adapting to current European racial distortions.[21]

Man Ray moved to Paris in 1925. With Marcel Duchamp he had earlier founded a New York Dada movement. In Paris, he became associated with surrealism, under André Breton, who later on would promote Aimé Césaire's *Cahier de retour au pays natal* for its surrealistic, not its anti-colonial, thrust. Man Ray's *Les champs délicieux* ("The Delightful Fields") was published in 1922, when his experimental photographs fit comfortably into the cosmopolitan, pluralistic world of Paris.[22] As early as 1919, Sidney Bechet, the great saxophonist, toured Europe. Bechet was a veteran musician, born in New Orleans, and his style was praised by classical European conductors. Again, he too settled permanently in Paris in the 1940s, living there until his death.[23]

Josephine Baker and Sidney Bechet were but two examples of the curiosity that Europe, and particularly France, took in the Black world. This interest in France had gone back some time: for instance, in the early part of the nineteenth century a hot debate had flared up between F. R. de Tussac and Abbé Henry Grégoire. The latter, with his 1808 publication of *De la littérature des nègres* had successfully shown that Black writing could be traced back to the sixteenth century. De Tussac would have none of this; he responded in *Cri des Colons* (1810) that, as the Black writers had written in the borrowed languages of England, France, Holland, Portugal, and Spain, then "les Africains n'ont point de littérature" (Africans do not have a literature).[24]

Empire might explain some of the French interest in non-European culture. But the British response was different, for there was no debate about indigenous literature, only about the need to save savages. What interest did exist in Africa before Marcus Garvey was put forward by colonials—Edward Blyden, as early as 1850, and later George Padmore and H. Sylvester Williams. And when they chose a site for their Second Pan African Congress in 1919 (ironical though it may be), they selected Paris.[25]

For both African Americans and Euro Americans, therefore, France seemed the embodiment of what they sought and wanted. However, I wish to stress that, whether they went to Paris seeking to avoid "race" or not, they found it. True, it was different: the polarities were no longer there, but a new myth of the exotic Black had been substituted instead.

Blaise Cendrars had brought out his *Anthologie nègre* in 1927, which was followed less than two decades later by Damas's and Sengor's. All of them introduced contemporary-world Black writers to a French public. New movements in France during the first decades of the twentieth century meant at least trying to rediscover, understand, and depict the Black world. Europe had sanctioned the approval of African and even African American culture. The latter was most prominent, particularly after World War I, with ragtime music.

Europe had gone in search of an Africa it had itself rejected, and it accepted Africa now, as it did many other things non-European. Picasso, Matisse, and Georges Braque began their experimentation with Dogon sculpture. They would hang the masks in their studio, use them as models for their own work, or copy them outright. More traditional European art had been naturalistic and representational; the Dadaists, cubists, and surrealists shifted definition from outer surface forms to the unseen. Their most effective period is 1910–1914. Some scholars like Roland Penrose show that Picasso's interest in African art was the initiative for "proto-cubism." Even Picasso's self-portraits in 1906 predate this period and yet show a definite traditional African style. Part of the explanation might lie in the fact that Picasso and Matisse were avid collectors from much earlier on.[26]

Interestingly enough, this activity, through which Europe dabbled in Africa, had the effect of popularizing and elevating African experience in the United States itself. Perhaps this is one reason that could be given for the Harlem Renaissance, especially Euro American interests in things African American. The myth of Europe had come full circle, as Euro Americans became part of this new European interest. Stravinsky produced "Piano Rag Music" in 1919; Vachel Lindsay published *The Congo and Other Poems* in 1914; Eugene O'Neill wrote *Emperor Jones* (1919) and *All God's Chillun Got Wings* (1924). Of course it was all still very fanciful and far-fetched, but it seemed almost mandated by the time.

Clichés and stereotypes abounded in "The Congo" and *Emperor Jones*. Lindsay's poem owed much to Poe's verses such as "Annabel Lee," "Ulalume," and "The Bells." But whereas Poe tended to employ sheer technical virtuosity, Lindsay claimed a more solemn purpose: "America," he stated with his usual profundity, "needs the flamboyant to save her soul." The problem was that the soul of African America was traded in for the sounds of a fanciful Euro America. Lindsay utilizes the stereotypes of drums, colors, idleness, and drunkenness, as in "Fat black bucks in a wine-barrel room/ Barrel-house kings with feet unstable ... /Boom, boom, boom." And after he relegates the African past to this simplistic state, he does much the same for the African American present: Words like "crap-shooters," "negro fairyland," "baboon butler," "cake-walk princes" are interspersed in the second part of the work. Truthfully, the poem does not make much sense, for it is a long sound of farce, an enormous screech of the misunderstood, the inane, and the crude. However, in 1914 "The Congo" was important; Yeats praised it, and Lindsay was in great demand for his recitals.[27]

Seven years later, when Eugene O'Neill published *The Emperor Jones* (1921), the equations are perhaps a little less macabre but still evident. Brutus (Brute?) Jones is also stereotypical: he is a Black criminal, slightly superstitious, easily fooled, cruel toward his fellow Blacks. Yet, he is able to rule an island of delightful Friday-like primitives. Here, as in Lindsay, the drum is disturbing, frightening, signaling the end to his power and savagery.[28]

Why "The Congo" and *Emperor Jones* received such wide Euro American approval at home must be understood. Both works confer a subhuman, yet exotic, status on Blacks. What is, however, not so easily comprehended is that later African American writers also accepted the stereotypes as valid—as a way of saying that this was the true and proper way to project themselves. Both Langston Hughes and Countee Cullen tapped into these stereotypical formats and borrowed certain impressions that resonate in their own work.

At another level it seemed surprising, although it should not, that Paul Robeson, one of the foremost champions of race pride in America, should have established an early reputation with *Emperor Jones*. Robeson did both the 1920 play and the 1933 movie version. He obviously did not feel degraded by portraying Brutus Jones, con man and savage, king and villain. For Brutus Jones, like some of the people fictional and real so far discussed, Paris was a means of escape to an ultimate freedom. There, he reflects, he will live off his riches. For him, France promises both material and human rewards, where he will live well and be respected. Perhaps Robeson saw some worth in this.

Van Vechten, later to became the executor of Gertrude Stein's estate, published *Nigger Heaven* in 1924, three years after *Emperor Jones*. Now the "brute" of Lindsay's "Congo" and O'Neill's *Emperor Jones* gives way to the Black self-hater, Byron Kasson, a would-be chronicler of African American experience. This is the Harlem that Byron observes:

> To Byron the atmosphere was vaguely distasteful. You want to be a writer, he adjured himself, and this is probably first-class material. Nevertheless, his immediate pendent thought was that he would never write about this life, that he could never feel anything but repugnance for these people, because they were black. I can't bear to think of myself as a part of this, he sighed.

And Lasca, with whom Byron falls in love tells him outright, "I loathe the race. Niggers are treacherous and deceitful. You'll never get anywhere if you depend on them."[29]

At the end Byron, like Lindsay's savage and O'Neill's brute, is destroyed by the sound of the drum, as it becomes intertwined with his racial revulsion: "Tum-tum! Tum-tum! Tum-tum. . . . Would that drummer never stop? Jungle! Savages!" The point is the same: The drum, symbol of the ancient art of Black Africa, stands for the destroyer of the African American soul. Since Afrocentricity is intrinsically destructive, these writers suggest that the "savage" must turn to Europe in order to really fulfill himself.

Black and White students, scholars, travelers, and musical casts all headed toward Europe. David Lewis writes in *When Harlem Was in Vogue* that in the summer of 1929:

> Afro-American travel to Europe had set a record that summer, with the casts of *Blackbirds* and *Porgy* booked into London theatres, jazz musicians answering the booming demand of Paris and Berlin night clubs, students and scholars bound for some serious enterprise.

Even after the Depression, Lewis continues, "Harlem gossip was . . . spiced by news of Afro-Americans in Europe." *Tatler* readers, he says, knew of Jules Bledsoe's Paris concert at the Salle Gaveau. The *Defender* wrote about Nora Holt at the Coventry Street restaurant, and other papers like *The Amsterdam News*, the *Defender*, and the Pittsburgh *Courier* regaled its Black readers with Ethel Waters's appearances at the London Palladium and the Café de Paris.[30] Europe was definitely in for African Americans as a place of acceptance, even fulfillment.

In the final analysis, for our purposes, therefore, scant differences existed between American artists who stayed home and those who lived abroad. Their major point of contact was a Europe that was either unrealized or imaginary. Edna St. Vincent Millay and Edgar Lee Masters used evergreen themes like death and rebirth to state safe concerns—Leon Howard refers to them as "sterile."[31] I suspect that this response merely criticizes their failure to update their craft by using contemporary European forms.

Ford Maddox Ford searched for American writers for his *transatlantic review*. But, as Kenneth Lyn shows,

> thanks to Hemingway's machinations inside the office and Pound's harassments from outside, the *review* actually ran a total of sixty British pieces, forty French and ninety American, the latter by such writers as William Carlos Williams, Lincoln Stephens, H. D., Natalie Barney, John Dos Passos, Nathan Asch, Djuna Barnes, and Gertrude Stein.[32]

The expatriates were thus caught up in new roles as American patrons to European arts. George Wiekes explains that they also drew heavily from the French environment:

> Paris meant something different to each of them, a pleasant ambiance, a sense of freedom, a foreign temperament that challenged and complemented their own, or a way of life conducive to creation. All of them found it a good place to work. Naturally they learned about their art and craft from the artists they encountered. What they produced cannot be called French, though one or two adopted a Parisian style, and none was unaffected. Chiefly they felt the all-pervasive classical spirit of France, even in an iconoclastic age. Under this influence they became more conscious of form, style, language, or medium than any previous generation of Americans.

For Gertrude Stein, Wiekes continues, it was an opportunity to imitate the Cubist painters in words; for Cummings, Dos Passos, Hemingway, and others, "the armistice left them both disengaged from society and restless for further adventures"; and, later, for Henry Miller, Paris "satisfied his emotional, intellectual and creative needs." Man Ray, Wiekes adds, was different, "surrounded by French poets and artists" and, for musical composers like Virgil Thomson and George Antheil, there existed the "modern influence of Erik Satie and the neoclassicism of Stravinsky."[33] Malcolm Cowley warns, though, "They were never united into a single group or school."[34]

Pound's role, as Hoffman sees it, was to encourage "other Americans who felt intimidated or stifled." Hoffman adds:

> The insistent refrain of criticism, both native and expatriate, was that America lacked taste, was crude, vulgar, pretentious; that it crushed the sensitive soul, rewarded the unscrupulous and the thickskinned, drove its artists and writers into retreats on the margins of its prosperous cities and towns.[35]

Therefore, the need existed to cast off old America—Longfellow and Whittier, for instance, and become quite selective about the American past to promote Melville and Whitman.

For rushing toward Europe definitely did not mean discarding everything American. Writers had to understand, with Stein, to "realize our parents, remember our grandparents, and know ourselves and our history is complete."[36] This is the partial equivalent of Eliot's "pastness of the past and its presence."[37] For Stein, living in France, which had undertaken the serious exploration of non-Europe, meant that she had to recall her own American experience of Blackness in "Melanctha" of *Three Lives* (1909), trying her best to elevate what she terms the "subtle, intelligent, attractive, half white girl" to heroic status.[38] She does not succeed, because Melanctha is a creature of the exoticism of Europe.

Receiving some approval, albeit a trifle far out, from D. H. Lawrence could only help writers feel that they were on the right track. In his *Studies in Classic American Literature* (1923), his obvious admiration for the frank openness of some American writers was apparent. Lawrence's poetry at times even imitated the translucence of Whitman:

> He was everything and everything was in him. He drove an automobile with a very fierce headlight, along the track of a fixed idea, through the darkness of this world. And he saw everything that way. Just as a motorist does in the night.
>
> I who happen to be asleep under the bushes hoping a snake won't crawl on my neck; I, seeing Walt go by in his great fierce poetic machine, think to myself: What a funny world that fellow sees.[39]

In a letter to Aldous Huxley, he praises Whitman as one of the "grand perverts."[40] So Europe opened up to American letters in the 1920s, pushed it out of its obsessions with mythical Eurocentricity, and gave it new life. Freedom from parochialism meant, at least for the Black author Jessie Fauset, that she did not have to be always concerned with color: "nobody cares—not even Americans, it seems—whether an artist is white, black or yellow."[41] But for many of the writers, the illusion soon passed. "The so-called 'lost generation,' " Sylvia Beach wrote, "had grown up and become famous."[42] By the start of World War II, the fling with European romance and African primordialism was practically over.

Also over at this time was the naive flirtation of African American writers with European-imposed prescriptions. The spokesperson for the author Wallace Thurman in his bitter attack on the Harlem Renaissance, *Infants of the Spring* (1932), lays it all out:

> That ninety-nine and ninety-nine hundredths per cent of the Negro race is patiently possessed and motivated by an inferiority complex. Being a slave race actuated by slave morality, what else could you expect? Within themselves and by their every action they subscribe to the doctrine of Nordic superiority and the louder they cry against it the more they mark themselves inferiors.[43]

The judgment is harsh, but it addresses disappointed hopes rather than total disillusionment. In reality, the 1930s and the beginning of World War II mark a true loss of hope. America could no longer pretend to be neutral, feeding off the cast-off culture of an ancient Europe. No longer could the United States exist in Europe's shadow. A call for leadership had sounded: Euro Americans would go back home with their old images and try to resuscitate their dying ancestor.

Despite apparent official reluctance on America's part, both world wars effectively thrust it onto the European scenario. So, even though the country heeded Senator Henry Cabot Lodge, and appeared to turn away from Europe, in truth and fact the linkage remained. At one level, economic realities were forged out of global reality. As noted, the stock market crash was not confined to Wall Street, but was felt in England, France, and Germany. At a second level, there was no way in which American investment abroad and the wealth of the trans-Atlantic millionaires of steel and oil could be confined here. Along with the birth of the corporate empire came the accompanying problems of unionization, employee versus employer, fought out on both sides of the Atlantic. The newsreels brought the continents even closer, and no stronger evidence could be shown of economic leverage than when Michael Meehan launched a stock market brokerage firm on a passenger line, the "R. M. S. Berengaria," before the stock market crash.

To some extent, the illusion of America going its separate way might be argued in the post-1929 New Deal. But Franklin Delano Roosevelt's New Deal could be seen as a pragmatic effort to utilize what then appeared as successful

Soviet efforts at centralized planning and control. Under the National Recovery Administration, prices were fixed and wages frozen. The federal government handed out loans for public works. Writers were employed to write guidebooks, and actors could survive in theater companies.

In addition, in the midst of "isolationism" after World War I, the United States could not and did not sever its ties with Europe despite the refusal of the allies to pay their war debts. Even the peace movement had counterparts on both sides of the Atlantic, and nothing in the Neutrality Act prevented the relaxation of laws that would permit the sale of material mainly to Britain on a "cash-and-carry" basis.

From the late 1930s on, the United States seemed to have known exactly on which side of the European conflict it would position itself. As early as 1938, the U.S. Ambassador to Germany had been withdrawn; Germany had also recalled its own representative. In 1939, Roosevelt had asked Congress for $552 million and had sought safeguards that Germany and Italy would not attack. The orders from Europe boosted the U.S. economy, but the government still played favorites, choosing eventually to extend favorable credit terms to Britain. On the other hand, a year before Pearl Harbor, the United States had frozen German and Italian assets in this country.

Despite Roosevelt's public statements ("Your boys are not going to be sent to any foreign war"), he bypassed Congress, sending American destroyers to Britain in exchange for bases. Churchill's letters to him were now desperate. The Land Lease Bill freed up millions of American dollars for British use and provided U.S. navy and U.S. patrol planes as escorts. When Roosevelt and Churchill met for four days in Newfoundland (singing "Onward Christian Soldiers" in unison), they planned for the unity concretized in the Atlantic Charter.[44]

How did Roosevelt accomplish a volte-face? The answer was simple—Pearl Harbor. Recent evidence suggests though that the Dutch, French, and certainly the British knew of the impending attack. Some historians have even suggested that Churchill told Roosevelt of the probability of Pearl Harbor. Roosevelt, however, realized that he had to have a demonstrable and dramatic act that would shake the nation out of its composure. In any event, the day of infamy, December 7, 1941, was a just rallying cause. Hitler obliged by declaring war on December 11, 1941. Again, the United States was lined up with its Anglo European allies, and on D-Day American troops invaded Europe once more. History had replayed itself.

Visibly, in an age of increasingly quicker communications, the picture told a thousand words. The "Big Three" were now the "Big Four," with the United States as biggest player. Roosevelt was catapulted to world leader: at Quebec, with Mackenzie King and Churchill; at Yalta with Churchill and Stalin; again at Teheran, with Churchill and Stalin. After 1945, when Roosevelt had won the war, Harry S. Truman secured the peace. At Potsdam, in 1945, he conferred with Churchill, and later with Clement Atlee and Stalin.[45] America established itself as indispensable to the post-1945 world, creating a financial institution, the World Bank. John D. Rockefeller donated over $8 million to help secure a permanent base for the United Nations. Indeed, some might argue that the superpower mantle was not so much undertaken by the United States as imposed on it by bankrupt colonial European powers. Most recently this may be noted in the case of the Persian Gulf and Somalia.

American economic control of Europe begins slowly, first with the passage of the Marshall Plan Act in 1948 and later the U.S. Foreign Assistance Bill. Millions of dollars were directed toward Europe. Additionally, a demonstrable and awesome new power was revealed, made more powerful in newsreel and newspaper footage, when the United States released the atomic bomb on Hiroshima and Nagasaki. If today we speak of a superpower, this is where its origins lie, for Europe had expended itself.

NOTES

1. John U. Nef, *The United States and Civilization* (Chicago: University of Chicago Press, 1967), 422–423. Emphasis added.

2. William Dean Howells, *The Minister's Charge* [1887] in *Novels 1886–1888* (New York: Library of America, 1989), 256–259.

3. Howells, *April Hopes* [1888] in *Novels*, 355.

4. Howells, *Novels*, 643.

5. Howells, *Novels*. See "Chronology" at end, ed. Don L. Cook, 868–869.

6. Ibid, 871. Also see a thoughtful review by Edwin H. Cady, *The Realist at War: The Mature Years 1885–1920 of William Dean Howells* (Syracuse: Syracuse University Press, 1958).

7. Nef, *United States and Civilization*, 423.

8. Henry James, *The Notebooks of Henry James*, ed. F. O. Mattiessen and Kenneth B. Murdock (Chicago: Chicago University Press, 1947), xv, 20, 190–191. Emphasis added.

9. James, *Notebooks*, 191.

10. James, *Notebooks*, 190–191.

11. For information on Woodrow Wilson, consult Arthur Link, *Wilson: The Struggle for Neutrality 1914–1915* (Princeton:Princeton University Press, 1960), and especially *Woodrow Wilson: Revolution, War, and Peace* (Arlington Heights, Ill.: AHM, 1979).

12. George Wiekes, *Americans in Paris* (New York: Doubleday, 1969), 150–151.

13. Louis Simpson, *Three in the Tower: The Lives and Works of Ezra Pound, T. S. Eliot and William Carlos Williams* (New York: William Morrow, 1975), 4.

14. For some of the basic information on White writers in Paris, see Malcolm Cowley, *Exile's Return* (Dallas, Penn.: Penguin, 1969); Frederick J Hoffman, *The Twenties* (New York: Free Press, 1962); and Samuel Putnam, *Paris Was Our Mistress* (Carbondale: Southern Illinois University Press, 1947). For a good study of Black writers of the period, see Nathaniel Huggins, *The Harlem Renaissance* (New York: Oxford University Press, 1971); and David Lewis, *When Harlem Was in Vogue* (New York: Oxford University Press, 1979).

15. See Sylvia Beach, *Shakespeare and Company* (New York: Harcourt, Brace and Company, 1956). Republished Lincoln: University of Nebraska Press, 1991, with an introduction by James Laughlin.

16. Wiekes, *Americans*, 159–160.

17. For the best background information on Black writers and artists in Paris during this period, consult Michel Fabre, *Black American Writers in France 1840–1980* (Urbana: University of Illinois Press, 1991). Also see the imaginative interest that both Richard Wright and Lanston Hughes had in the Spanish Civil War. According to a recent writer, this acted as a kind of empathy, taking the place of an overall Black feeling for the plight of Ethiopia. See Danny Duncan Collum, ed., *African Americans in the Spanish Civil War* (New York: G. K. Hall, 1992), 33, 101–102.

18. Léon Damas, interviewed by author, February 18, 1977, and published in *Journal of Caribbean Studies*, 1, No. 1 (Winter 1980), 64.

19. Theodore F. Wolff, "The Year the Americans Took Paris," *Christian Science Monitor*, 15 October 15 1990, 16.

20. For this information I am indebted to background discussion provided for a ballet performance of "Shéhérezade" performed by the Louisville Ballet Company at the Kentucky Center for the Arts and broadcast on Kentucky Educational Television, May 28, 1990.

21. For information on Josephine Baker, see Josephine Baker and Jo Bouillon, *Josephine* (New York: Harper and Row, 1977), especially 116–125, 131–142, 148, 232–233, 255–256, 285–290; and Ronald Bogle, *Brown Sugar* (New York: Harper and Row, 1976). Also see the documentary film *Chasing a Rainbow: The Life of Josephine Baker*, narrated by Oliver Todd (1986). Two of her fims, available on video *Zou Zou* (1934) and *Princess Tam Tam* (1935), are both thin disguises for her exhibitionism and her carefully cultivated image as the embodiment of exotica.

22. Sidney Bechet, *Treat It Gentle* (New York: Da Capo Press, 1975). Also see Baker and Bouillon, *Josephine*, 46, 47, 51, 55.

23. Bruce Kellner, ed., *The Harlem Renaissance* (New York: Methuen, 1987), 29. Kellner's book is a handy reference guide for the period, with aphabetized biographies that are succinct and mostly accurate.

24. F. R. De Tussac, *Cri des colons contre un ouvrage de M. L'Éveque et Senateur Grégoire, ayant pour titre de la littérature des nègres* (Paris: De Launay Librarie, 1810).

25. Background on the Second Pan African Congress as well as on Edward Blyden, George Padmore, and H. Sylvester Williams may be found in Hollis Lynch, *Edward Wilmot Blyden— Pan Negro Patriot* (Oxford University Press, 1970) and *Black Spokesman* (New York: Humanities Press, 1971).

26. For some information on the African period of modern painters and artists in France, see Bruce Cole and Adelheid Gealt, *Art of the Western World* (New York: Summit Books, 1989), 266–267, 270–271. For specific information on Picasso, see *Picasso: Creation and Design* by Arianna Stassinopoulos Huffington (New York: Simon and Schuster, 1989), 89–90. Concerning the effect of African influence on both Picasso and Matisse, see *Matisse and Picasso* by Françoise Gilot (New York: Doubleday, 1991), 47 and 168 for Matisse and 47, 187, and 269–270 for Picasso.

27. Vachel Lindsay, *The Congo and Other Poems* (New York: Macmillan, 1914).

28. Eugene O'Neill. *The Emperor Jones* (Englewood Cliffs, N.J.: Prentice-Hall, 1921).

29. Carl Van Vechten, *Nigger Heaven* (New York: Alfred A. Knopf, 1926), 192, 257.

30. David Lewis, *Harlem in Vogue*, 254, 264.

31. Leon Howard, *Literature and the American Tradition* (New York: Doubleday, 1960).

32. Kenneth Lyn, *Hemingway* (New York: Simon and Schuster, 1987), 233.

33. Wiekes, *Americans*, 5, 6, 8, 78.

34. Cowley, *Exile's Return*, 7.

35. Frederick J. Hoffman, *The Twenties* (New York: Free Press, 1962), 53.

36. Gertrude Stein, *Three Lives* [1909] (New York: Vintage Books, 1936), 85–236.

37. T. S. Eliot, *Selected Prose* (Harmondsworth, U.K.: Penguin, 1953), 23.

38. Stein, *Three Lives*, p. 86.

39. D. H. Lawrence, *Studies in Classic American Literature* (London: Penguin, 1977), 175. I am never quite sure that Lawrence actually had to read Whitman to write this.

40. D. H. Lawrence, *The Letters of D. H. Lawrence,* ed. Aldous Huxley (London: Heinemann, 1932).

41. Hugh Ford, ed. and int. *The Left Bank Revisited: Selections from the Paris 'Tribune' 1917–1934* (University Park: Pennsylvania State University Press, 1972), 47–48.

42. Beach, *Shakespeare*, 206.

43. Wallace Thurman, *Infants of the Spring* (New York: Macaulay Company, 1932), 140.

44. Kenneth S. Davis, *FDR: Into the Storm* (New York: Random House, 1992). Davis shows that Roosevelt was very concerned about what he saw as a threat to Western civilization when Germany began its offensive.

45. See the study by David McCullough, *Truman* (New York: Simon and Schuster, 1992).

9
Steinbeck's European Audience —————————

D ust Bowl, lack of rain, drought, and economic poverty represent the cosmic background against which Steinbeck places *The Grapes of Wrath* (1939). To empathize with the characters, the reader must believe that life, liberty, and the pursuit of happiness are the rightful domain of Euro Americans, even poor ones. Natural disaster conspires against a God-centered universe.

Concomitant with the breakdown of natural order, a collapse of spiritual well-being also exists. The preacher, Jim Casy, is a fallen man questioning whether virtue and goodness actually exist in the world. Tom has no regrets over his homicide; the death of a man seemed to be the earthly manifestation of the demise of God.

The natural world, here particularized in the foreboding wind, plays an active role that portends destruction. At the beginning of the novel, the bleak scenery is unfamiliar and frightening, with its absence of a vital human society and the grim presence of solitary beings observing the devastation of the land. Muley's recollections of family are his attempts to piece together a society in disorder. The flight of the Joad family is in reality the dislocation of an entire society, with Tom's quest an attempt at either repairing or restoring order.

Sharecroppers have history on their side, for they had worked the land, fought and died for it. They feel a natural affinity with landscape and fail to understand how the forces of nature and rapacity have worked against them. Their stand is noble, even epic, in its posture, but they are doomed to become the refuse of a progress marked by the ruthless advance of Caterpillar tractors and greedy middlemen.

At the heart of the conflict is the ruthlessness of the capitalist system itself. Muley Graves is as homeless and mad as his name suggests, and he no longer has even basic relationships with his own society. The new owners are faceless company men, who do not belong to the land, nor the land to them. They are the new authorities, forerunners of what will plague the Joads.

The family's move to California is Steinbeck's fictional dramatization of historical westward expansion. California (like America itself) remains the stuff of dreams, high wages, and the better life. The idyllic life promised has less in common with earthly America and more in common with a heavenly paradise. The Joads' departure—hardly a Homeric odyssey with cyclical components—is instead, from the very start of the novel, the assured occurrence that phantom rather than substance awaits the family.

As Steinbeck has warned his readers of this in the intercalary chapters quite early in the novel, the stuff of the action has more to do with anguish, disappointment, and unfulfillment rather than joy, satisfaction, and achievement. Grampa has to be doped before he will set out, and the sight of the old man leaving his lost land is truly touching, almost funereal:

> "Come on," Tom said. "Le's get Grampa on." Pa and Uncle John and Tom and Al went into the kitchen where Grampa slept, his forehead down on his arms, and a line of drying coffee on the table. They took him under the elbows and lifted him to his feet, and he grumbled and cursed thickly, like a drunken man. Out the door they boosted him, and when they came to the truck Tom and Al climbed up, and, leaning over, hooked their hands under his arms and lifted him gently up, and laid him on top of the load. Al untied the tarpaulin, and they rolled him under and put a box under the tarp beside him, so that the weight of the heavy canvas would not be upon him.[1]

For he is not departing as a hero would; instead, he leaves crudely, scattered about among the odds and ends of the family's possessions. There is not much nobility here, and none is suggested.

The ramshackle odyssey of the family across America contrasts with the awe and dignity of Graeco-Roman and biblical heroes as they traversed their ancient world. Later on, Grampa's death evokes no nobility in either the family or the reader. "This here ol' man," Casy eulogizes over a make-shift grave, "jus' lived a life an' jus' died out of it."[2] More specifically, his death represents a lack of grace or caring in a society not even conscious of its own loss of faith. No ennobling spirit can elevate Grampa to the status of revered sire, as Casy's homily captures so well.

Compounded by this inability to speak to God, the irony of quest also demonstrates other variations of the Bible. The enactment of the biblical flood shows an absent God; humans are imprisoned, arklike, in a world at variance with their physical needs and aspirations. The turtle is an interesting symbol, first appearing in one of Steinbeck's chapter commentaries and later picked up and discarded by Tom. Its personal will to live has nothing to do with the blind contradictions of an impersonal fate. This is not the sound of the turtle that brings back life and the promise of love in the "Song of Solomon."

Particularly, references that stress a type of divine will show its constant opposition to human will. Observe the quest for water, which is not even materially self-fulfilling, for it destroys the few remaining possessions of the Joads. Also, the breakup of the extended family, despite Ma's tenacious hold, is further indication that humans survive without design or purpose. On the other hand, Casy does move from negative to positive concepts, from aloneness to unity. Indeed, his becoming part of the Emersonian Oversoul is the single most hopeful view that the novel projects. Only through Tom's Christ-like defiance of authority, does the reader comprehend Tom's discipleship after Casy's death.

The Grapes of Wrath achieves its novelistic purpose, but not because Steinbeck utilized real American-lived experience. Certainly a superficial understanding lies in the plight of the Joads seeking California, but the grander design invests the retelling of this in terms of the search for the Promised Land. Pa reminds one of Moses, Ma of Aaron; Rose of Sharon conveys the sensuality of the Queen of Sheba, even as she describes her love in the rich metaphors of the "Song of Solomon."

Because a new society is being founded, new laws have to be enacted and a new covenant made as Tom moves through an understanding of self, a concept of family and group, toward peoplehood. Steinbeck noted that the common outsiderdom of the Okies brings about both their unity and power. Theirs are the voices of the nation itself, the very echoes of Zora Neale Hurston's *Their Eyes Were Watching God*, published two years before:

And they listened while the tales were told . . .

And the people listened . . .

And the people listened and remembered . . .

And the people listened, and their faces were quiet with listening.

The story tellers, gathering attention into their tales, spoke in great rhythms, spoke in great words because the tales were great, and the listeners became great through them.[3]

These are the points where the novel elevates an invented ethnic past, achieving a commonality with its European counterpart. The idea of the novelist as commentator, describer, and foreteller of events is found most notably as early as Fielding's *Tom Jones* and as late as Tolstoy's *War and Peace*. Such clear associations help place *The Grapes of Wrath* within the European tradition even though Steinbeck attempts to strike a more personal nationalistic note in the intercalary chapters. The novelist becomes his own creation, and his created people and place pass into the history of all peoples.

Even if the predicament of the Joads had little interest for European readers, it becomes more meaningful when rendered in terms of religion. Some of the philosophical issues at the core of the book, such as the purposelessness of life and God's inability to alter it, would strike a familiar note. For in the 1930s, Europeans were also experiencing such issues, especially given the problems brought about by the Depression and the threat of another war.

Major European-Soviet influence occurs in the outright denunciation of the capitalist system. From beginning to end *The Grapes of Wrath* makes this point. Wicked company officials drive the Joads from the land. On their way to California, their need for the most basic sustenance was rebuffed either by landowners or by the bullying tactics of policemen and others who guarded the sanctity of President Hoover's Hooverville. Only in the government camps is the family secure enough to extend the boundaries of their inner circle to include the larger society, to make laws, and to provide political solutions to their economic plight.

Beyond the allegory, specific narrative developments and prophetic personages take the novel away from a merely local reference point. At the most basic level, the insignificant deaths of Granma and Grampa, two ancestral figures, emphasize a total lack of values. The West and America represented an absence of purpose; how else could the noble scions of the lineage die with no honor and be buried with little ritual? Similarly, if the past could offer no clue as to the significance of historical existence, then the future would also show little relevance for life. Rose of Sharon's baby is doomed; a religious zealot had foretold that it might be born black and dead, but instead it came into the world as a blue, shriveled mummy. Perhaps there is still hope for her. Perhaps the child is both ancient corpse and mother source, as may be deduced from the loaded word "mummy."

Three episodes are worth briefly mentioning, as they all extend the allegory into dimensions that would be easily understood outside America, helping to maintain Steinbeck's popularity with European readers. First, there is the figure of the Lazarus-like ragged man who warns the family of what lies ahead. He has seen his future and theirs, and he has rejected it, preferring to return home to starve. He says simply, "Me—I'm comin' back. I been there."[4] Pa begins to question the myth of the West, which the family had previously seen in handbills; it seems as if their search was for unearthly ideals. The speaker is nameless; one knows only that he too has been a sufferer, with a dead wife and two children who had starved to death.

Second, this is the equivalent to the equally shadowy figure of the woman who foretells the death of Rose of Sharon's child, although she is given concrete form later on. Her view of the world is that it is incessantly evil; as she speaks, she howls and her body seems to move independently of itself. Even though an explanation is given of her possible insanity, nevertheless her disembodied posture suggests that she belongs, like the ragged man on the porch, to a different array of characters. They, like Muley Graves, inhabit the netherworld of rejection rather than the more reassuring one of social acceptance.

Third, the cave plays a major role in Tom's realization of his real potentiality, because it is the prehistoric domicile of European (not Euro American) human beings. On the American continent, evolution did not play any role in the development of the Euro American population; indeed, it must be added that even Native Americans walked upright onto the continent. In a way, the nation was always a full-grown adult, born with its clothes on. For Tom to come to terms with Jim Casy's theories, he must undergo rebirth. He had rejected this condition at the novel's inception, seeing the cave then as one that he had himself dug. Toward the end of the story, after the primordial murder of one of Casy's tormentors, Tom's family hide him in a cave. When Ma goes there, the Freudian meaning is complete. Tom must be reborn if he is to lead his people. Thus the cave is an initiation into a new European group consciousness, completely contrary to individualistic conceptions of Euro American history.

Now both *magna mater* and new disciple are able, each in his or her own way, to understand Casy's teaching. Ma sums it up for Pa:

Man, he lives in jerks—baby born an' a man dies, an' that's a jerk—gets a farm an' loses his farm, an' that's a jerk. Woman, it's all one flow, like a stream, little eddies, little waterfalls, but the river, it goes right on. Woman looks at it like that. *We ain't gonna die out. People is going' on—changin' a little, maybe, but goin' right on.*[5]

Tom had already told Ma, after they had both rediscovered the womb in their journey through darkness and brush back to the cave, that Casy

says one time he went out in the wilderness to find his own soul, an' he foun' he didn' have no soul that was his'n. Says he foun' he jus' got a little piece of a great big soul. Says a wilderness ain't no good, 'cause his little piece of soul wasn't no good 'less it was with the rest, an' was whole.[6]

When the journey is complete, its resemblance also bears even more directly on New World European settlement than on westward expansion. The ingredients are magnified on a larger canvas, for the journey to the New World involved suffering and deprivation, separation from basic European family units, and severance from ancient customs and modes. Through unceremonial birth and death, the seekers who colonized America were in pursuit of a New World myth. *The Grapes of Wrath* explores in depth the shift from the dry wells of the homeland to the ritual baths of the Promised Land, especially with the acceptance of water as friend, not foe, as seen during the Joads' stay at a government camp. Hence, the "West" of *The Grapes of Wrath* expands into the Western world of Europe and America.

An almost idyllic treatment is given to the daily activities of communal concourse. Once people are free from the intrusive tactics of overzealous and authoritative bureaucrats, they can coexist in a peaceful and harmonious manner. They plan activities around labor and leisure, establish their own governance, and ensure its execution. Although happiness for the family is short-lived here, Steinbeck's argument definitely advocates such communalism as a way of life.

Europeans had escaped political and religious persecution much as the Joads fled from economic and spiritual ruin. In the West, official mythology had declared that the dream was secure. But for the Okies no such promise of fulfillment was assured, as it could not have been for European emigrants. The novel's journey peels away at layers of false expectations of America as old colonial territory and new colonized frontier. The Joads ascend to epic proportion and stature not because they have triumphed, but because they have newer and clearer insights about life. Their legendary status arises from their victory over the limitations of stereotype placed on them.

Each character exhibits aspects of the human race itself. Rose of Sharon's husband, Connie, is Judas-like in his betrayal of group aims and his denial of ethnic purpose. At the end, Ma Joad is elevated to the stature of leader and provider, as she succors the young, feeds the hungry, and comforts the dying. Casy, prophet and later union organizer, bequeaths his calling to the novice, Tom. Tom's hideout in the willows is but a little removed from Christ's retreat in the wilderness. Finally, Rose of Sharon's nursing a dying man back to life with the mother's milk of her dead baby concludes the novel at a point where resuscitation affirms the wholeness of life. *The Grapes of Wrath* supremely endorses life, for once humaneness is learned and becomes endemic to the whole person, all triumph.

Life discovered, rejected, rediscovered, explored, and finally overcome is the major issue of *East of Eden*. Again, the biblical frame of reference is apparent: A journey motif provides the parallel structure, with easily recognizable biblical names like Adam and Samuel or slightly altered names as with Cal and Aron, Abra and Cathy. European connection is noted in the character of Samuel Hamilton, an Irishman who lives out a European past in the American present, bequeathing to Lee a sympathetic understanding of his own and Lee's cultural dualism.

Lee helps to emphasize the colonial aspect within America. True, he belongs to the genre of "boys" found in E. M. Forster's *Passage to India*, Evelyn Waugh's *Black Mischief,* and especially Conrad's *Heart of Darkness* and Joyce Carey's *Mister Johnson*. But Lee is definitely not Conrad's ship boy or Carey's oafish layabout, for he had intentionally chosen to play the part of illiterate, until finally he reveals himself as a source of wisdom. Lee is the quintessential outsider; he is unable to change, for as he tells the Irishman "in a few years you can almost disappear; while I, . . . have no chance of mixing."[7]

The servant role for Lee is the thinker's mask, what he terms "the refuge of the philosopher." Through this he exerts influence and control on the Trask family. Tradition in *East of Eden* is pragmatic and always relevant. When Cathy gives birth to her twins, a rope is used to alleviate the labor. This is both a handy device and symbol of linkage, between mother and children and particularly between Cal and Aron. Steinbeck seemingly suggests, with Cathy's rejection of her children, her attempted killing of Adam, and her departure, that the ties are not tangible. What does exist as indisputable proof is that generational impulses will always control humans for good or ill.

Quite intentionally, values are inverted in the work to establish the point that association with Europe is not real. Therefore, the events of the early parts of the novel, such as the initial family tragedies, Adam's rivalry with half brother Charles, and so on, demonstrate both disintegration of family and separation from Europe. Land defines the new heritage:

> *When people first came to the West, particularly from the owned and fought-over farmlets of Europe,* and saw so much land to be had for the signing of a paper and the building of a foundation, an itching land-greed seemed to come over them. *They wanted more and more land*—good land if possible, but land anyway. *Perhaps they had filaments of memory of feudal Europe where great families became and remained great because they owned things.* The early settlers took up land they didn't need and couldn't use; they took up worthless land just to own it. *And all proportions changed.* A man who might have been well-to-do on ten acres in Europe was rat-poor on two thousand in California.[8]

The change of values is rooted in the very existence of a different land.

Tragedy initiates this inverse epic, with the gonorrhea of Adam's father, the suicide of his mother, and the hasty acquisition of a new wife for his father with "a number of admirable qualities. She was a deep scrubber and a corner-cleaner in the house."[9] Therefore the presence of a real and supportive tradition is intentionally discarded. No rituals are described for the funeral of Mrs. Trask or the marriage of Adam's father. Birth, marriage, and death do not indicate milestones in life but only show the markers of a meaningless and abject existence.

Cal and Aron's tempestuous relationship is obviously meant to suggest Cain and Abel's. Little individuality and distinctiveness are accorded them, and Cal is depicted as a kind of primordial hunter and fighter; on the other hand, Aron is shown as gentle and sensitive, with little ability for physical prowess. In a way, Cal is an American frontiersman and Aron a European idealist. The clash between them is fundamental, as it arises out of American Civil War experience, and also symbolic, deriving itself from the archetypal contention of good and evil. Actuality would work itself out into the larger meaning. As Steinbeck notes in *Journal of a Novel*, the detailed almost day-by-day account of the writing of *East of Eden*: "I am not going to put artificial structures on this book. The real structures are enough. I mean the *disciplines imposed by realities and certain universal writers*."[10]

Love, unfulfilled, sought for, and either won or never attained, is a major theme of the novel. So deep and passionate is the affection between Cal and Aron that it excludes the intervention of a female presence. When Abra does come into the story, she is the medium for the completion of an almost homosexual love between the two brothers. Adam's love for Aron and his ultimate grief over his death form still another theme in which love is uppermost. Adam's deathbed forgiveness of Cal is yet another instance of the male-gender affection and passion that the novel asserts. Not that the relationships are all male centered, but the men seem incapable of forming real and lasting attachments to women.

Women become, therefore, the means through which men are able to achieve ultimate fulfillment. But women destroy men in the process. After Sam's death, Adam visits Cathy (now Kate), holed up in a brothel. She confesses her plans to move to New York, to "find a man, if he's still alive, and very slowly and with the greatest attention to pain I will take his life away."[11] Love between the sexes is pointless: Dessie falls into despair over a thwarted love affair, and Abra confesses that she had outgrown Aron's affection. Lee, as mediator between Adam and Cal, exhibits deep and poignant affection for both. He sends Cal to Abra, urges Adam to forgive his son, and brings the two generations together. Thus Lee's synthesis of the cultural dualism extends beyond ethnicity into a commingling of male/female and older/younger extremes.

As the epic is turned upon itself, it establishes a new way of creating a dialogue between the traditions of Europe and the experiences of America. Steinbeck alluded to the need to "give an impression not so much of the physical life of the country as of the kind of spiritual life—the thinking life—the state of mind—the plateau of thought."[12] When he achieves this, he is closest to a merging of Europe and America.

East of Eden, somewhat like *The Grapes of Wrath*, is also concerned with fertility. In the former instance, the issue moved beyond concerns regarding sterile soil to deal with broader human implications of fecundity. They are interrelated in *East of Eden*: Cathy seeks the barrenness of the bleak landscape, even as Adam (like his father before him) searches for fertile ground to grow crops. "What I really want is water," he tells Samuel but confesses a trifle morosely, "I mean to make a garden of my land. Remember my name is Adam. So far I've had no Eden, let alone been driven out."[13] At this point, the author wishes the reader to understand how the inversion of the epic is accomplished;

in America, despite appearances, any vital connection between faith and assurance through the Judaeo-Christian God cannot be assumed.

Adam Trask is thus unable to symbolize Adam, as Cathy is equally incapable of representing Eve. Cathy seeks and meets death, not life; Adam yearns for a lineage and loses the pride of his life when Aron dies in battle. Adam himself is paralyzed and finally dies. None of them contributes toward a positive construction, only a rather negative destruction. "It is using the Biblical story as measure of ourselves," Steinbeck explains.[14] J. Paul Hunter surmises that "the method serves to nullify too literal a reading, while at the same time drawing in a whole new range of suggestions."[15] The symbols are not permitted to have easy Eurocentric interpretations: The discovery of oil presages the death of Adam's real mother, and the finding of water occasions the shooting of Adam by Cathy.

Little dignity is accorded the participants of the counter-epic. Note the monstrous manner in which Cathy gives birth to the twins, her crudeness in addressing Adam, the fatal meeting between a reluctant mother and her son, Aron, as well as his violent response. He seems afraid to discover the truth about himself and his past. As Cal tells Abra, "He went mad—just crazy. He yelled at her. Outside he knocked me down and ran away. Our dear mother killed herself; my father—he's—there's something wrong with him. Now you know about me. Now you have some reason to walk away from me."[16] Cal has summed up in a few words the tragedy of the novel. No lofty reasons are asserted, for there are none. But located within his condemnation of Aron are issues pertaining to the truly archetypal. In the brother/brother conflict may be found not just Cain and Abel, but the internecine struggles of European states, the War of Independence, and the Civil War. In Aron's "madness" may be seen the insanity that harks back to central characters on the Graecian and Elizabethan stage. In Cathy's and Adam's deaths are found the indispensable tragic ends of the villainous and the virtuous. And in Cal's guilt, there exists the figure of Oedipus, as in Cal's pursuit of his mother, in her responses to him, and even in her thoughts about Aron: "There was something frigidly beautiful about him, something untouched and untouchable."[17] This is actually where the Eurocentric equation lies, one that would be recognizable on both sides of the Atlantic, as it is as old as the Bible and Greek drama.

Homoerotic, incestuous, and transsexual implications abound in the story. One of the minor characters, Mary, wants Tom to alter her sexually. The conversation between the mother and her son Cal hints strongly at sexual attraction in the following exchange:

"All right. What *do* you want?"

"Nothing, ma'am."

"Just wanted to look at me?"

"Yes, ma'am."

"Are you satisfied?"

"Yes, ma'am."

"How do I look?" She smiled crookedly at him and showed her sharp white little teeth.

"All right."[18]

Cathy, Steinbeck writes, "is a little piece of the monster in all of us." Levels of sexual interplay are meant to utilize yet another pointer toward the resolution of epic into a European concept of universality.

In *East of Eden* Steinbeck invented a past for America. Lee, witness and interpreter, stands out because he is obviously not part of the European past, nor does he realistically belong to the story of the Trask family. Steinbeck wanted a universal mouthpiece that would move beyond the traditional role of a Greek chorus. In his words because "it is the duty of the writer, to lift up, to extend, to encourage,"[19] then the dismal chronology of Euro Americans must somehow be alleviated. Steinbeck wrote to his publisher:

> Now you are going to like Lee. He is a philosopher. And also he is a kind and thoughtful man. And beyond all this he is going to go in the book because I need him. The book needs his eye and his criticism which is more detached than mine. . . . Lee's attitudes will if anything be clearer than mine.[20]

The introduction of such an extra-authorial figure, a kind of super-narrator, is a bold invention. He stands outside the borders of the narrative, so that later on we can affirm his faith as our own: "I wanted Lee's statement of faith to be so simple and so beautiful that there could be no doubt of its truth."[21] And so we accept Lee's affirmation that "every man in every generation is refined" and never doubt that "whatever made us . . . would stop trying."[22] This is a sublime affirmation that undoes the viewpoint that life is pointless and leads to no satisfactory end. There exists, the novel implies, always hope for ultimate redemption.

Cathy's words to Aron, "You have me in you," had attempted to dismiss Lee's version of history as a process of constant renewal. Abra and Cal (at least this seems to have been Steinbeck's intention) are not imprisoned within their Euro American, Judaeo-Christian heritage but are free to act individually in the process of constant renewal. Lee is able to help Cal free himself of his burden of guilt, for Lee not only theoretically empathizes but practically shows Cal the way toward ultimate self-understanding.

Finally, Lee is able to separate Cal from his adherence to the mythology of Europe and its inherited guilt. By including himself in the general condemnation, Lee makes a point of great importance and of particular interest to us as he addresses Cal:

"And are you taking pleasure from this whipping you're giving yourself? Are you enjoying your despair?"

"Lee!"

"You're pretty full of yourself. You're marveling at the tragic spectacle of Caleb Trask—*Caleb the magnificent, the unique. Caleb whose suffering should have its Homer.* Did you ever think of yourself as a snot-nose kid—mean sometimes, incredibly generous sometimes?[23]

The exchange relegates the "Homeric" hero to the status of crybaby. Lee, as outsider, is best equipped to denounce such a perversion of true nobility. Instead, Lee indicates the direction of the American hero, away from the self-torture and pity associated with Eurocentric virtue. In the final analysis, he contends:

We're a violent people, Cal. Does it seem strange to you that I include myself? *Maybe it's true that we are all descended from the restless, the nervous, the criminals, the arguers and brawlers, but also the brave and independent and generous.* If our ancestors had not been that, they would have stayed in their home plots in the other world and starved over the squeezed-out soil.[24]

We are back to infertility and lack of growth, but Lee points out that barrenness exists elsewhere—in Europe. Then Lee concludes, in the statement over which Steinbeck exercised such great care:

That's why I include myself. We all have that heritage, no matter what old land our fathers left. All colors and blends of Americans have somewhat the same tendencies. It's a breed— selected out by accident. And so we're overbrave and overfearful —we're kind and cruel as children. We're overfriendly and at the same time frightened of strangers. We boast and are impressed. We're oversentimental and realistic. We are mundane and materialistic—*and do you know of any other nation that acts for ideals?* We eat too much. We have no taste, no sense of proportion. We throw our energy about like waste. *In the old lands they say of us that we go from barbarism to decadence without an intervening culture. Can it be that our critics have not the key or the language of our culture?* That's what we are, Cal—all of us. You aren't very different.[25]

The "minority" voice asserts the valid distinction of America, away from Europe. Perhaps Steinbeck would not have agreed with these views once he grew interested in genetic theories and misplaced race concepts. But here he speaks to a demand for the separateness of America. He even admits to some of Henry James's negatives, but in his wonderful manner he embraces everything.

Steinbeck, like Hemingway and Eliot, represents varied aspects of American literature, for in all their work, they turn Eurocentricity toward a new direction, seeking to find out ways in which the European world can, even if only slightly, come to terms with American experience. In other words, they do not merely reach out toward Europe, but rather (in varying degrees) manipulate Europe, its religions and rituals, its myths and its truths, into understandable American metaphor. At one end is Eliot, utilizing the huge component of Anglican religion and English and French thought. At the other end is Steinbeck, more homegrown, always intent on establishing verisimilitude through the liberal juxtaposing of American experience and biblical archetype. All of them use the journey, often without a hero or with a wounded hero, to describe the divisions between America and a Europe both real and imagined, and demonstrate how Euro American characters attempt to bridge this gap.

NOTES

1. John Steinbeck, *The Grapes of Wrath*, (New York: Viking Press, 1939), 154–155.

2. Ibid., 196.

3. Zora Neale Hurston, *Their Eyes Were Watching God* (Greenwich, Conn.: Fawcett Publications, 1969), 444–445.

4. Steinbeck, *Grapes*, 257.

5. Ibid., 577.

6. Ibid., 570.

7. John Steinbeck, *East of Eden* (New York: Bantam Books, 1962), 143. Emphasis added.

8. Ibid., 9. Emphasis added.

9. Ibid., 12.

10. John Steinbeck, *Journal of a Novel: The "East of Eden" Letters* (New York: Viking Press, 1969), 118.

11. Steinbeck, *East of Eden*, 287–288.

12. Steinbeck, *Journal*, 31.

13. Steinbeck, *East of Eden*, 148.

14. Steinbeck, *Journal*, 105.

15. J. Paul Hunter, "Steinbeck's Wine of Affirmation in *The Grapes of Wrath*," in *The Grapes of Wrath: A Collection of Critical Essays*, 41, ed. Robert Con Davis (Englewood Cliffs, N.J.: Prentice-Hall, 1982).

16. Steinbeck, *East of Eden*, 510.

17. Ibid., 452.

18. Ibid., 409.

19. Steinbeck, *Journal*, 115.

20. Ibid., 73.

21. Ibid., 115, 531, 532.

22. Steinbeck, *East of Eden*, 531, 532.

23. Ibid., 504. Emphasis added.

24. Ibid., 504–505. Emphasis added.

25. Ibid., 505. Emphasis added.

10
European "Tradition" and American Literature ——————————

In the early twentieth century, American writers responded so well to Europe seemingly because the European environment had been painstakingly preserved for them. The myth of Europe, even when realized in fact by their very presence there, continued to have a nurturing effect. Europe was recognizable, for it had been described over and over again, relayed partly through American literature itself and, of course, through the national literatures of Europe. In many respects, therefore, Europe became both the ideal and idealized, in that its parameters had been charted and American writers merely had to exercise selectivity: To which aspects did they want to lay claim and which did they wish to reject? Thornton Wilder, Ernest Hemingway, T. S. Eliot, and John Steinbeck will be considered to see in what ways they provide responses.

For Henry Adams, even though the British could admit to the superiority of the American rifle, "In the face of the spontaneous outburst of genius which at that moment gave to English literature and art a character distinct even in its own experiences, Americans might have been excused for making no figure at all."[1] But he does identify "a slow variation from European types" in writers such as William Ellery Channing and Washington Irving. Actually, American writers sought not so much for a variation as for a new and distinct identity. The basic problem was that this became well nigh impossible, given the close language affinity, cultural ties, and mutually accepted models.

Whitman's *Democratic Vistas* (1871) and *Passage to India* (1871) sought to continue the Emerson/Thoreau exploration of East and West to bring about a reformation of the human spirit. But even Whitman has to concede that "America has yet morally and artistically originated nothing." Whitman's poetry does attempt to originate: He opens up his lines; he equates "I" with "we," thereby assembling a type of personal epic for his land. Whitman also frees his poetry from European prudery: phallic symbols abound in "Song of Myself," and he takes a beautiful, very un-English, delight in the body. However, the mere writing of an epic such as *Leaves of Grass*, especially in its final form, owes a great deal to the parallel construction and long cadences of the King James Bible. Hence, even though Whitman's Civil War experiences are real, in the search for universal statement, Whitman did of necessity fall back on Homeric and biblical references.

One senses Whitman's need to globalize his poetry—hence his resort to frequent itemizing of place names, personal names, and so on. But it is not enough merely to articulate globalism; surely, to be effective it must be intrinsic to the poetry itself. Take for instance these lines, "I see the regions of snow and ice/ I see the sharp-eyed Samoiede and the Finn/ I see the seal-seeker in his boat poising his lance." Or even further on, "I am a real Parisian . . . I am of London, Manchester, Bristol, Edinburgh, Limerick."[2] The lines ignore what Whitman says he aspires to accomplish—"to speak to America"—what nowadays we would praise as addressing the multicultural nature of the society. When he does try for cultural mix and seeks to incorporate Africans, more often than not Eurocentric stereotypes emerge. For instance, "Yon Hottentot with clicking palate! you woolly-hair'd hordes! . . . / Yon human forms with the fathomless ever-impressive countenances of brutes!"[3] does not exactly objectively address non-Whites in the society. Even in "Pioneers! O Pioneers!," the youths and women who become heroes as they push westward are a "beloved race" of Caucasians. Every other race is absent.

Strong Eurocentric words introduce the presence of African Americans into America's epic; they are "savage," "heavy-lipped," "sold at the stand," voices of the intermediate generations of slaves." Perhaps his own question in "O'er Travel'd Roads" applies not only to the poets of the time but also to Whitman himself:

> Of the great poems receiv'd from abroad and from the ages, and today enveloping and penetrating America, is there one that is consistent with these United States, or essentially applicable to them as they are and are to be? Is there one whose underlying basis is not a denial and insult to democracy?[4]

And, one can easily agree with the conclusion that "as long as the States continue to absorb and be dominated by the poetry of the Old World, and remain unsupplied with autochthonous song . . . so long will they stop short of first-class nationality and remain defective."[5]

One may interpret the epic in America as a modified genre intended to reach out to what John Crowe Ransom termed "the world body" but which in reality was the European continent. Certainly, no one in Africa would have recognized anything vaguely familiar in the wild cavortings of Lindsay's savages in "The Congo," nor would anyone on a Caribbean island have seen himself in O'Neill's *Emperor Jones*. As stated, in reaching out to Europe, American writers had to opt quite intentionally to incorporate the mistaken fabrications of Europe and to continue to assemble stereotypes in a European convention.

Even the few attempts at compromise were often not enough for European writers. Both T. H. Huxley's *American Addresses* (1877) and Matthew Arnold's *Civilization in the United States* (1889) found that the large physical scope of landscape and the glorification of the "average" man were, as they saw it, disadvantages. The British writers did not suggest solutions, but their inherent assumption indicated that for American literature to became global, it would have to negate American experience—a truly absurd contention. Was this not, in essence, Henry James's major quarrel with Hawthorne?

American writers therefore persisted in attempting to furnish their literature with recognizable universals. Both Edgar Lee Masters' *Spoon River Anthology* (1915) and Thornton Wilder's *Our Town* (1938) use small-town America as the backdrop, but both writers endeavor to establish similarities with European norms by utilizing various devices. Masters moves beneath the surface to explore inner, even hidden, distant lives. Thornton uses Grovers Corner as a place somewhere, anywhere, in the world—hence his use of a bare stage, his intentional artifice of having a stage manager speak to the audience, and the flexible manner in which "characters" are sketches to be filled in, somewhat like Luigi Pirandello's 1921 play, *Six Characters in Search of an Author*. Both Masters and Wilder begin with the local but attempt to justify it in terms of a European "universal."

Our Town is particularly relevant, as it demonstrates one American writer's use of these European universals to achieve effect. First, there is an almost Aristotelian sense of time constraint, as well as the more obvious one of place. Second, localized scenes, characters, and references lend authenticity but suggest larger meanings. Third, the format of Greek drama is used: a narrator's voice serves as a chorus, allowing for control of action and manipulation of time. Fourth, larger-than-life figures assume symbolic importance, at times suggesting gods. The audiences may participate because they recognize each other but at the same time, it is hoped, they can adjust to an agreed-upon European universal. Finally, also helpful in the translation of this American drama into a European dimension is its intentional sparseness. Little use is made of scenery or props and, as everyone would be expected to understand, the development of mundane daily life is meant to express a larger experience beyond the United States.

As with Whitman, a major problem still exists. The characters of small-town Anglo America seriously inhibit any possible expansion. Obviously, the Polish section of the town is a mere appendage, and there are no African Americans or any other ethnic group to truly Americanize the play. For instance, when Professor Willard is summoned by the narrator, he dashes off (in his bumbling fashion) dates and place names, relegating indigenous Indians to extinction. He can, however, speak quite authoritatively about the "blue-eyed stock" of immigrants who arrived in the seventeenth century. When Julia Gibbs confesses her longing to travel, her desire to visit Paris and to establish the European link is even more explicit. The play's undoubted popularity in America was most likely due to the opposite of what Wilder hoped for—not universal attainment, but recognition of themselves by small-town White Americans.

Wilder was obviously plotting a course that would take him into a more direct relationship with European modes of thought. *The Skin of Our Teeth* (1942) has no pretensions at presenting Smalltown, U.S.A. The play is directly concerned with the biblical flood and the possibility of human redemption. In this instance, as George Antrobus and his family battle an inimical environment, Wilder has created elemental characters. There can be little confusion with the Webbs and Gibbs of *Our Town*. Here Wilder is more like Steinbeck.

With *Theophilus North* (1973), Wilder uses the short-story form to return to the concerns of his first work, *The Cabala* (1926), about the decay of a noble Italian family. In *Theophilus North*, the rot is within American society itself. Through North's eccentricities and nonconformity, the stupidities and pretensions of the anglicized rich at Newport, Rhode Island, become the subject of laughter. If North has Eurocentric leanings (and he certainly does, given his background and training), at least his Bohemian humanity secures him within the lower orders of the society and separates him from the upper class. Wilder seems to be suggesting that Eurocentrism becomes a danger when it ceases to be an expression of personal idiosyncrasy and assumes the proportions of compulsory stances and pretentious modes of conduct. We laugh, not at North's antics, as he can be quite beguiling, but at what he castigates—the artifice that makes all things European into a cultural sounding board.

Flood, death, resurrection, flagging hope, and omnipresent despair are often vehicles through which American writers as different as Faulkner and Poe seek to "universalize" (actually Europeanize) their work. As already noted, the Bible plays an important part, for as text it has recognizable hierarchical values on both sides of the Atlantic. For instance, Melville's *Moby Dick* (1851) and Hemingway's *The Old Man and the Sea* (1952) utilize biblical themes beneath the narrative layer. Names, events, words, all significantly placed within the narrative flow, are expected to conjure up this kind of recognition. For instance, in *Moby Dick* the *Pequod* sets sail on Christmas day. Numerous language references consolidate the religious connotation; even at the end, the ship is said to be like Satan, because it seeks to drag all its occupants down to hell. Melville thus moves from the strictly fictional to the allegorical, thereby establishing an important device that would aid in trans-Atlantic empathy.

Equally allegorical is Santiago's struggle in Hemingway's *The Old Man and the Sea*. The name "Santiago" is rife with meanings, not only suggesting Spanish cities in Cuba and Chile but, more important, conjuring up the notion of "saint." Indeed, the true parallel with biblical lore is to be found in the whale/marlin focus of both *Moby Dick* and *The Old Man and the Sea*. For they conjure up the words of Christ: "I shall make Ye fishers of men." Thus, the search on which both Captain Ahab and Santiago embark is more in keeping with inner quest than outer fulfillment. But Hemingway's actual experiences in Europe gave him the ability to move beyond Europe and to provide an almost objective stance: the posture of the novelist, in Joyce's words, "above God's handiwork [in this case, America] paring His nails."

Hemingway's *The Sun Also Rises* (1926) attempts to "de-Americanize" the novel. For a start, with the exception of diarist Jake Barnes, whose written novel this really is, most of the characters are outside mainstream Euro American society. Robert Cohn, a Jewish writer, a little in keeping with the period, is the eternal "outsider," never welcome in Brett's circle. Brett herself is English, a more recent version of James's Daisy Miller, with her short hair, hats, and the constant flouting of all traditions. Her fiancé, Mike Campbell, is Scotch, and Pedro Romero the matador, with whom she has an ill-fated affair, is, of course, Spanish. Count Mippipopolous is Greek, and Harris is English. Add to this the assortment of people Barnes encounters—whores, innkeepers, writers—and one begins to obtain a feel for Hemingway's point—total immersion in the European world.

Within this very European context, Americans come off very badly. They are tourists who gape and peer and exult over the foreign landscape. Or they exist in some kind of illusory past, like Spider Kelly, a Princeton boxing coach who can vouch for Cohn's pugilistic ability, or else, like the Braddocks, loudmouthed and vulgar. There is a singular exception, Barnes's friend Bill Gorton, who is really a kind of alter ego of Barnes.

One gets the feel of expatriate life in the twenties. The postwar situation had condemned the characters to an eternal doom. They wander about aimlessly, disillusioned by love, by life itself. Barnes's war wound symbolizes his own impotence as well as their inability to act, to move in any specific and definitive direction with assuredness. Barnes's wound is physical, as is Romero's when Cohn fights him over Brett, but Cohn's wound is deeper and more significant, for he realizes that this battle, his personal showdown, cannot really resolve deep human conflict.

Hemingway's Europeans and Euro Americans seek, like F. Scott Fitzgerald's, alternatives to confrontation with danger and death. They drink and whore, not only for the supposedly macho qualities frequently mentioned by critics but also because they try to find quick and easy remedies to compensate for their feeling of abandonment. Dancing and music are part of their escape, although these are also obviously meant to describe their activities at a realistic level. But Hemingway, as an American writer, Hemingway brings his prejudices with him: Homosexuality disgusts Brett, as do the Black musicians who embarrass her with ribald songs.

An alternative to this despair is achieved in two remarkable places. First, when Gorton and Barnes go fishing together in Basque country and, second, in the fiesta at Pamplona. In both instances, the action takes place outside time. In these two "moments," Hemingway allows for reflection on the nature of the European world in which his characters find themselves. Mark Spilka notes this about the fishing trip: "As Barnes and Gorton approach 'the good place,' each item in the landscape is singled out and given its own importance." Later, the techniques of fishing are treated with the same reverence for detail: "These men have left the wasteland for the green plains of health, they have traveled miles, by train and on foot, to reach a particular trout stream. The fishing there is good, the talk free and easy."[6] At these times, Hemingway's American characters can escape from even the Englishness with which they are forced to speak, write, and clothe their thoughts.

Language becomes a barrier, because it is Anglo-Saxon and must be stripped down to bare essentials. Witness the conversation between Frederic Henry and Count Greffi in *A Farewell to Arms* (1929):

> "Oh but when you are tired it will be easier for you to talk English."
>
> "American."
>
> "Yes, American. You will please talk American. *It is a delightful language.*"[7]

One could view this, were it not for Hemingway's total interest in the non-American world, as a bid for some kind of American linguistic monopoly. Actually, it is an attempt to move away from Anglo American prejudices and to reclaim language as something indigenous to America. Instances abound in *The Sun Also Rises*, as careful attention is paid to the fact that New York novelist Robert Prentiss had "some sort of an English accent." Jake expresses both his anti-English and anti-aristocratic feelings when he affirms: "When you were with the English, you got into the habit of using English expressions in your thinking. The English spoken language—the upper classes, anyway—must have fewer words than the Eskimo."[8]

In this way, Hemingway parts company with Emerson, Hawthorne, Whittier, and others, for they wrote, as he saw it in *Green Hills of Africa*, "like exiled English colonials from an English of which they were never a part to a newer England that they were making."[9] One does not have to agree with the examples or even with the result in Hemingway's work—after all, Catherine Barkley (Henry's lover) and Lady Brett (Jake's admirer) are all English. But one realizes that Hemingway was attempting to rid American literature of its Anglo concerns and sounds, of what has been termed "the polite occasional, literary, pictur-esque, Europe-imitating school-room poets."[10]

Ironically, however, Hemingway wrote both within and against the background of English and European conflict. In his early stories, there is an attitude of sparseness and emotional distancing, later developed in *The Sun Also Rises* and *A Farewell to Arms*. Later on, he would return to Spain, Africa, Cuba, and Paris. In large measure, after stories like "Up in Michigan," the settings are nearly always outside the United States. Hemingway says he wrote this story in Paris in 1921,[11] and although there are signs of the later Hemingway in the use of American English, in Jim's love for "the taste and the feel of whiskey," yet he seems inhibited by the setting—reducing the lovemaking between Liz and Jim to something that reads almost like rape, were it not for its crude comicality:

> "Don't, Jim," Liz said. Jim slid the hand further up.
>
> "You mustn't, Jim. You mustn't." Neither Jim nor Jim's big hand paid any attention to her.
>
> The boards were hard. Jim had her dress up and was trying to do something to her. She was frightened but she wanted it. She had to have it but it frightened her.
>
> "You mustn't do it, Jim. You mustn't."
>
> "I got to. I'm going to. You know we got to."
>
> "No we haven't, Jim. We ain't got to. Oh, it isn't right. Oh, it's so big and it hurts so. You can't. Oh, Jim. Jim. Oh."[12]

If then this is an attempt, albeit early, at locating action at home, at "Americanizing" fiction, it fails dismally.

Even though Hemingway dismissed Anglo-Saxon mannerisms, as he points out in *A Moveable Feast* (1964), Paris did free him as a novelist, for his job as foreign correspondent to the *Toronto Star* gave him access to important political leaders in Europe such as Lloyd George, Georges Clemenceau, and even Benito Mussolini. Sherwood Anderson helped bring about Hemingway's introduction to Gertrude Stein, through whom he would meet many other expatriates of the period. But he was not pinned down to a single spot, and with typical American aplomb, noted particularly in Ezra Pound, he regarded all Europe as his cultural birthright. In 1937, for instance, he went to Spain to cover the Civil War for the North American Newspaper Alliance. Even when, in 1928, he moved to the United States, he established himself at the furthest point south, at Key West, moving in 1940 to Cuba, where to this day he continues to be revered. After his "liberation" of the Hotel Ritz and another marriage, he lived first in Venice and still later in Cuba. The beautiful, sensitively wrought *The Old Man and the Sea* (1952) grew out of the Cuban experience. Even now, the official Cuban newspaper *Granma* never forgets to publicize the birthday and reminiscences of the man on whom Santiago was based. It is not without irony that when, as an older man, Hemingway did return to the United States, he committed suicide.

In *The Old Man and the Sea*, Hemingway achieves a novel of epic proportions, because he had managed to distance himself from American parochialism. Here, the American novel truly deals in global proportions by rendering a parable of the constant struggle of humans to overcome environment. Santiago and the boy Manolin represent not only age and youth, but the mature and growing vitality of the non-European world. As the aged Santiago fights and pits his human skill against the marlin, he is a long way removed from earlier Hemingway heroes in the European environment. For the reader instinctively knows that Santiago cannot win and that his triumph will not be in material gain, but in spiritual conquest. So although, at the end, he sails home to port with a skeleton, the young boy marvels at his accomplishment. True enough, the epic posture derives from classical European tradition, but the story Hemingway recounts is little to do with Europe or America unless these are the forces against which Santiago battles.

In typical Hemingway fashion, the oppressor is feminized very much like a country, but within the context of Latin American machismo:

> He always thought of the sea as la mar which is what people call her in Spanish when they love her. Sometimes those who love her say bad things of her but they are always said as though she were a woman. Some of the younger fishermen, those who used buoys as floats for their lines and had motorboats, bought when the shark liners had brought much money spoke of her as el mar which is masculine. They spoke of her as a contestant or a place or even an enemy. But the Old Man always thought of her as feminine and as something that gave or withheld great favors, and if she did wild or wicked things it was because she could not help them. The moon affects her as it does a woman.[13]

One could accuse Hemingway here of being the "village-explainer," which Gertrude Stein pronounced was fine, if one were a village. Or one could see a bristling sexism in Santiago's thoughts. But, at the deeper level, beyond the spoken words, is a great empathy; victim and victor recognize a common humanity. As Clinton Burhans suggests:

> Santiago comes to feel his deepest love for the creature that he himself hunts and kills, the great fish which he must catch not alone for physical need but even more for his pride and his profession. The great marlin is unlike the other fish which the old man catches; he is a spiritual more than a physical necessity. . . . and during his long ordeal, Santiago comes to pity the marlin and then to respect and love him.[14]

Santiago's task is to prove once and for all that he can accomplish something, however intangible. This is the heroization of the New World victim.

One treads warily, or ought to, especially given Hemingway's comment that he did not want to discuss symbols in his novels, as "it deprives the explainers of work."[15] But in this epic, as it cannot be read as a short story or novel in the traditional sense, some room must be made for allegorical interpretation.

Hemingway's success in dealing with the worldview of others, as found in *The Old Man and the Sea,* was anticipated earlier in "The Snows of Kilimanjaro," first published in *Esquire* in August 1936. As Harry dies, he recalls a life that seems to have been a combination of ineptitude and sloth. Like Santiago, Harry dreams, and the context of the dream is important. For here, in the third decade of the twentieth century, Harry and Hemingway accorded to the Gikuyu people of Africa a degree of understanding not usually found in Eurocentric thought, plus a recognition of Mount Kilimanjaro as the House of God, where Harry dreams the plane will take him.

Not until 1959 does Canadian-born Saul Bellow attempt anything even vaguely similar. In *Henderson the Rain King,* Bellow's Gene Henderson opts out of his materialistic millionaire world, in urgent answer to a greater plea—"I want, I want"—but even here Bellow cannot resist giving to his questing hero the Crusoe-like quality of conqueror. As soon as Henderson arrives in Africa, he becomes a heroic figure, rising to the stature of tribal chief and rainmaker. His role has been termed "escapist machismo" by Charles Molesworth.[16] Hemingway is more subtle and sincere, for Harry conquers no one, not even himself. Santiago does not dominate either the ocean or the fish, for this would simply reverse the agent, not the role, of victim and victimizer. In a way, this puts the lie to "nada," to the supposed insignificance of humans and events, and to the religious vacuum of Hemingway's work. In *The Old Man and the Sea,* Hemingway finalizes the ritual of guilt and redemption, which had been left virtually unresolved in his major novels.

By shifting his experience away from Europe, Hemingway thus constructs a novel for the Americas—not just an American novel. Because he is a realist and the story is set in Catholic Cuba, the Christian instances are multifold. For instance, names demarcate the first indication of this direction: Santiago is St. James, the fisherman; Manolin is, more likely than not, St. Manuel. Instances of other Christian references abound in the supper scene between Martin (St. Martin de Porras from Peru?), in Christ/Santiago as fisherman; in the significance of the three days of sailing; in the bird (albatross or Christian dove or both?); in Santiago's crippled hands, reminding one of crucifixion, as well as the references to pain, fasting, and calling the fish his "brother." For Santiago, the ultimate realization is in his visions, free of suffering—where he dreams of Africa, of the African lion, and his place in the world. The work moves beyond Christian sermonizing to involve an alien humanity that has seldom been described so vividly.

Names are also given significance, because only in their Christian context could Western readers glean their other-worldliness. But the core of the story has, among other things, to do with the way that the old bequeath knowledge to the young. The Old Man enacts some of the deeds of a Christ-figure because Hemingway is conscious of his readers' penchant for instant recognition. Therefore, one ought not to miss the part where Santiago is resting, but thinks of himself as if his hands had gone through nails and wood.

In *The Hero with a Thousand Faces*, Joseph Campbell was not necessarily referring to Hemingway when he affirmed that the hero monomyth was made up of three essentials— departure, initiation, and return. But, for Hemingway, these elements of a global myth exist, not in the early Michigan stories nor in the novels set in Europe, but quite definitely in *The Old Man and the Sea*. Like Santiago, Campbell's mythical heroes *depart* on an adventure that approximates life itself, coming to terms with the forces of the world and the heroes' basic aloneness; *initiation* takes the form of the trials they endure, which take them backward and forward in time and space, so that they comprehend infinity itself, recognizing their own affinity with the cosmos; *return* occurs, for Santiago, not with a physical "boon" such as Campbell describes but with a new understanding of his place in the cosmos. The novel does not end with an interrogative, as in *The Sun Also Rises*, or with death as in *For Whom the Bell Tolls* (1940) or *A Farewell to Arms*. Instead Hemingway's *The Old Man and the Sea* includes the world, because both writer and protagonist are free of the need for Eurocentric approbation. Triumphant then is the overall global archetype of human birth, initiation, and old age paralleling, as Santiago well knows, dawn, midday, and sunset—what Leo Gurko has termed, "the culmination of Hemingway's long search for disengagement from the social world and total entry into the natural."[17] For "social world" I prefer to read "European," and for "nature" I prefer to substitute "pan-American reality." In his quest, Santiago anticipates the *magico-realismo* of modern Latin American writers, for he returns to the "good town" for the plaudits of a human society he recognizes, needs, and knows.

At the core of Hemingway's work is the issue of quest, personal and national. Surely this is also the major meaning of Eliot's *The Waste Land* and Pound's *Cantos*. The search is for basic human validation of worth. Expressed in a European metaphor, these works seek to suggest that such an effort is quite in keeping with America's political ascendancy. Just as Woodrow Wilson would project his own vision of a League of Nations or Franklin Delano Roosevelt his version of a Europe, unified and peaceful, so these writers try to dissect and reassemble Europe. They attempt to be creators of Europe but try not to be bound in by this; they seek to placate Europe but hope not to be conscribed by this.

Eliot is the major purveyor of the European canon and relater of its image— both securely located within the European frame of cultural reference. He tells us in "Tradition and the Individual Talent" that the "historical sense" compels an artist "to write not merely with his own generation in his bones, but with a feeling that the whole of the literature of Europe from Homer and within it the whole of the literature of his own country has a simultaneous existence and composes a simultaneous order."[18] In *The Waste Land* (1922), the entire movement of the poem is couched in the overall allegory of a search for water. French and German, Cockney idiomatic patter, references to Hindu scripture, are all meant to promote the poem as "universal," much as Pound had used the Chinese idiogram, along with Italian and Provencal references, to accomplish much the same. In addition, *The Waste Land* (once it was not only Eliot trying out his dexterity as in "He Do the Police in Different Voices") became a kind of sermon that used past European culture to demolish contemporary European lifestyle.[19]

Images of water and aridity are used as ways of contrasting spiritual life and physical death, in the larger sense, and ordinary human life and death, in general. At the beginning of the poem, images are used with their immediate meanings, but as the poem expands they incorporate opposites and contradictions. Water, with its association of cleansing and the ritual of baptism, is contrasted with aridity, with its suggestion of foulness and the symbol of the damned. The drama of various *personae* moves from the barrenness of Part I, "The Burial of the Dead," to the suggestion of fertility and growth in Part V, "What the Thunder Said."

At the beginning of the poem, the bleak European landscape represents an environment in which the protagonist does not feel at ease. The life he lives is one opposed to the natural cycle. Therefore, not unnaturally, he is surprised by summer, as well as rain. At one level, the situation being described is that of a culturally divided individual, ill at ease with the seasons and unable to function as a full and complete person.

Religious images enforce this as a predicament of all modern human beings. The prophet Isaiah had foretold that the coming of Christ would be like a river in a dry place. However, here there are only images of ruin and little hope for the purifying water. People exist in a limbo state in which they are said to be neither alive nor dead; hence, they know fear of death, indeed, of the possibility of the reduction to dust, but are clearly unable to alter their situation and opt for a better spiritual state. Ancient European vegetation myths are intentionally used in the poem, particularly in the first part, to reinforce the theme of aridity. The hope for the renewal of life in spring is not realized. The world will not come to life again, because Europeans are not in tune with the life cycle, have neglected to observe the appropriate rituals, Christian or pagan, and have opted instead for a vulgar and popularized interpretation of the Tarot cards and false attachment to the mechanical. Eliot writes that the crowds going to work all seemed dead, initially referring to English clerks on their way to work in the City but harking back to Danteesque implications of death.

In "A Game of Chess," one notes the manner in which Europeans all share a common predicament. Upper, middle, and lower classes are all part of the same emptiness—the manner in which the life flow has been locked off. In the Shakespearean Cleopatra-like figure, there is reference to rape; in the lower-class bar scene (appropriately edited by Eliot's English wife), there is an allusion to abortion; in the dialogue between the middle-class *personae*, there is reference to pearls that used to be eyes, a refrain that will reoccur in the next section of the poem.

Water is now not merely a cleansing agent, but also suggests destruction. Part IV, "Death by Water," dramatizes a dualism that is most likely also Eliot's. He writes about Phlebas the Phoenician and how the undersea currents pickled him. A nice point is made here. The image of water not only suggests Christian hope, but also indicates pagan despair. Equally, images apparently relating to destruction are also inverted. As noted in Part I, there is a need for water, but there is also a desire to escape the fire-like heat. Quite intentionally, Eliot chooses the Buddha's "Fire Sermon" to show the manner in which fire can be both destroyer and savior. Fire, not water, is needed to destroy the heat and passion of the immoral "nymphs" and their depraved companions.

Fire is also necessary to consume the sensuous passion of Sweeney, who lusts after both Mrs. Porter and her daughter. Fire is needed to give meaning to the empty sexual encounter between the typist and the realtor (Eliot prefers the English term "houseagent"). Note that water is no purifier at this point and that the flirtatious encounters between the women and the men occur on the *Thames*. There is reference to "soda water" in the allusion to Sweeney and Mrs. Porter, and Queen Elizabeth and the Earl of Leicester are "boating" as they indulge in their fruitless flirtation. The anglicisms are, of course, quite intentional, but they also show us an American poet striving to have an authentic English voice.

In "The Fire Sermon," water is the accompaniment of sexual immorality related in the crassest of terms. For as Eliot himself may have thought when he went to the seaside town of Margate to recuperate from a nervous breakdown, he was unable to establish the most basic relationships in his own life. "Margate Sands," where connection cannot take place, seems to suggest both the sea and the desert, thus preparing the reader for the moral predicament of St. Augustine, burning with lust as if on fire.

In Part V, rain seems to fall. At first, there is only the hope that it might. The paradox of water and aridity again occur in lines and images that continue to exploit their many meanings. Here the "rock" could be the Christian church, as well as aridity. Other related images have possible double meanings. As the cock crows before rain falls, the reference could anticipate spiritual renewal or connote the betrayal of Christ by St. Peter, the "rock" on whom the Christian church was supposedly founded.

As Europeans cannot be sure of redemption, the poem ends on a note that reinforces the duality of the images of water and aridity. The words of the thunder become Sanskrit interrogatives that recall previous *personae* of the poem and their meaningless lives. So "Datta" (give) might ironically conjure up the English typist; "Dayadhvam" (sympathize) could remind the reader of the empty dialogue in "A Game of Chess"; and "Damyata" (control) perhaps bitterly suggests the flirtation of Elizabeth and Leicester. For even though the thunder indicates the possibility of rain and renewal, the "broken images" return as reminders that Europeans are still at odds with their world.

The Fisher King demonstrates the bitter predicament of humans and the manner in which water and aridity each suggest varying combinations of hope and despair. At the end Eliot describes a predicament that is both personalized and personal. There is hope and despair, salvation and damnation. Christ had called upon his disciples to be "fishers of men," but "the arid plain" that is the backdrop of the scene is the contradiction in the human psyche that prefers barrenness to fertility, abortion to birth, shadow to light, or even death to life. The reader is back in the grim, haunting world of "The Burial of the Dead." Revival is possible but scarcely probable.

The images of aridity and water are intentionally interchangeable. *The Waste Land* relates the problems of Europeans who grope toward solutions but can be sure of nothing. Eliot merges these images as indications of modern European confusion. Ancient assurances from the European past, whether religious or mythical, are neither understood nor credible. Instead, there is only the narrow borderline that people inhabit—one that is neither shadow nor substance, neither water nor aridity.

Of course, as critics have demonstrated ad nauseam, there are multiple meanings to *The Waste Land*. For my purpose here, I merely wished to view it as an exercise in the tactics of crossover appeal. At center is a body of European literature, the Bible, and the quest. Throughout the poem, the religious theme of Christian redemption is reinforced although, in keeping with "The Movement," there are also multicultural references, Pound-like, to eastern philosophy and culture. The recipe of *The Waste Land* could not fail, for it served as an inter-Atlanticist device that sought to link European cultures across continents.

Not unnaturally, Eliot returned to the self-same formula time and time again. In "The Hollow Men," "Journey of the Magi," "Gerontion," "A Song for Simeon," and so on, at center is the recognizable and mutually acceptable Bible. Liturgical phrases from the Anglican High Church find a place in "The Hollow Men." Echoes of St. Luke may be easily located in "Journey of the Magi" and "A Song for Simeon." Along with this, is the Jew-bashing (very European and Euro American, very much meant, and very reflective of the time) found in *The Waste Land*, "Gerontion," and other poems. Indeed, the most blatant example occurs in an earlier piece, "Burbank with a Baedeker; Bleistein with a Cigar" where positioned beneath a pile (perhaps suggesting garbage) "The jew [*sic*] is underneath the lot." As noted, these sentiments were not peculiar to Eliot alone but were very much in keeping with Eurocentric belief at that time.

Earlier poems by Eliot had attempted to describe the American experience, but not very successfully. Poems such as "Preludes," "Rhapsody on a Windy Night," and "The *Boston Evening Transcript*" do not work, because Eliot's Euro American audience is parochial and fail to see themselves. His poetry could have gone in the direction of "Mr. Apollinax," whose "laughter tinkled among the teacups" when he visited the United States. In other words, most of his work could have been in the amusing, witty genre of *Old Possum's Book of Practical Cats* (1939). Indeed it could even be argued that earlier versions of *The Waste Land* demonstrate interesting aspects to this comicality. But Eliot seemed intentionally to pull back from laughter—perhaps because of the sad events of his first marriage. In any case, he was much more concerned with something that no other American writer had ever attempted—the exploration of English culture from within. In a way, this was no mean task; but it was, put differently, a type of deliberately cultivated parochial ethnocentrism that would later have him make the proud assertion that he was Anglican, English, and Royalist. Surely this declaration placed him most outside the ranks of American poets; he had grown English plumes.

Four Quartets (1943) takes the spoken sermon of *The Waste Land* into inward meditation. With the exception of "The Dry Salvages," the other three poems all center round English place names: "Burnt Norton" is an English country house, "East Coker" an English village, whence Eliot traces his ancestry, and "Little Gidding" was the center of an Anglican community in the seventeenth century. Departing from these intentionally local British settings, *Four Quartets* concern themselves mainly with time (past, present, and future) and place (ideal or actual). Again, Eliot is establishing a careful medium for transcultural interaction.

"East Coker" permits us to understand a little of how the American-turned-Englishman sees himself as a person in the middle, attempting to understand and fashion a new diction. At a personal level, the "words" are the newly acquired English of England, the new experiences of living on the other side of the Atlantic. There can be no turning back, Eliot says, for "home" (the United States) is the point of departure. The journey (and such it is once more) demarcates a return to the initial point of departure. Thus Europe becomes "home" too, for this Eliot would argue is where culture begins and ends.

Eliot does not prescribe for others or lay down mandates (at least not in his poetry), but he does seem to suggest that artistic fulfillment for a Eurocentric American writer must lie in a final return back to the point of origin in the past traditions of Europe itself. Such a retreat to cultural origins means that "originality" is neither feasible nor possible. In his introduction to Pound's *Selected Poems*, Eliot categorically affirms:

Poets may be divided into those who develop technique, those who imitate technique, and those who invent technique. When I say "invent," I should use inverted commas, for invention would be irreproachable if it were possible. *Invention is wrong only because it is impossible. . . . True originality is merely development.*[20]

Thus the American artist enters the European cultural context in a tabula rasa state. Eliot took this quite literally, if one is to judge by the number of anglicisms in his writing, his very British manner and dress, and his "development" of the "technique" of relying on European, but mainly English, writers—varying from Shakespeare to the Metaphysicals, from Dryden to the Romantics. Again (the point is made in "Tradition and the Individual Talent"), all that a new poet can do is to respond to the order that is already laid down, what today we would refer to as the "canon." Stanley Sultan asserts that:

> In treating influence as a benign historical relation of the past (Tradition) with the evolving future (Development), he [Eliot] was applying what seems to me one of his fundamental beliefs: that the instrumental generational process in literary history is a dialect of reciprocal interactions between the old and the truly new.[21]

One can only partly agree with Sultan to make any sense of Eliot's poetic methodology, but both "tradition" and "development" are situated (for both Eliot and Pound) in European cultural norms. Pound had stated his own view in equally categorical terms when he said that "many dead men are our grandchildren's contemporaries."[22]

These are some of the theories Eliot applies to his poetry. For instance, on the physical level, "Little Gidding" suggests that patriotism itself (to America?) may be a hindrance, for it merely emphasizes a desire for the familiar and the known. Memory, both for historical events and for individual attachments, must not be blind patriotic compliance, or what Eliot terms "servitude"; instead, the true purpose of individual accounting and group chronicling should involve liberation from any proscribed future arising out of a past over which one had little control. Hence, from the very outset, the journey involves a great deal of abandonment. This is not to be lightly undertaken. Eliot must have understood the painstaking nature of being without a legacy and of having to construct a heritage—after all, it is the quandary of any colonial. But the suggestion is that belonging to a specific country, at a given moment in time, does seem to carry with it too much of an adherence to particular norms and values. Casting the familiar aside recognizes that it is mandatory to discard birthright, the usual cultural baggage with which one is born, leading to the final realization that a people without a past seem to have slight chance of redemption. Did not Henry James also express a similar viewpoint?

The journey in "Little Gidding" operates on a number of other levels, which are made apparent as the poem progresses. The spiritual, or the search for a very

Western and Christian God, is at the core. There is the additional search for the "tribe," not only to write and improve its language but also to seek for new universal group norms and values. This is why no assured "I" exists in the poem. Instead, from Part I the reader is made the central focus of exploration. The two long passages, both beginning "If *you* came this way" (emphasis added), bear close examination.

These passages, almost prosaic, and containing long flowing lines without indentations, suggest that they should be read almost like prose tracts. In the first one, there seems to be a greater concern with place, whereas in the second there seems a greater interest in space. Together they identify the nature of the journey, at both the physical and spiritual levels, not for the individual, but for the nation. The word "if" is very important, as it suggests a condition that might or might not occur. However, the earlier and later parts of the poem have prepared the reader for the inevitability of the passage, for it is a *rite de passage* of a major social group, not merely an individual. Europe becomes the place where America is initiated into adulthood.

"The" route in the earlier part gives way to "any" route in the later part, and sensuous gratification merges into the absence of all sense in the second segment. Thus, from the very beginning of the journey, there are indications of other possibilities beyond mere sensual apprehension. This is why the specifics in the first part are replaced by mere hints in the second. For example, concrete references to the road, the pig-sty, and the tombstone are replaced by prayer and the awakening of the group. "You" (now with its clear suggestion of plurality), might have been easily satisfied with its own specific geography of place and the exact chronology of time. However, the concept of a larger space brings back the realization that the synthesization of timelessness and place-lessness occurs at a specific period and area in Europe, quite naturally for Eliot in England. Although Eliot is not so crude as to fashion a mere paean for England, and England is not symbiotic with absolute Time, yet it is through England's present and past, that universal time and place may be fully compre-hended. Of course, the British were flattered, although I do recall that at least one native-born English poet, William Empson, had always felt that Eliot made him a trifle uncomfortable in his constant need to spiritualize the British countryside.[23]

A number of issues come together at this point in the poem. Time and space, timelessness and the particularity of time, the physical quality of place and the insubstantial nature of space, all blend to connect the end with the beginning, life with death, history with myth, and any wrongful national identification with correct European awareness. One cannot seek to know Truth, Eliot asserts, unless the specifics of individual desires and needs are submerged beneath larger national wishes and expectations, thus leading toward a more profound understanding of what Eliot terms "purpose." Such a need to identify with the entire universe must expand beyond the immediacy of sensual experience, however poignant. Such an understanding cannot be within the province of any one "generation" (with the intentional double meaning of procreation and people living at the same time). The poem states, quite explicitly, that the cyclical quest involves both the individual and the social group in a new understanding of the natural cycle.

Questions asked quite early in the poem seem, at the end, to offer no conclusions, for the search for answers must be like the eternal succession of lives, followed nirvana-like by death and life again. At this point, "Little Gidding" is concerned with the search for order in the universe, involving spiritual goodness, physical perfection, love, and understanding, as well as excellence in literary craftsmanship. Also the protagonist seeks the knowledge of how life, in the Hindu sense previously stated in *The Waste Land*, becomes a part of this natural cycle.

The elements all pass to nothingness. Part of initial recognition itself is that everything is transitory. The death of air is the end of human life and human effort as well as the end of nature. The end of earth is the way that flood and drought mock at the insignificant efforts of humans to feed themselves. The demise of water and fire seemingly symbolizes a total destruction of all life. Fire and water, as observed in *The Waste Land*, are images that suggest both cleansing and destruction; likewise, at this point in "Little Gidding," they provide a hint of possible redemption.

Classical elements of the search—departure, initiation, and return— are elements all found in "Little Gidding." Pointers to the departure occur in the sections, already cited, beginning "If you came this way. . . . " The initiation is found in the visionary section in Part II, which relates in almost biblical terms a meeting with the Dante-like, very European, figure/ artist. The return occurs at the end, where the poet/protagonist has gained new knowledge. The journey is also cyclical, for at the end the seeker goes back to the place of origin. He knows of his origins now in a new and different way, not because the place has changed but because he has undergone profound alteration as a person and as a representative of his Euroethnic group. He sets out yet again on further explorations.

Encountering the Dantean "dead master" is a type of extraterrestrial experience, lending added significance to the journey, both to its spiritual nature (as it is enacted *in space and out of time*), and to its physical attribute (as it is enacted *in place and within time*). The encounter described at this point of the poem relates the nature of the artist's quest in universal, but very European, terms. The other person, the heritage, is protean, both singular and plural, recognizable and strange. This represents the multilayered quality of European American inheritance. The Dante/Virgil encounter thus takes on a personal significance here, in that Dante had consciously chosen to write in the language of Italy but nevertheless owed a tremendous debt to the long-dead Latin poet. Eliot is himself writing in a new language, actually a hybrid, strengthened by its association with American English, although Eliot himself would have strongly denied any such relationship.

Later lines point out that any type of self-encounter, perhaps with a former national group psyche, lay in returning to European origins, home, the point from which the journey started. The culturally divided protagonist has to assume a double part, being both himself and someone else. By beginning from within and moving outward, at both a personal and a national level, the artist attempts to achieve some understanding of the nature of the world and the meaning of his place in the universe. Eliot suggests that such a journey in taking the seeker back to his European past provides an attempt at understanding himself. But this new self is not the recognizable, familiar self; there is mutual recognition, yet the two selves are both friend and stranger. The encounter between two cultures can be quite confounding, as Eliot himself knew too well.

Therefore, revolutionary change is essential for the individual/artist to achieve success on the journey. Yet it is not enough merely to borrow from the past, since there must need be revolution of the inner self if the writer hopes to bring about outer change. In addition, the journey back to origins, to the beginning of culture, a real self, the world and its universal vision, means that there must be a realization that the past must provide not mere solace, but the desire for change. For the only assurances of old age, of the demise of an old tradition, are "expiring sense," of both intelligence and sensuality; impotence, both individual sexual inability and group physical inability; and, pointless and useless reiteration of what little had previously been accomplished.

These harsh images, which reiterate the journey as returning to the place of departure, abjectly concern themselves with the hapless condition of an alien in some vain quest to know and understand a host culture. The choice for the Euro American artist and individual is either to be "consumed" by fire (the inevitability of cultural destruction) or "redeemed" by fire (the possibility of spiritual preservation). In any case, both European atavism and American nativeness seem lost.

Logically, Part V returns us to the beginning of the poem. In Part I the fire imagery had been externalized, seemingly unrelated to an internal predicament. Images are scattered, almost in haphazard fashion. References to sun and ice, fire and growth, and "pentecostal fire" are startling and disturbing. As the reader, at this early stage of "Little Gidding," lacks the context of the development of these images, he must wait for their expansion and the fruition of argument at a later stage in order to understand how the poem turns itself around in on itself to achieve meaning.

After the spiritual and physical experiences, individual and national quests, concerns with local and national place and space, everyday and universal time, the poem therefore reaches back on itself. The ideal is never found, for it has to remain ever mysterious and elusive. At least there exist some definite signposts. No longer is it the middle of an unidentifiable season but, instead afternoon in winter. No longer is it "never" and "always," coexisting at the same time but, instead, *"now and England"* (emphasis added). This is a seemingly satisfactory state, but one should not surrender to delusion and thus refuse to undertake further expeditions. In the imagery of Columbus's "discovery" of America, Eliot continues the parallel between inner and external exploration. So, perhaps for the very reason that we truly understand for the very first time, the challenge for further exploration remains. Eternity may be glimpsed by mortals in sudden flashes, which ironically emulate the play of children as they dodge between bushes.

Although final conclusions are not easily attained, yet the knowledge exists that the lives of people and nations are made up of a series of repetitive beginnings. "Little Gidding" stresses the need for this search to commence over and over again, with the seeker content only in the knowledge that each cycle will bring about a different and deeper revelation. Thus, Eliot provides the reader with a profound manifestation of the nature of cyclical movement, not from beginning to end but from beginning to beginning. The form and meaning of the poem crystallize this as both the predicament and the motivation of the Eurocentric writer in exile as he seeks to find origins that are, indeed must be, forever elusive and as he comes to terms with a new sense of place and his own significance within the European frame of reference.

Both *The Waste Land* and "Little Gidding" fall seriously short of what are truly universal meanings. Despite the global preoccupations with issues that do concern humans everywhere, despite the allusions to non-European references, they both narrow themselves to a single issue—concern with Europe and its predicaments in the 1920s, yet the possibility to bring about redemption of all humans and particularly (if the narrator's voice may be personalized as I have attempted to do) to move American letters toward a new possibility, one that takes all Europe as the province of its heritage. Because of this, it may speak for Europe because it has now refined and redefined itself. It takes, on the one hand, an enormous dose of inferiority to agree to surrender a national birthright, but an equally huge injection of superiority, on the other, to be able to advocate, as no insular European could, a panacea that addressed itself to the entire continent of Europe. The brashness was ill-directed, even illogical, but the gravest criticism of Eurocentrism must reside here, in the manner in which these works selfishly and disproportionally discarded the needs and aspirations of large segments of the nation at home. In the final analysis, this is what makes Eurocentrism socially unjust and morally wrong.

NOTES

1. Henry Adams, *History of the United States of America during the Administration of Jefferson and Madison* (Chicago: University of Chicago Press, 1967), 398.

2. Walt Whitman, *Leaves of Grass*, ed. with an introduction by Jerome Loving (New York: Oxford University Press, 1990), 117.

3. Ibid., 119.

4. Ibid., 431.

5. Ibid., 438.

6. Mark Spilka, "The Death of Love in *The Sun Also Rises*," in *Hemingway and His Critics*, ed. Carlos Baker (New York: Hill and Wang, 1961), 85.

7. Ernest Hemingway, *A Farewell to Arms* (New York: Scribner's, 1929), 269. Emphasis added.

8. Ernest Hemingway, *The Sun Also Rises* (New York: Scribner's, 1926), 149.

9. Ernest Hemingway, *Green Hills of Africa* (New York: Scribner's, 1935), 21.

10. Daniel Fuchs, "Ernest Hemingway: Literary Critic," *Ernest Hemingway: A Collection of Criticism*, ed. Arthur Waldhorn, (New York: McGraw-Hill, 1973), 101.

11. Ernest Hemingway, *The Short Stories of Ernest Hemingway* (New York: Scribner's, 1938), Preface, v.

12. Ibid., 84.

13. Ernest Hemingway, *The Old Man and the Sea* (New York: Scribner's, 1952), 27.

14. Clinton Burhans, "*The Old Man and the Sea*: Hemingway's Tragic Vision of Man," in *Hemingway and His Critics*, ed. Carlos Baker (New York: Hill and Wang, 1961), 261.

15. George Plimpton, "An Interview with Ernest Hemingway." *Paris Review* no. 18 (Spring 1958): 60–89. Reprinted in *Writers at Work*. [The "Paris Review" Interviews, second series], (New York: Viking, 1963), 76.

16. Charles Molesworth, "Culture Power and Society," in *Columbia Literary History of the United States*, ed. Emory Elliott et al. (New York: Columbia University Press, 1988), 1030.

17. Leo Gurko, "The Old Man and the Sea," *College English* 17 (October 1955): 15.

18. T. S. Eliot, *Selected Prose* (Harmondsworth, Middlesex: Penguin, 1953), 23.

19. See the edition of the early manuscript, which includes Eliot's revisions, Pound's corrections, and Eliot's first wife's assistance with parts, Valerie Eliot, ed., *T. S. Eliot: The Waste Land* (London: Faber and Faber, 1971).

20. T. S. Eliot's Introduction to Ezra Pound's *Selected Poems* (London: Faber and Faber, 1948) 9. Emphasis added.

21. Stanley Sultan, *Eliot, Joyce and Company* (New York: Oxford University Press, 1987), 29.

22. Ezra Pound, *The Spirit of Romance* (1910), cited by Lillian Feder, "The Literary Scene," in *The New Pelican Guide to English Literature*, 9 vols., ed. Boris Ford (London: Penguin Books, 1988), 9:316.

23. William Empson has a witty, wicked, and yet fascinating piece in *Using Biography* (London: Chatto and Windus, 1984), 189–200.

Bibliography

Abbott, Edith. *Historical Aspects of the Immigration Problem.* Chicago: University of Chicago Press, 1926.

———. *Immigration: Select Documents and Case Records.* Chicago: University of Chicago Press, 1924.

Abrahams, Roger. *Deep Down in the Jungle: Negro Narrative Folklore from the Streets of Philadelphia.* Hatboro, Pa.: Folklore Associates, 1964.

Abrams, M. H. *Natural Supernaturalism: Tradition and Revolution in Romantic Literature.* New York: Norton, 1973.

Adams, Henry. *History of the United States of America during the Administration of Jefferson and Madison.* Chicago: University of Chicago Press, 1967.

Adams, John Quincy. *Argument of John Quincy Adams before the Supreme Court of the United States in the Case of the United States, Appellants, vs. Cinque and Other Africans Captured in the Schooner Amistad.* New York: S. W. Benedict, 1841.

Adler, Mortimer. *Great Ideas from the Great Books.* New York: Washington Square Press, 1961.

Ajayi, J. F., and Ian Espie. *A Thousand Years of West African History.* Ibadan, Nigeria: Ibadan University Press, 1965.

Akenhurst, Michael. *A Modern Introduction to International Law.* London: Allen and Unwin, 1970, 1987.

Albert, Judith. *The Sixties Papers.* New York: Praeger, 1984.

Alcott, Louisa May. "Transcendental Wild Oats." In *Bronson Alcott's Fruitlands,* by Clara Endicott Sears, 146–174. Boston: Houghton Mifflin, 1915.

Alger, Horatio. *Ragged Dick and Mark the Match Boy.* [1868]. New York: Collier Books, 1962.

Anastaplo, George. *The Constitution of 1787.* Baltimore and London: Johns Hopkins University Press, 1989.

Anderson, Margaret C. *My Thirty Years War: An Autobiography.* New York: Covici, Friede Publications, 1930.

Arnold, Matthew. "Civilization in the United States." In *Matthew Arnold,* edited by Miriam Alcott and Robert H. Super, 489–504. Oxford: Oxford University Press, 1986.

Arvin, Newton, ed. *The Heart of Hawthorne's Journals*. New York: Barnes and Noble, 1967.

Asante, Molefi. *The Afrocentric Idea*. Philadelphia: University of Pennsylvania Press, 1981.

Backman, Melvin. "Hemingway: The Matador and the Crucified." In *Hemingway and His Critics*, edited by Carlos Baker, 245–258. New York: Hill and Wang, 1961.

Bailey, Thomas Pierce. *Race Orthodoxy in the South and Other Aspects of the Race Question*. New York: Neale Publishing, 1914.

Bailey v. Alabama, 219 US 219, January 3, 1911.

Bailyn, Bernard. "The Central Themes of the American Revolution: An Interpretation." In *Essays on the American Revolution*, edited by Stephen G. Lurtz and James H. Houtson. Chapel Hill: 1973.

———. *The Origins of American Politics*. New York: Knopf, 1967.

Baker, Carlos, ed. *Hemingway and His Critics*. New York: Hill and Wang, 1961.

Baker, Josephine, and Jo Bouillon. *Josephine*. Translated by Mariana Fitzpatrick. New York: Harper and Row, 1976.

Barbour, Brian. *American Transcendentalism*. South Bend, Ind.: University of Notre Dame Press, 1973.

Beach, Sylvia. *Shakespeare and Company*. New York: Harcourt, Brace, 1956. Also Lincoln: University of Nebraska Press, 1991.

Bechet, Sidney. *Treat It Gentle*. New York: Da Capo Press, 1975.

Beecher, Lyman. *A Plea for the West*. Cincinnati: Trumann and Smith; New York: Leavitt, Lord, 1835.

Benét, Stephen Vincent. "A Creed for Americans." In *Great American Stories and Poems*, compiled by Hugh Graham. New York: Gallahad Books, 1987.

Benstock, Shari. *Women of the Left Bank: Paris, 1900–1940*. Austin: University of Texas Press, 1986.

Bernal, Martin. *Black Athena: The Afroasiatic Roots of Classical Civilization*. 2 vols. to date. New Brunswick: Rutgers University Press, 1987 (vol.1), 1991 (vol. 2).

Black, Henry Campbell. *Black's Law Dictionary*. St. Paul, Minn.: West Publishing, 1979.

Blackstock, Nelson. *COINTELPRO*. Introduction by Noam Chomsky. New York: Vintage Books, 1976.

Blassingame, John W. *The Slave Community: Plantation Life in the Antebellum South*. New York and Oxford: Oxford University Press, 1979.

Bloom, Allan, and Roger Kimball. *The Closing of the American Mind*. New York: Simon and Schuster, 1987.

Bogle, Ronald. *Brown Sugar*. New York: Harmony Books, 1980.

Bontemps, Arna. *The Harlem Renaissance Remembered*. New York: Dodd, Mead, 1972.

Boorstin, Daniel. *America and the Image of Europe*. Cleveland, Ohio: World Publishing, 1960.

Bork, Robert H. *The Tempting of America: The Political Seduction of the Law*. New York: Free Press, 1990.

Boswell, James. *The Life of Samuel Johnson*, 2 vols. London: Swan, Sennenschein, 1888.

Bourne, Randolph. "Trans-National America." *Atlantic Monthly* 118 (July 1916): 86–97.

Bremner, Robert H. *American Philanthropy*. Chicago: University of Chicago Press, 1988.

Brenner, Michael J. "Finding America's Place." *Foreign Policy* 79 (Summer 1990): 25–43.

Bridge, J. H. *Millionaire and Grub Street*. New York: Brentan's, 1931.

Brinnin, John Malcolm. *Dylan Thomas in America*. New York: Paragon House, 1989.

Brown, Charles Brockden. "Why the Arts Are Distorted in American Life." *Literary Magazine*, July 1806, 76–77.

Brown, Roger H. *Republic in Peril: 1812*. New York: Columbia University Press, 1964.

Buell, Lawrence. *Literary Transcendentalism: Style and Vision in the American Renaissance*. Ithaca, N.Y.: Cornell University Press, 1975.

Burhans, Clinton. "*The Old Man and the Sea*: Hemingway's Tragic Vision of Man." In *Hemingway and His Critics*, edited by Carlos Baker. 259–268. New York: Hill Wang, 1961.

Burt, A. L. *The United States, Great Britain, and British North America*. New Haven: Yale University Press, 1940.

Cable, Mary. *Black Odyssey: The Case of the Slave Ship Amistad*. New York: Viking Press, 1971.

Cady, Edwin H. *The Realist at War: The Mature Years 1885–1920 of William Dean Howells*. Syracuse: Syracuse University Press, 1958.

———. *The Road to Realism: The Early Years 1837–1885 of William Dean Howells*. Syracuse: Syracuse University Press, 1956.

Callahan, Joseph P., and Leonard H. Clark. *Introduction to American Education*. New York: Macmillan, 1977.

Calleo, David P. *Beyond American Hegemony*. New York: Basic Books, 1987.

Campbell, Joseph. *The Hero with a Thousand Faces*. Princeton, N.J.: Princeton University Press, 1968.

Campbell, Penelope. *Maryland in Africa: The Maryland State Colonization Society, 1831–1857*. Urbana: University of Illinois Press, 1971.

Carlyle, Thomas. *Occasional Discourse on the Nigger Question*. London: T. Bosworth, 1853.

Carnegie, Andrew. *The Negro in America*. Inverness, Scotland, 1907.

———. "Wealth." *North America Review* 148 (June 1889): 653–654 and 149 (December 1889): 682–698. Reprint of *The Gospel of Wealth and Other Timely Essays*, edited by Edward C. Kirkland. Cambridge, Mass., 1962.

Chalmers, David M. *Hooded Americanism: The History of the Ku Klux Klan*. Durham, N.C.: Duke University Press, 1987.

Chase, Richard. "Melville and Moby Dick." In *Melville: A Collection of Critical Essays*, edited by Rubard Chase. Englewood Cliffs, N.J.: Prentice-Hall, 1962.

Cheek, William. *Black Resistance before the Civil War*. Beverly Hills, Calif.:Glenco, 1970.

Claiborne, Robert. *The Roots of English*. New York: Times Books, 1989.

Clausen, Henry C., and Bruce Lee. *Pearl Harbor: Final Judgment*. New York: Crown Publishers, 1992.

Clebsch, William A. *American Religious Thought: A History*. Chicago: University of Chicago Press, 1973.

Clifford, James. *Commentary on Margaret Mead. Times Literary Supplement*, May 13, 1983, 475–476.

Cockburn, Alexander. "Beat the Devil: Redwood Summer: Chico Mendez in the First World," *The Nation*, July 2, 1990, 6–7.

Cole, Bruce, and Adelheid Gealt. *Art of the Western World*. New York: Summit Books, 1989.

Coles, Harry L. *The War of 1812*. Chicago: University of Chicago Press, 1965.

Collum, Danny Duncan, ed. *African Americans in the Spanish Civil War*. New York: G. K. Hall, 1992.

Columbus, Christopher. *The Journal of Christopher Columbus*. Translated by Cecil Jane. New York: Bonanza Books, 1960.

Conrad, Peter. *Imagining America*. New York: Oxford University Press, 1980.

Cooper, James Fenimore. *The American Democrat; or, Hints on the Focal and Civic Relations of the United States of America*. Cooperstown: H. & E. Phinney, 1838.

———. *The Pathfinder; or, The Inland Sea*. New York: A. P. Putnam's Sons, n.d [1840].

———. *The Redskins; or, Indian and Injin*. New York: A. P. Putnam's Sons, n.d [1846].

Cowley, Malcolm. *Exile's Return*. Dallas, Pa.: Penguin, 1969.

Crèvecoeur, J. Hector St. John. *Letters from an American Farmer* [1782]. London: Penguin Books, 1981.

Crosskey, William Winslow, and Jeffrey William. *Politics and the Constitution in the History of the United States*, 3 vols. Chicago: University of Chicago Press, 1953–1980.

Cunard, Nancy. *Negro: An Anthology*. Edited and abridged by Hugh Ford. New York: Frederick Ungar Publishing, 1970.

Damas, Léon G. "Léon Damas: Interviewed February 18, 1977." *Journal of Caribbean Studies* 1, no. 1 (Winter 1980): 63–73.

Dance, Daryl Cumber. *Shuckin' and Jivin': Folklore from Contemporary Black Americans*. Bloomington: Indiana University Press, 1978.

Daniel, Pete. *The Shadow of Slavery: Peonage in the South, 1901–1969*. Urbana: University of Illinois Press, 1971.

Dathorne, O. R. *The Black Mind*. Minneapolis: University of Minnesota Press, 1974.

Davis, Kenneth S. *FDR: Into the Storm*. New York: Random House, 1992.

De Reincourt, Amaury. *The American Empire*. New York: Dell Publishing, 1968.

Desalvo, Louise. *Nathaniel Hawthorne*. Atlantic Highlands, N.J.: Humanities Press International, 1987.

De Tussac, F. R. *Cri des colons contre un ouvrage de M. L'Éveque et Senateur Grégoire, ayant pour titre de la littérature des nègres* (Paris: De Launay Librarie, 1810).

Dickens, Charles. *American Notes* [1842]. New York: St. Martin's Press, 1985.

———. *Dickens on America and the Americans*, edited by Michael Slater. Austin: University of Texas Press, 1975.

Dickinson, John. *Letters from a Farmer in Pennsylvania to the Inhabitants of the British Colonies* [1768]. St. Clair Shore, Mich.: Scholarly Press, 1969.

Dillingham Commission. *Report of the United States Immigration Commission*. 41 vols. 1911. 1st vol. (S. doc. 747, 61st Congress, 3d Session)–40th vol. (S. doc. 761, 61st Congress, 3d Session).

Dimbleby, David, and David Reynolds. *An Ocean Apart*. New York: Random House, 1988.

Donner, Frank. *The Age of Surveillance: The Aims and Methods of America's Political Intelligence System*. New York: Knopf, 1980.

Dooley, Roger. *From Scarface to Scarlett: American Films in the 1930s*. New York: Harcourt, Brace, 1984.

Drake, William. "Walden." In *Thoreau: A Collection of Critical Essays*, edited by Sherman Paul, 71-91. Englewood Cliffs, N.J.: Prentice-Hall, 1962.

D'Souza, Dinesh. *Illiberal Education: The Politics of Race and Sex on Campus*. New York: Free Press, 1991.

Du Bois, W. E. B. *Dusk of Dawn: An Essay Toward an Autobiography of a Race Concept*. New York: Harcourt, Brace, 1940.

———. *The Philadelphia Negro: A Social Study. Together with a Special Report on Domestic Service, by I. Eaton*. Political Economy and Public Law Series, No. 14. Philadelphia: University of Pennsylvania Press, 1899.

Dumond, Dwight. *Anti-Slavery Origins of the Civil War*. Ann Arbor: University of Michigan Press, 1959.

Dundes, Alan, ed. *Mother Wit from the Laughing Barrel*. Englewood Cliffs, N.J.: Prentice-Hall, 1973.

Dye, Thomas. *Who's Running America?* 6th ed. Englewood Cliffs, N.J.: Prentice-Hall, 1986.

Edmonds, Robin. *The Big Three: Churchill, Roosevelt, and Stalin in Peace and War*. New York: Norton, 1991.

Eisenhower, Dwight D. *Crusade in Europe*. New York: Doubleday, 1948.

Eliot, T. S. *The Complete Poems and Plays: 1909–1950*. New York: Harcourt, Brace and World, 1971.

———. *Selected Prose*. Harmondsworth, Middlesex: Penguin, 1953.

Eliot, Valerie, ed. *The Letters of T. S. Eliot*, vol. 1. New York: Harcourt Brace Jovanovich, 1988.

———. *T. S. Eliot: The Waste Land*. London: Faber and Fab er, 1971.

Ellis, John Tracy. *American Catholicism*. Chicago: University of Chicago Press, 1956.

Emerson, Ralph Waldo. *The Collected Works of Ralph Waldo Emerson*, 4 vols., edited by Robert E. Spiller and Alfred R. Ferguson. Cambridge, Mass.: Belknap Press of Harvard University Press, 1971.

———. *The Collected Works of Ralph Waldo Emerson*, edited by Joseph Slater and Douglas Emory Wilson. 4 vols. Vol. 2. *Essays: First Series*, edited by Joseph Slater, Alfred R. Ferguson, and Jean Ferguson. Cambridge, Mass.: Belknap Press of Harvard University Press, 1979.

———. *Essays and Lectures*. New York: Library of America, 1983.

Empson, William. *Using Biography*. London: Chatto and Windus, 1984.

Eyre, Ronald, ed. *London Assurance,* by Dion Boueicault. London, Methuen, 1971.

Fabre, Michel. *Black American Writers in France 1840–1980*. Urbana: University of Illinois Press, 1991.

Fairchild, Hoxie Neale. *The Noble Savage: A Study in Romantic Realism*. New York: Columbia University Press, 1928.

The Federalist Papers. Introduction by Clinton Rossiter. New York: New American Library, 1961.

Felder, Cain. *Troubling Biblical Waters*. New York: Orbis Books, 1989.

Ferrell, Robert H. *Woodrow Wilson and World War I*. New York: Harper and Row, 1985.

Fischer, David Hackett. *Albion's Seed: Four British Folkways in America*. New York: Oxford University Press, 1989.

Fitzgerald, F. Scott. *The Great Gatsby*. New York: Charles Scribner's Sons, 1953.

Fogel, Robert William, and Stanley L. Engerman. *Time on the Cross: The Economics of American Negro Slavery*. New York: Norton, 1989.

Ford, Boris, ed. *The New Pelican Guide to English Literature*, 9 vols. London: Penguin Books, 1988.

Ford, Hugh, ed. and int. *The Left Bank Revisited: Selections from the 'Paris Tribune' 1917–1934*. University Park: Pennsylvania State University Press, 1972.

Franklin, Benjamin. "Observation Concerning the Increase of Mankind, Peopling of Countries, etc." 10 vols. In *The Writings of Benjamin Franklin*, edited by Albert H. Smyth. New York: 1905.

Frazier, E. Franklin. *Black Bourgeoisie*. Glencoe, Ill.: Free Press, 1957.

———. *The Negro in the United States*. New York: Macmillan, 1957.

Freeman, Michael. *Edmund Burke and the Critique of Political Radicalism*. Chicago: University of Chicago Press, 1980.

Friedman, John Block. *The Monstrous Races in Medieval Art and Thought*. Cambridge, Mass.: Harvard University Press, 1981.

Fuchs, Daniel. "Ernest Hemingway: Literary Critic." In *Ernest Hemingway: A Collection of Criticism*, edited by Arthur Waldhorn, 92–111. New York: McGraw-Hill, 1973.

Fyfe, Christopher. *History of Sierra Leone*. London: Oxford University Press, 1962.

Garko, Leo. "The Achievement of Ernest Hemingway." *College English* 12 (April 1952): 368–375.

Garvey, Amy Jacques, ed. *Philosophy and Opinions of Marcus Garvey or Africa for the Africans*. Vols. 1 and 2, [1923 and 1925]. Dover, Mass.: Majority Press, 1986.

Garvey, Marcus. *The Marcus Garvey and Universal Negro Improvement Association Papers*, edited by Robert A. Hill. 7 vols. Los Angeles: University of California Press. Vol. 1, 1826–August 1919 (1983); Vol. 2, 27 August 1919–31 August, 1920 (1983); Vol. 3, September 1920–August 1921 (1984); Vol. 4, September 1921–September 1922 (1985); Vol. 5, September 1922–August 1924 (1987); Vol. 6, September 1924–December 1927 (1989); Vol. 7, November 1927–August 1940 (1990).

———. *Message to the People: The Course of African Philosophy*, edited by Tony Martin. Dover, Mass.: Majority Press, 1985.

Getty, J. Paul. *How to Be Rich*. Chicago: Playboy Press, 1965.

Gilot, Françoise. *Matisse and Picasso*. New York: Doubleday, 1991.

Glassman, Steve, and Kathryn Lee Seidel. *Zora in Florida*. Orlando: University of Central Florida Press, 1991.

Gore, Al. *Earth in the Balance*. Boston: Houghton Mifflin, 1992.

Grady, Henry W. *The New South*. New York: Robert Bonner's Sons, 1890.

Graham, Hugh, compiler. *Great American Stories and Poems*. New York: Galahad Books, 1987. Originally published 1919.

Grant, Madison. *The Passing of the Great Race in America*. New York: Charles Scribner's Sons, 1916.

Greene, Jack P. "An Uneasy Connection: An Analysis of the Pre-Conditions of the American Revolution." In *Essays on the American Revolution*, edited by Stephen G. Kurtz and James H. Huston. Chapel Hill: University of North Carolina Press, 1973.

Grégoire, Abbé Henry. *De las littérature des nègres*. Paris: Makadan, 1808.

Gura, Philip F., and Myevson, Joel. *Critical Essays on American Transcendentalism*. Boston: G. K. Hall, 1982.

Gurko, Leo. "The Old Man and the Sea." *College English* 17 (October 1955): 11–15.

Hakluyt, Richard. *Voyages and Discoveries*, edited by Jack Beeching. Harmondsworth, U.K.: Penguin Books, 1972.

Hawthorne, Nathaniel. *The Blithedale Romance* [1852]. London: Penguin Books, 1923.

Hemenway, Robert. *Zora Neale Hurston: A Literary Biography*. Chicago: University of Chicago Press, 1977.

Hemingway, Ernest. *A Farewell to Arms*. New York: Scribner's, 1929.

———. *Green Hills of Africa*. New York: Scribner's, 1935.

———. *A Moveable Feast*. New York: Scribner's, 1964.

———. *The Old Man and the Sea*. New York: Scribner's, 1952.

———. *The Short Stories of Ernest Hemingway*. New York: Scribner's, 1938.

———. *The Sun Also Rises*. New York: Scribner's, 1926.

Hirsch, E. D., Jr. *Cultural Literacy: What Every American Needs to Know*. New York: Vintage Books, 1988.

Hitchens, Christopher. *Blood, Class, and Nostalgia: Anglo-American Ironies*. New York: Farrar, Strauss and Giroux, 1990.

Hoffman, Frederick J. *The Twenties*. New York: Free Press, 1962.

Horsman, Reginald. *The Causes of the War of 1812*. Philadelphia: University of Pennsylvania Press, 1962.

Horwill, Herbert W. *The Usages of the American Constitution*. Oxford: Oxford University Press, 1925.

Howard, Leon. *Literature and the American Tradition*. New York: Doubleday, 1960.

Howe, Kay Seymour. *Cooper's Americans*. Columbus: Ohio State University Press, 1963.

Howells, William Dean. *Annie Kilburn* [1889]. Reprinted in *Novels 1886–1888*. New York: Library of America, 1989.

———. *April Hopes.* [1888]. Reprinted in *Novels 1886–1888.* New York: Library of America, 1989.

———. *The Minister's Charge.* [1887]. Reprinted in *Novels 1886–1888.* New York: Library of America, 1989.

Huffington, Arianna Stassinopoulos. *Picasso: Creation and Design.* New York: Simon and Schuster, 1989.

Huggins, Nathan. *Harlem Renaissance.* New York: Oxford University Press, 1971.

Hunter, J. Paul. "Steinbeck's Wine of Affirmation in *The Grapes of Wrath.*" In *The Grapes of Wrath: A Collection of Critical Essays,* edited by Robert Conn Davis, 36–47. Englewood Cliffs, N.J.: Prentice-Hall, 1982.

Hurston, Zora Neale. *Dust Tracks on a Road.* [1942]. With an introduction by Larry Neale. Philadelphia and New York: J. B. Lippincott, 1971.

———. *Their Eyes Were Watching God.* Greenwich, Conn.: Fawcett Publications, 1969.

Iacocca, Lee (with William Novak). *Iacocca: An Autobiography.* New York: Bantam Books, 1984.

James, Henry. "The Beast in the Jungle," "The Jolly Corner," and "The Turn of the Screw." In *The Novels and Tales of Henry James,* 26 vols. New York: Charles Scribner's Sons, 1907–1917.

———. "Nathaniel Hawthorne." *Literary Criticism.* New York: Library of America, 1984.

———. *The Notebooks of Henry James,* edited by F. O. Matthiessen and Kenneth Murdock. Chicago: University of Chicago Press, 1947.

Jefferson, Thomas. "Notes on the State of Virginia." In *The Portable Thomas Jefferson,* edited by Merrill D. Peterson. New York: Penguin, 1975.

Jenks, Jeremiah W., and W. Jelt Lauck. *The Immigration Problem,* in *Encyclopedia,* 6th ed., by Funk and Wagnall, 1926.

Jensen, Arthur R. "Environment, Heredity and Intelligence." Summarized from *Harvard Educational Review* in *U.S. News & World Report* (March 10, 1969): 48.

Johnson, Charles S. *Growing Up in the Black Belt: Negro Youth in the Rural South.* Washington, D.C.: American Council on Education, 1941.

Jones, Howard. *Mutiny on the Amistad.* Oxford: Oxford University Press, 1987.

Jones, Maldwyn Allen. *American Immigration.* Chicago: University of Chicago Press, 1960.

Karp, Walter. "Henry Ford's Village." In *A Sense of History, the Best Writings from the Pages of the American Heritage.* New York: American Heritage, 1985.

Kellner, Bruce, ed. *The Harlem Renaissance: A Historical Dictionary for the Era.* New York: Methuen, 1987.

Kennedy, Paul M. *The Rise and Fall of the Great Powers.* New York: Random House, 1987.

Kerner, Otto. *The Report of the National Advisory Commission on Civil Disorders.* New York: Bantam Books, 1968.

Kimball, Roger. *Tenured Radicals: How Politics Has Corrupted Higher Education.* New York: Harper and Row, 1990.

Knight, Franklin W. "Cuba: Politics, Economy, and Society, 1898–1985." In *The Modern Caribbean,* edited by Franklin W. Knight and Colin A. Palmer. Chapel Hill: University of North Carolina Press, 1989.

Koster, Donald N. *Transcendentalism in America.* Boston: G. K. Hall, 1975.

Lasch, Christopher. *The True and Only Heaven: Progress and Its Critics.* New York: Norton, 1991.

Lawrence, D. H. *The Letters of D. H. Lawrence,* edited by Aldous Huxley. London: Heinemann, 1932.

———. *Studies in Classic American Literature.* London: Penguin, 1977.

Legum, Colin. *Pan Africanism: A Short Political Guide.* London: Pall Mall Press, 1962.

Lerner, Max. *America as a Civilization: Life and Thought in the United States Today*. New York: Henry Holt, 1987.

Levine, Bruce, Stephen Brier, David Brandage, et al., *Who Built North America? Working People and the Nation's Economics, Politics, Culture and Society*. New York: Pantheon Books, 1989.

Lewis, David Levering. *When Harlem Was in Vogue*. New York: Oxford University Press, 1979.

Lincoln, C. Eric. *The Black Church Since Frazier* [with E. Franklin Frazier's *The Negro Church*] New York: Schocken Books, 1974.

Lindbergh, Charles A. *We*. New York: G. P. Putnam's Sons, 1927.

Lindsay, Vachel. *The Congo and Other Poems*. New York: Macmillan, 1914.

Link, Arthur S. *Wilson: The Struggle for Neutrality 1914–1915*. Princeton: Princeton University Press, 1960.

————. *Woodrow Wilson: Revolution, War, and Peace*. Arlington Heights, Ill: AHM, 1979.

Little, Kenneth. *Negroes in Britain: A Study of Racial Relations in English Society*. London: Kegan Paul, 1947.

Lloyd, P. C. *Africa in Social Change*. Harmondsworth, UK: Penguin, 1987.

Locke, John. *The Second Treatise of Civil Government and a Letter Concerning Toleration*, edited with an introduction by J. W. Gough. Oxford: Basil Blackwell, 1946.

Loewenheim, Frances L., Harold D. Langley, and Manfred Jonas. *Roosevelt and Churchill: Their Secret Wartime Correspondence*. New York: Saturday Review Press and E. P. Dutton, 1975.

Long, Edward. *History of Jamaica*. London: Printed for T. Lowndes, 1774.

Louis, William Roger, and Hedley Bell. *The Special Relationship: Anglo-American Relations since 1945*. Oxford: Oxford University Press, 1986.

Luhman, Reid, and Stuart Gilman. *Race and Ethnic Relations: The Social and Political Experience of Minority Groups*. Belmont, Calif: Wadsworth, 1980.

Lundberg, Ferdinand. *America's Sixty Families*. New York: Vanguard Press, 1937.

————. *Cracks in the Constitution*. Secaucus, N.J.: Lyle Stuart, 1980.

Lyn, Kenneth. *Hemingway*. New York: Simon and Schuster, 1987.

Lynch, Hollis. *Edward Wilmot Blyden: Pan-Negro Patriot, 1832–1912*. London: Oxford University Press, 1967.

Malcolm X. *By Any Means Necessary: Speeches, Interviews and a Letter by Malcolm X*, edited by George Breitman. New York: Pathfinder Press, 1970.

Mandelbaum, Maurice. "Societal Facts." In *Theories of History*, edited by Patrick Gardiner. New York: Free Press and London: Collier-Macmillan, 1959.

Martin, Christopher. *The Amistad Affair*. New York: Tower Publications, 1970.

Martin, Edmond B. *All We Want Is Make Us Free: La Amistad and the Reform Abolitionists*. Lanham, Md.: University Press of America, 1986.

Martin, Tony. *The Pan African Connection*. Canton, Mass.: Majority Press, 1983.

Marx, Leo. *The Machine in the Garden: Technology and the Pastoral Idea in America*. New York: Oxford University Press, 1964.

Mast, Gerald, ed. *The Movies in Our Midst*. Chicago: University of Chicago Press, 1982.

Mbiti, John. *African Religions and Philosophy*. Oxford: Heinemann, 1969.

————. *Introduction to African Religion*. Oxford: Heinemann, 1975.

McClelland, Peter D., and Richard J. Zeckhauser. *Demographic Dimensions of the New Republic*. Cambridge, Mass.: 1982.

McCullough, David. *Truman*. New York: Simon and Schuster, 1992.

McCullough, N. V. *The Negro in English Literature*. Ilfracombe, England: Stockwell Printers, 1962.

McKay, Claude. *Banana Bottom*. New York: Harper, 1933.

————. *The Negroes in America*. Port Washington, New York: Kennikat Press, 1979.

McKitrick, Eric L. *Slavery Defended: The Views of the Old South*. Englewood Cliffs, N.J.: Prentice-Hall, 1963.

McLaughlin, Jack. *Jefferson and Monticello: The Biography of a Builder*. New York: Henry Holt, 1988.

Mead, Margaret. *Coming of Age in Samoa*. New York: William Morrow, 1928. Edition used published by American Museum of Natural History, 1973. Preface by Franz Boas.

Miller, Perry. *The Transcendentalists*. Cambridge, Mass.: Harvard University Press, 1950.

Molesworth, Charles. "Culture, Power and Society." In *Columbia Literary History of the United States*, edited by Emory Elliott et al., 1023–1044. New York: Columbia University Press, 1988.

Monaghan, E. Jennifer. "Literary Search and Gender in Colonial New England." *American Quarterly* 40 (1). (March 1928).

Monk, Maria. *Awful Disclosures of the Hotel Dieu Nunnery of Montreal*. New York. Privately published by author, 1836.

Moore, Stephen. "Flee Market: More Refugees at Lower Cost." *Policy Review*. No. 52 (Spring 1990): 64–68.

Morgan, Edward S. "Revisions in Need of Revising" In *The Challenges of the American Revolution*, 50–52. New York: W. W. Norton, 1976.

Morrison, Toni. *Playing in the Dark*. Cambridge, Mass.: Harvard University Press, 1992.

Morse, Samuel F. B. *A Foreign Conspiracy against the Liberties of the United States*. New York: Leavitt, Lord & Co., 1834.

Moses, Wilson Jeremiah. *The Golden Age of Black Nationalism, 1850 to 1925*. New York: Oxford University Press, 1978.

Myrdal, Gunnar. *An American Dilemma*, 2 vols. New York: McGraw-Hill, 1964.

Naipaul, V. S. *A Turn in the South*. New York: Alfred A. Knopf, 1989.

National Association for the Advancement of Colored People. *Thirty Years of Lynching in the United States, 1889–1918*. New York: NAACP, 1919.

Nef, John U. *The United States and Civilization*. Chicago: University of Chicago Press, 1967.

Nicholas, H. G. *The United States and Britain*. Chicago: University of Chicago Press, 1975.

Nietzsche, Friedrich. *The Birth of Tragedy*. Translated by Walter Kaufmann. New York: Random House, 1967.

North, Oliver. "Reagan Aides and the Secret Government." *Miami Herald*, Sunday, 5 July 1987, 1 and 14A.

Nye, Joseph. *Bound to Lead: The Changing Nature of American Power*. New York: Basic Books, 1990.

Olmsted, Frederick Law. *The Papers of Frederick Law Olmsted*, 5 vols. edited by Victoria Post Panney, Gerard J. Rauluk, and Carolyn F. Hoffman. Baltimore: Johns Hopkins University Press, 1990.

————. *Walks and Talks of an American Farmer in England*, 2 vols. New York: G. P. Putnam, 1852.

O'Flaherty, Wendy, trans. *Hindu Myths*. London: Penguin, 1975.

O'Neill, Eugene. *The Emperor Jones*. Englewood Cliffs, N.J.: Prentice-Hall, 1921.

O'Reilly, Kenneth. *Racial Matters: The FBI's Secret File on Black America 1960–1972*. New York: Free Press, 1989.

Oring, Elliott. *Folk Groups and Folklore Genres: An Introduction*. Logan: Utah State University Press, 1986.

Padmore, George. *Pan Africanism or Communism*. Garden City, New York: Doubleday, 1971.

Page, Thomas Nelson. *The Negro: The Southerner's Problem*. New York: Charles Scribner's Sons, 1904.

Paine, Thomas. *The Complete Writings of Thomas Paine*, 2 vols. New York: Citadel Press, 1945.

Paul, Sherman, ed. *Thoreau: A Collection of Critical Essays*. Englewood Cliffs, N.J.: Prentice-Hall, 1962.

Pearce, Roy Harvey. *The Savages of America: A Study of the Indian and the Idea of Civilization*. Baltimore: Johns Hopkins University Press, 1953.

Peets, Elbert. "Landscape Design." *American Mercury* 4 (1925).

————. "The Landscape Priesthood." *American Mercury* 10 (1927).

Penrose, Roland. *Portrait of Picasso*. New York: Museum of Modern Art, 1971.

Perkins, Bradford. *Prologue to War: England and the United States, 1805–1812*. Berkeley and Los Angeles: University of California Press, 1961.

Plimpton, George. "An Interview with Ernest Hemingway." *Paris Review*, no. 18 (Spring 1958), 60–89. Reprinted in *Writers at Work*. [The "Paris Review" Interviews, second series], 215–239. New York: Viking, 1963.

Power, Thomas. *New York Review of Books*. 13 May 1993, 49-55.

Putnam, Samuel. *Paris Was Our Mistress*. Carbondale: Southern Illinois University Press, 1947.

Quarles, Benjamin. *The Negro in the Making of America*. London: Collier-Macmillan, 1964.

Randall, John Herman. *The Career of Philosophy*, 3 vols. Columbia University Press, 1962.

Ratner, Lorman. *Powder Keg: Northern Opposition to the Anti-Slavery Movement*. New York: Basic Books, 1968.

Read, Jan. *The Moors in Spain and Portugal*. London: Faber and Faber, 1974.

Rensberger, Boyce. "Margaret Mead: The Nature-Nurture Debate." Reprint from *Science 84 Magazine*. American Association for the Advancement of Science, 28–33.

Rerkus, Cathy, ed. *COINTELPRO: The FBI's Secret War on Political Freedom*. New York: Monad Press, 1975.

Rieff, David. "The Transformation of America." *Times Literary Supplement*, no. 4547 (25–31 May 1990): 543–544.

Rose, Anna C. *Transcendentalism as Social Movement, 1830–1850*. New Haven: Yale University Press, 1981.

Rosenzweig, Roy, and Elizabeth Blackmar. *The Park and the People: A History of Central Park*. Ithaca, N.Y.: Cornell University Press, 1992.

Rousseau, Jean Jacques. *Émile*. Woodbury, N.Y.: Barron's Educational Series, 1964.

Said, Edward W. *Orientalism*. New York: Vintage Books, 1979.

St. John, J. Hector. See Crèvecoeur.

Sandiford, Keith A. *Measuring the Moment*. Cranbury, N.J.: Susquehanna University Press, 1988.

Schlesinger, Arthur. "When Ethnic Studies Are Un-American" *Wall Street Journal*, 23 April 1990, 14A.

Schulte Nordholt, J. W. *Het Volk dat in duisternis wandelt*. Arnhem, Netherlands, 1956.

Sears, Clara Endicott. *Bronson Alcott's Fruitlands*. Boston: Houghton Mifflin, 1915.

Sen, K. M. *Hinduism*. New York: Viking Penguin, 1962.

Shyllon, Folarin. *Black People in Britain 1555–1833*. London: Oxford University Press, 1977.

Silverberg, Robert. "And the Mound Builders Vanished from the Earth." In *A Sense of History: The Best Writings from the Pages of the American Heritage*. New York: American Heritage, 1985.

Simpson, Louis. *Three on the Tower: The Lives and Works of Ezra Pound, T. S. Eliot, and William Carlos Williams*. New York: William Morrow, 1975.

Sklar, Robert. *Movie-Made America*. New York: Vintage Books, 1975.

Smith, Houston. *The Religions of Man*. New York: Perennial Library, 1965.

Snowden, Frank. *Blacks in Antiquity*. Cambridge: Belknap Press of Harvard University Press, 1970.

Sowell, Thomas. *The Economics and Politics of Race*. New York: William Morrow Books, 1983.

Spann, Edward K. "The Greatest Grid: The New York Plan of 1811." In *Two Centuries of American Planning*, edited by Daniel Schaffer. Baltimore: Johns Hopkins University Press, 1988.

Spencer, Benjamin. *Quest for Nationality*. Syracuse, N.Y.: Syracuse University Press, 1957.

Spilka, Mark. "The Death of Love in *The Sun Also Rises*." In *Hemingway and His Critics*, edited by Carlos Baker, 80–92. New York: Hill and Wang, 1961.

Spratlin, Valaurez B. *Juan Latino: Slave and Humanist*. New York: Spinner Press, 1938.

Stanton, Bill. *Klanwatch*. New York: Grove Weidenfeld, 1991.

Steele, Shelby. *The Content of Our Character*. New York: St. Martin's Press, 1990.

Stein, Gertrude. *Three Lives*. [1909] New York: Vintage Books, 1936.

Steinbeck, John. *East of Eden*. New York: Bantam Books, 1962.

——— . *The Grapes of Wrath*. New York: Viking Press, 1939.

——— . *Journal of a Novel: The "East of Eden" Letters*. New York: Viking Press, 1969.

Stoddard, Lothrop. *The Rising Tide of Color against White World Supremacy*. New York: Charles Scribner's Sons, 1920. Reprinted Miami: Mnemosyne, 1989.

Stoeht, Tylor. *Nay-Saying in Concord: Emerson, Alcott and Thoreau*. Hamden, Conn.: Archon Books, 1979.

Stoller, Leo. "Thoreau's Doctrine of Simplicity." In *Thoreau: A Collection of Essays*, edited by Sherman Paul, 37–52. Englewood Cliffs, N.J.: Prentice-Hall, 1962.

Sultan, Stanley. *Eliot, Joyce and Company*. New York: Oxford University Press, 1987.

Summers, Anthony. *Official and Confidential: The Secret Life of J. Edgar Hoover*. New York: G. P. Putnam's Sons, 1993.

Sypher, Wylie. *Guinea's Captive Kings: British Anti-Slavery Literature of the Eighteenth Century*. Chapel Hill: University of North Carolina Press, 1942.

Tannenbaum, Frank. *Slave and Citizen: The Negro in the Americas*. New York: Knopf, 1946.

Thomas, Lamont D. *Paul Cuffe*. Urbana: University of Illinois Press, 1988.

Thoreau, Henry David. *A Week on the Concord and Merrimack Rivers. Walden; or, Life in the Woods. The Maine Woods. Cape Cod*. New York: Library of America, 1985.

Thurman, Wallace. *Infants of the Spring*. New York: Macaulay, 1932. A.M.S. Press Reprint, 1975.

Tocqueville, Alexis Compte de. *Democracy in America* [1899]. Edited by J. P. Mayer. New York: Harper and Row, 1969.

Toppin, Edgar A. *A Biographical History of Blacks in America since 1528*. New York: David McKay, 1971.

Toynbee, Arnold. *The World and the West*. New York: Oxford University Press, 1953.

Trollope, Anthony. *North America*. New York: Alfred A. Knopf, 1951.

——— . *The Timeless Traveler: Twenty Letters to the "Liverpoole Mercury"* [1875]. Edited with an introduction by Bradford Allen Booth. Berkeley: University of California Press, 1941.

Trollope, Francis. *Domestic Manners of the Americans* [1832]. New York: Alfred A. Knopf, 1949.

Trump, Donald J. (with Tony Schwartz). *Trump: The Art of the Deal*. New York: Warner Books, 1987.

Tucker, Robert W., and David C. Hendrickson. *The Fall of the First British Empire*. Baltimore: Johns Hopkins University Press, 1982.

Tyler, Moses Coit. *The Literary History of the American Revolution 1763–1783*. 2 vols. New York: G. P. Putnam's Sons, 1897.

"United States versus the Libelants and Claimants of the Schooner Amistad." (1841). *United States Reports*, vol. 40. Collected by Richard Peters. Washington, D.C.: U.S. Government Printing Office, 1941, 588–596.

Urofsky, Melvin I. *A March of Liberty*. New York: Knopf, 1988.

Van Vechten, Carl. *Nigger Heaven*. New York: Alfred A. Knopf, 1926.

Veblen, Thorstein. *The Theory of the Leisure Class: An Economic Study of Institutions*. New York: Macmillan, 1899. Reprinted with an introduction by C. Wright Mills, vi–xix. New York: Mentor, 1953.

Waite, Edward F. "The Negro in the Supreme Court." *Minnesota Law Review* 30 (March 1946): 219–304.

Walker, David. *Walker's Appeal in Four Articles with a Preamble to the Concerned Citizens of the World but in Particular and Very Expressly for Those of the United States*. Boston 1830. In *One Continuous Cry*, by Herbert Aptheker. New York: Humanities Press, 1965.

Wall, Joseph Frazier. *Andrew Carnegie*. Pittsburgh: University of Pittsburgh Press, 1970.

Washington, Booker T. *The Booker T. Washington Papers*, 9 vols. Edited by Louis R. Harlan. Urbana, Ill.: University of Illinois Press, 1972–1980.

Watkins, J. W. N. "Historical Explanation of the Social Sciences." *Theories of History*, edited by Patrick Gardiner. New York: Free Press and London: Collier-Macmillan, 1959.

Wattenberg, Ben J. *First Universal Nation*. New York: Free Press, 1992.

Waugh, Evelyn. *Brideshead Revisited*. Boston: Little, Brown, 1945.

———. *The Loved One*. Boston: Little, Brown, 1977.

Weatherford, Jack. *Indian Givers*. New York: Fawcett, 1988.

———. *Native Roots*. New York: Fawcett, 1992.

Weisbuch, Robert. *Atlantic Double-Cross: American Literature and British Influences in the Age of Emerson*. Chicago: University of Chicago Press, 1986.

Wexler, Immanuel. *The Marshall Plan Revisited: The European Recovery Program in Economic Perspective*. Westport, Conn.: Greenwood Press, 1983.

Wheatley, Phillis. *The Collected Works of Phillis Wheatley*. Edited by John Shields. New York: Oxford University Press, 1988.

———. *The Poems of Phillis Wheatley*. Edited by Julian D. Mason. Chapel Hill: University of North Carolina Press, 1966.

Whitman, Walter. *Democratic Vistas* [1891]. Garden City, N.Y.: Doubleday, Doran and Company, 1935.

———. *Leaves of Grass*. Edited with an introduction by Jerome Loving. New York: Oxford University Press, 1990.

Wiekes, George. *Americans in Paris*. New York: Doubleday, 1969.

Wilder, Thornton. *Our Town*. New York: Harper and Row, 1960.

———. *The Skin of Our Teeth*. New York: Samuel French, 1944.

———. *Theophilus North*. New York: Harper and Row, 1973.

Williams, John. *The Man Who Cried I Am*. Boston: Little, Brown, 1967.

Wills, Gary. *The Second Civil War: Arming for Armageddon*. New York: New American Library, 1968.

Winthrop, John. *Winthrop's Journal "History of New England" 1630–1649*, 2 vols. Edited by James Kendall Hosmer. New York: C. Scribner's Sons, 1908.

Wolff, Theodore F. "The Year the Americans Took Paris." *Christian Science Monitor,* 15 October 1990, 16.

Wright, Richard. *Black Power*. New York: Harper, 1954.

Yette, Samuel F. *The Choice: The Issue of Black Survival in America*. New York: Berkley Medallion Books, 1972.

Index

ABOUT THE AUTHOR

O. R. DATHORNE is Professor of English at the University of Kentucky and Executive Director of the Association of Caribbean Studies. His latest publications include two seminal studies, *Black Mind* (1974) and *Dark Ancestors* (1981); a novel, *Dele's Child* (1986); a book of poems, *Songs for a New World* (1988); and most recently *Imagining the World* (Bergin & Garvey, 1994). Dr. Dathorne is also the editor of *Journal of Caribbean Studies*.

ISBN 0-89789-397-2

EAN

HARDCOVER BAR CODE